"TO MAKE AMERICA"

"TO MAKE AMERICA"

*European Emigration in the Early
Modern Period*

EDITED BY
IDA ALTMAN AND JAMES HORN

UNIVERSITY OF CALIFORNIA PRESS
BERKELEY   LOS ANGELES   OXFORD

University of California Press
Berkeley and Los Angeles, California

University of California Press
Oxford, England

Copyright © 1991 by The Regents of the University of California

Library of Congress Cataloging-in-Publication Data

"To make America" : European emigration in the early modern period / edited by Ida Altman and James Horn.
  p. cm.
  Includes bibliographical references and index.
  ISBN 0-520-7233-2 (cloth)
  1. Europeans—America—History. 2. America—Emigration and immigration—History. 3. Europe—Emigration and immigration—History. 4. America—History—To 1810. I. Altman, Ida. II. Horn, James P. P.
E29.E87T6   1991
970.004—dc20   91-7918
                                                      CIP

1 2 3 4 5 6 7 8 9

Contents

	Acknowledgments	vii
1.	Introduction Ida Altman and James Horn	1
2.	A New World in the Old: Local Society and Spanish Emigration to the Indies Ida Altman	30
3.	Legal and Illegal Emigration from Seville, 1550–1650 Auke Pieter Jacobs	59
4.	"To Parts Beyond the Seas": Free Emigration to the Chesapeake in the Seventeenth Century James Horn	85
5.	Recruitment of French Emigrants to Canada, 1600–1760 Leslie Choquette	131
6.	Indentured Servants Bound for the French Antilles in the Seventeenth and Eighteenth Centuries Christian Huetz de Lemps	172
7.	Harnessing the Lure of the "Best Poor Man's Country": The Dynamics of German-Speaking Immigration to British North America, 1683–1783 Marianne Wokeck	204

Contributors 245
Index 247

Acknowledgments

The editors acknowledge with gratitude the contributions of Leslie Choquette, Christian Huetz de Lemps, A. Pieter Jacobs, and Marianne Wokeck not only for the high quality of their work and ideas but also for the responsiveness and patience that helped bring this collaborative effort to completion. During the initial phase of the project we solicited advice regarding potential contributors from a number of scholars; we thank them for their help along the way. We also thank Scott Mahler, until recently editor at the University of California Press, for his encouragement and consistent support. We wish him luck in his future endeavors.

We dedicate this volume to the people who first "made" America, as well as to those who came later, of whom we write here.

One

Introduction

Ida Altman and James Horn

The movement of peoples from Europe to the Americas in the early modern period was fundamental to the formation of New World society. Providing the manpower for exploration, conquest, and settlement, hundreds of thousands chose to leave their homelands to make the long and arduous journey across the Atlantic to the developing Euro-American societies of the Caribbean and North, South, and Central America. From Nova Scotia to Peru, within two centuries significant elements of European civilization had been transplanted and adapted to suit conditions in the radically different context of the New World. American society reflected the heterogeneous origins of immigrants, the variations in timing and motivations for colonization, the degree of state support for colonizing enterprises, and the adaptations that settlers made to the novel conditions they encountered. Formal institutions—agencies of government and church—generally followed rather than preceded substantial emigration to new areas. Laws and state policy regulating emigration likewise took shape in response to the movement of people already under way, and governmental efforts to channel or control emigration often met with only partial success in the face of socioeconomic and demographic realities in both homeland and colony. Society in America, in all its diverse forms, was an accommodation between two very different worlds, old and new.[1]

Given their crucial role in the formation of new societies in

America, one might expect emigrants to occupy center stage in the history of the New World and to play a key part in accounts of European history of the same era. Yet early modern emigration as a whole has elicited relatively little scholarly attention, and the individuals who participated in this movement have attracted even less. To date, discussions of emigration have largely concentrated on its quantitative and legal aspects, together with some focus on the origins, destinations, and basic demography (age and sex) of settlers. While important, such studies provide only a starting point for further research. Detailed examination of the background and motivations of emigrants, the effects of state intervention, the role of commercial interests, and the maintenance of important social and economic connections between people on both sides of the Atlantic can shed light on some of the most crucial factors that shaped the development of early American societies and conditioned their relations with, and impact on, the Old World.[2]

The articles in this volume address a number of these issues and represent some of the most recent approaches to the study of early modern emigration. Included are studies of emigration from four countries—Spain, England, France, and Germany—to virtually every part of the Americas. The authors treat the complexity and diversity of motivation and background; the variety of recruitment practices; the currents and cross-currents of movement that encompassed temporary migration, journeys back and forth across the Atlantic, and return migration to Europe. Taken together, they reveal important differences in the form and character of emigration in this period but also point to the coherence of the movement as a whole. They demonstrate the interconnections between society in Europe and the New World which ensured that only rarely would colonies become culturally isolated enclaves. These studies offer a comparative framework that allows an understanding of both the rich variety of experience that characterized the background of emigrants and some of the general forces that influenced the movement of all colonists, no matter from which country they came or where they settled in America. From this perspective, differences in migratory patterns hinge more on the relative strength or weakness of certain common factors rather than on radically different configurations. While patterns of emigration might appear superficially to be quite different, the differences were more often those of degree rather than kind.

European Diaspora: The Magnitude and Pace of Emigration

There are no reliable sources from which accurate estimates of the numbers of emigrants who settled in America can be constructed. The following figures are intended to convey an impression of the relative magnitude of movements and the timing of emigration from different countries; naturally, they must be treated with caution.

Approximately one and a half million Europeans settled in the New World between 1500 and 1800.[3] (See table 1.1.) Although dwarfed by the scale of importations of African slaves in the same period, and Lilliputian compared to emigration in the nineteenth and early twentieth century, nevertheless the sheer size of the movement in terms of early modern populations is impressive.[4] During the sixteenth century, as Spain and Portugal colonized vast areas of Central and South America together with the larger Caribbean islands, there was a steady flow of government and church officials, members of the lesser nobility, people from the

TABLE 1.1. *Approximate Numbers of European Emigrants to America, 1500–1783*

Country of Origin	Number	Date
Spain	437,000	1500–1650
Portugal	100,000	1500–1700
Britain	400,000	1607–1700
Britain[1]	322,000	1700–1780
France	51,000	1608–1760
"Germany"[2]	100,000	1683–1783
Total	1,410,000	1500–1783

Sources: Bailyn, *Voyagers to the West*, 24–26; Gemery, "Markets for Migrants," 35–40; Altman, Choquette, Horn, Wokeck, articles in this volume.

[1] Includes between 190,000 and 25,000 Scots and Irish.

[2] Germany refers to emigrants from southwestern Germany and the German-speaking cantons of Switzerland and Alsace Lorraine.

working classes, and their families averaging roughly three thousand people per year from a total population of around eight million. About 437,000 left Spain in the period from 1500 to 1650, and 100,000 left Portugal between 1500 and 1700. France contributed something like 51,000 colonists between the early seventeenth century and 1760 out of an average population of 20 million, of whom about 27,000 went to Canada and a slightly smaller number to the West Indies.[5]

Emigration rates from Britain were proportionally much higher than from other parts of Europe. In the seventeenth century alone, roughly 400,000 settlers left Britain (principally England), "a ratio of emigrants to domestic population almost twice that of Spain's."[6] By 1660, England had established five substantial overseas settlements: Ulster and Munster, the Chesapeake, Bermuda, Barbados and the Leeward islands, and New England. During the peak period of emigration, 1630 to 1660, as many as six and a half to eight thousand migrants left the country annually. Put differently, the equivalent population of a sizable provincial town took ship every year. Most settled in the plantation colonies. Between 1630 and 1700, over 220,000 people (59%) went to the Caribbean, 116,000 (31%) to the southern mainland, and 39,000 (10%) to the northern and middle colonies. Approximately 60 percent migrated as servants (poor laborers who contracted to work in the tobacco and sugar fields in return for their passage across the Atlantic, food and lodging, and certain "freedom dues").[7]

Gross national figures, however, disguise the importance of differential regional participation in—and therefore the impact of—emigration from other countries. Spanish emigration, for example, was largely Castilian, with only negligible input from the eastern kingdom of Aragon (Catalonia, Valencia, and Aragon); in fact, in the first part of the sixteenth century, Spanish emigrants overwhelmingly came from the south and southwest (Andalusia and Extremadura) and, in the earliest decades, even more specifically from Seville and environs.[8]

Regional emigration rates could vary considerably from the national figures. The sparsely populated region of Extremadura, with only 7 percent of Spain's population in the sixteenth century, produced approximately 17 percent of the emigrants to America.

The findings of Leslie Choquette, Christian Huetz de Lemps, and Marianne Wokeck suggest similar patterns of local and regional concentrations of emigrants from France and Germany, respectively. Furthermore, private recruitment and the tendency to follow relatives and compatriots to particular destinations linked certain European regions firmly to specific locales in the New World. Well over half of all emigrants from the Extremaduran cities of Trujillo and Cáceres went to Peru (although Mexico received the largest numbers of Spanish emigrants in the sixteenth century overall). Almost half of the emigrants to Chile in the seventeenth and eighteenth centuries were Basques, while most German emigrants settled in the middle colonies of North America.[9]

The pace of European emigration may have slackened in the period from 1660 to 1783, but there are virtually no estimates of Spanish emigration for the seventeenth and eighteenth centuries. Roughly 600,000 settlers arrived in North America in the seventeenth century compared to about 450,000 between 1700 and the end of the American Revolution. The ethnic composition of emigrants changed significantly. Of the 322,000 settlers who left Britain, between 190,000 and 250,000 were Scots and Irish. Migration from England therefore declined rapidly, although there were occasional spurts, for example, in the 1770s. The direction of movement also changed significantly. Henry Gemery estimates that only 20 percent of emigrants during the period 1700–1780 settled in the Caribbean compared to 54 percent in the south and 26 percent in the northern and middle colonies.[10] During the same period, a little under 100,000 German-speaking immigrants arrived, mainly in Pennsylvania, and there were several thousand French Huguenot immigrants, who settled in the Chesapeake and Carolinas. While the great majority of the white population of North America remained British in origin until 1800, the eighteenth century saw much greater ethnic diversity, especially in the middle and southern colonies.[11]

Notable, too, is the inverse relationship between the timing of European migrations and slave importations. As European emigration declined and the plantation system and transatlantic economy matured, the number of slaves transported to the Americas increased dramatically. Links between the development of colonial economies, European markets, and labor demands are complex;

why and how planters switched from white to slave labor has generated much speculation.¹² This is not the place to rehearse these arguments, but there can be little doubt that the enormous increase in black immigration in the eighteenth century irrevocably altered the social and racial morphology of colonial society throughout the New World, adding a potentially explosive ingredient to the already complex social mix of Europeans and indigenous peoples.¹³

Diverse Multitudes: The Character of Emigration

Hidalgos, servants, redemptioners, seigneurs-commerçants, artisans, farmers, soldiers, and *filles du roi* were among those of diverse background who moved to America in the early modern period. The means by which they were able to undertake the move varied considerably as well, with the result that the legal and economic status of emigrants could fall anywhere along the spectrum from "unfree" to "free."

In general, free emigrants were those who were able to fund their own (and their families') journey to America and did not owe a fixed period of labor service to any other party. They included government officials, clergymen, merchants, artisans, farmers, and members of the gentry and lesser nobility, all of whom typically had a skill, profession, or some capital that could facilitate entrance into colonial society. The possession of these, as well as personal or political connections, allowed them, at least potentially, to take advantage of opportunities in the New World immediately. Usually established in their trades or professions, they tended to be older than those who arrived in America under some sort of labor contract. In many cases, free emigrants were able to draw on the support and advice of friends and kin either in their native communities or in America to help them make the move across the Atlantic and settle in their new country. Ida Altman (chap. 2) shows clearly the paramount importance of such connections in generating movement from Extremadura. Similar principles governed free emigration from Britain and parts of Germany. No doubt, kin and friendship networks influenced free migration, to one degree or another, from most countries in this period; but their significance in encouraging emigration from particular regions, dictating the direction of movement and influencing the development of colonial society in a transatlantic context has been little studied.

Between these "free" emigrants and the large numbers of "unfree" emigrants fell individuals whose status shared some characteristics of both categories. Men and women departing Spain as servants (*criados*) in the entourage of an official, priest, or noble generally obligated themselves for some period of service; but the term could vary widely, from a few months to a few years, and was determined by the agreement negotiated between employer and employee. Thus, service in this context need not imply any significant loss of status or the conditions of work endured by "unfree" laborers. Continued dependency on a patron once in America was in most cases voluntary rather than a result of binding legal constraints. Similarly, whereas Choquette (chap. 5) shows that soldiers sent to French Canada had to sign on for periods of service a good deal longer than the three-year term of the engagés, Pieter Jacobs (chap. 3) has found that enlistment in military contingents bound for the New World from Spain could allow men to avoid the legal and financial requirements of emigration if they successfully deserted on arrival in an American port, a not uncommon practice. The arrangements by which some German redemptioners repaid relatives, friends, or patrons the cost of their passage provide another example of emigrants whose status in terms of continuing financial obligations was indeterminate; they were neither entirely free nor unfree.[14]

The vast majority of unfree laborers emigrated as indentured servants (British), engagés (French), and redemptioners (German), serving from two or three years to seven or eight, but there were also large numbers of convicts and political prisoners who served much longer terms. It is impossible to be precise about the proportion of the total migrant stream who found their way to America as unfree laborers. Indentured servants comprised between 75 and 85 percent of settlers who emigrated to the Chesapeake in the seventeenth century. Tobacco planters, as one authority has recently written, lived in "a sea of servants." The same was true of sugar planters, since the bulk of servants who left Britain between 1630 and 1660 went to the West Indies. Perhaps 60 percent of emigrants to all British colonies in America in the seventeenth century arrived under some form of labor contract.[15] Similarly, most French- and German-speaking emigrants had their passages to America wholly or partially paid. In British and French North America, cheap white labor was vital to the early development of colonial economies and predated the adoption of slavery by several generations. The Chesapeake "tobacco industry," for example, depended on a steady supply of white servants throughout the seventeenth century; slaves did not arrive in significant numbers until the 1680s and 1690s. "White servitude," Eric Williams comments, "was the historic base upon which Negro slavery was constructed."[16]

The evolution of the colonial indenture system has received a good deal of attention. As David Galenson points out, "Fundamentally, indentured servitude was an institutional arrangement that was devised to increase labor mobility" from Europe to America.[17] There were several key elements in the development of the system. First, "the marginal productivity of labor in many parts of colonial America" was much greater than in Europe and sufficiently high to allow bound workers to repay the cost of their passage across the Atlantic in four or five years. Second, the purely practical problem of how to arrange loans for poor workers unable to afford the cost of passage was overcome by the adoption of contracts that placed the principal responsibility for the enforcement of the servants' obligations, specified in the indenture or provincial laws, on the planters who purchased them. Merchants involved in the servant trade were not obliged to supervise laborers in the colonies, becoming instead the essential go-betweens supplying labor, like any other commodity in demand, to those who wanted and could afford it. Consequently, the risk to the exporter was minimized (in terms of the death or escape of servants). Third, planters could buy and sell the labor of servants, detailed in the indenture, which gave them considerable flexibility in meeting their labor needs. Finally, servants were encouraged to emigrate by the prospect of regular work, board and lodging in the short term, and the possibility of establishing themselves as planters after their service was completed.[18]

That, at least, was the ideal. Promoters stressed that the poor and unemployed in overpopulated Europe could find work and land of their own in the sparsely settled (i.e., by Europeans) expanse of colonial America. Without doubt, the attraction of cheap and abundant land was a powerful magnet for many poor settlers who had little reason to remain in their native countries. The reality proved quite different, however. Planters were usually determined to get as much work as possible out of their servants before their contracts expired. Colonial laws provided little protection for servants. The buying and selling of indentures meant that servants had no say in who they worked for or the day-to-day conditions of servitude. Cut off from kin and friends and far away from home, they were virtually powerless in the face of abuses. Pere du Tertre's comments about the harsh treatment of French servants in the West Indies in the mid-seventeenth century recall Richard Ligon's description of English and Irish servants' conditions in Barbados:

> The Island is divided into three sorts of men, viz. Masters, Servants, and Slaves. The slaves and their posterity being subject to their Masters for ever, are kept and preserved with greater care than the servants, who are theirs but for five years, according to the law of the Island. So that for the time, the servants have the worser lives, for they are put to very hard labour, ill lodging, and their diet very slight. . . . As for the usage of the Servants, it is much as the Master is, merciful or cruel.

In early Virginia, planters "dealt in servants the way Englishmen dealt in land or chattels" even though the "buying and selling [of] men and bois," John Rolfe noted in 1619, was "held in *England* a thing most intolerable."[19]

Harsh treatment of servants did not result solely from planters' avarice or abuses of the system but reflected the low esteem in which they were held. Virginia and Barbados, Sir Josiah Child believed, "were first peopled by a sort of loose vagrant People, vicious and destitute of a means to live at home (being either unfit for labour, or such as could find none to employ themselves about, or had so misbehaved themselves by Whoreing, Thieving or other Debauchery, that none would set them to work)." Public opinion changed little over time. According to William Eddis in 1770, most inhabitants of Maryland "conceive an opinion that the difference is merely nominal between the indented servant and the convicted felon."[20]

An unusually rich outpouring of recent research allows us to examine the social origins of English indentured servants in some detail.[21] Analysis of lists of settlers leaving major ports in the seventeenth and eighteenth centuries suggests that indentured servants came from a broad cross section of society, embracing paupers and vagrants, unskilled laborers, those employed in low-grade professional and service trades, smallholders, domestic and agricultural servants, textile workers, and even a few sons of gentlemen.[22] The vast majority were young, single, and male. Over three-quarters of the servants who left England in the seventeenth century were male, rising to over 90 percent between 1718 and 1775. Most, male and female, emigrated between the ages of sixteen and twenty-five. There were, however, significant fluctuations in age distribution, which suggests important changes in the social composition of servants across the period. Since, for obvious reasons, planters and merchants preferred to recruit mature, able-bodied men for labor in the colonies, the increasingly youthful profile of servants, especially males, suggests that by the late seventeenth and early eighteenth centuries, supplies of the most highly prized laborers were drying up.[23]

The picture for British emigration is complicated by the fact that many servants arrived in the colonies without indentures and were not recorded in lists from the major ports. They tended to be younger, were more likely to be illiterate, and generally came from lower social origins than indentured servants. Length and terms of service were in these cases regulated by the colonial courts and were usually severer than for servants indentured in England. Servant emigration was therefore multilayered. From time to time, the most desirable laborers, English men in their early twenties, were in short supply, and hence recruiters rounded up workers less in demand: women, unskilled youths, convicts, and the Irish. The peak periods of "high-quality" servant emigration appear to have been from roughly 1630 to 1690 and 1773 to 1776, but across the entire period, there was a steady flow of low-status migrants entering British America.[24]

As already mentioned, many fewer women servants emigrated from Britain than men. Men and boy servants were far more attractive to merchants and planters because their labor potential was considered greater. Women were sometimes put to work in the fields alongside the men, but it is unlikely that they consistently produced as much as male hands. Their primary duties revolved around "Howsholdworke" and all sorts of light tasks and errands. Little is known about their backgrounds. Of the 226 women who left Bristol between 1654 and 1686, and whose status was recorded, 214 were described simply as spinsters, 10 were widows, and 2 were wives of male servants. The London lists occasionally reveal a glimpse of their lives before leaving England. Mary Read, formerly a servant of Jane Corfield, had been committed to the Bridewell for "pilfering" two chickens from the shop of her master, John Corfield. Presumably, this was why her mistress consented "freely to part with her." Elizabeth Day bound herself for four years in Virginia with the consent of her husband, Stephen Day, sawyer; Hester Speed's husband had been "slaine in the rebellion in the West," a reference to Monmouth's uprising.[25] Throughout the seventeenth century, approximately 30 percent of women left England when under the age of twenty and a further 50 percent below twenty-five. Given that the average age of first marriage was around twenty-four, it appears that the great majority of female servants emigrated at or below the average marrying age. The idea that the colonies were a lively marriage mart was familiar to contemporaries. Describing Maryland, George Alsop believed that "the Women that go over into this Province as Servants, have the best luck here as in any place of the world besides; for they are no sooner on shoar, but are courted into a Copulative Matrimony, which some of them (for aught I know) had they not come to such a Market with their Virginity, might have kept it by them untill it had been mouldy."[26] As in much else relating to servant experience, the reality was very different from the puffery of promotional literature. Women servants were even more vulnerable to abuse than their male counterparts.

Servants came from towns and villages scattered throughout Britain, but by far the largest numbers were from London and southern England. In the seventeenth century, London and the Home Counties, followed by Bristol's hinterland and the area around Liverpool, stand out as the most important regions. Large numbers also emigrated from Ireland, particularly to the West Indies, where by the 1650s they formed the majority of laborers in Barbados. During the eighteenth century, as the numbers of

English servants declined, those from Scotland and Ireland dramatically increased. Well over 100,000 Scots-Irish emigrated from 1700 to 1760, and a further 55,000 Protestant Irish and 40,000 Scots left for America in the fifteen years before the Revolution. As Bailyn suggests, "The magnitudes of these figures become clear when they are seen in their local contexts: 40,000 Scots represent 3 percent of the entire population of Scotland in 1760; 55,000 Irish represent 2.3 percent of the Irish population."[27]

Emigration was, in the main, a two-stage process, shaped by the same general social and economic forces that influenced broader internal migratory patterns. Recent research on the relationship between migration within England and emigration has shown that they "were intimately linked," representing, as David Souden says, "joint but lagged responses to current circumstances, and the extension and retraction of the margin of migration."[28] Servants were a subset of a much larger group of young and single people who moved from village to town and town to city in search of greater opportunities than were to be had at home. Arriving in the major ports and cities—London, above all—they found there were plenty of people like themselves looking for work and precious little of it. Some eked out a living as best they could; others moved elsewhere or returned to their native communities; still others took ship for America. Moving to the colonies in this sense was a spectacular form of subsistence migration—a means of keeping alive hopes for eventual prosperity, modest comfort, or at least survival.[29]

How does the British experience compare to other countries? In the French West Indies, servants played an essential role in the beginnings of colonization since, like their counterparts in the British islands, they provided the bulk of the labor force before the arrival of slavery. Most, according to Gabriel Debien, were recruited in French ports of embarkation or surrounding countryside, although a substantial number came from farther afield. The migratory patterns of emigrants from Le Havre, Dieppe, La Rochelle, Honfleur, and Nantes appear to have more in common with those of English servants from the outports—Bristol and Liverpool, for example—than emigrants who sailed from London. Migration fields were less extensive and rural origins more prominent than in the case of emigrants from the English capital. Like British servants, French engagés tended to be young, male, and from the lower strata of society. Huetz de Lemps has found that nearly 70 percent leaving Bordeaux between 1713 and 1717 were between 15 and 19, while another 20 percent were under 25. The average age was 20.2 years, which compares to between 17.5 and 20.4 for servants leaving London from 1718 to 1729.[30] All were male, and the great majority had no specified trade. Later in the century, servants were typically older and more often had a designated occupation.

Servant emigration to the French West Indies was organized on the same principles as those governing British emigration. In return for the cost of their passage across the Altantic, board and lodging, and a small sum on completion of service, engagés contracted to serve usually for three years. Merchants in the colonial ports funded their transportation to the islands where they were sold to planters who then had the responsibility of enforcing the contract. Despite the servere conditions under which servants lived and worked, there appears to have been a steady flow of emigrants throughout the colonial period, in contrast to French Canada, which struggled to attract settlers and where the State was forced to involve itself actively in the recruitment and transportation of indentured servants, soldiers, and *filles du roi*.[31]

German emigrants exhibited somewhat different characteristics. The majority settled in the middle colonies of British America rather than the staple-producing islands or Chesapeake. While many arrived as bound laborers during the eighteenth century, the redemptioner system was different from indentured servitude in several respects. The system allowed variable terms of service in America according to how much or little the emigrant was able to contribute toward the cost of transportation. Redemptioners were also given time after arrival to raise the outstanding sum and so redeem any service owed. These features, Wokeck points out, were particularly suited to family emigration since teenage children could take on indentures to defray part of the overall cost of the passage. Because the great bulk of German-speaking emigrants settled in Pennsylvania, there was a good chance that relatives or friends already in the colony would help pay off some of the debts incurred during the move. Thus, at least down to the Seven Years

War, the incidence of family migration was high. Rather like English emigration to New England, families were headed by mature men who were able to capitalize on their resources partially to finance the move. After 1763, as the number of German emigrants declined, family migration decreased and the proportion of young, single males arriving as indentured servants rose steadily. The servant trade between Rotterdam and Pennsylvania, in its final phase, took on the same impersonal and exploitative features that characterized the British and French trades.[32]

Of the movements treated here, the Spanish case was distinctive in that emigration was not conditioned by the need to recruit large amounts of European labor for the development of American enterprises. Spain alone among the colonizing nations of the early modern period controlled and settled regions of the New World that were densely populated by indigenous peoples who practiced intensive agriculture and had highly organized political, social, and economic systems. In taking over such civilizations, the Spanish were able to take advantage, both directly and indirectly, of the productivity of Indian labor despite the catastrophic loss of Indian populations owing to the ravages of epidemic disease following contact. In the principal centers of Spanish colonization—above all, in Mexico and Peru, which from the 1540s flourished as a result of the immensely profitable silver mines and a virtually self-sufficient agricultural base—Spaniards depended on their retainers and African slaves to provide not mass, menial labor (which they extracted from the Indians) but rather European skills and, as a by-product of their skills and training, supervision for Indian labor.

The rapid and precocious development of society and economy in Spanish America created a situation in which the extent and variety of opportunities available to potential emigrants from all levels of society generally sufficed to sustain a fairly high rate of emigration requiring little or no systematic governmental or commercial organization and intervention. Thus, while it was easy enough for officials, entrepreneurs, and other individuals of means to find servants and employees to fill their entourages, they seldom retained their services for long in the face of the ample opportunities even relatively humble emigrants encountered in the Indies.

Continued dependency was usually assured only through positive incentives rather than negative constraints. The result was an immigrant group in Spanish America remarkably free of legal obligations (such as labor contracts) that might restrict their liberty of movement and choice, although they were, of course, often influenced by continuing ties of patronage, kinship, or debt.[33]

Poverty and Profit: Motives for Emigration

Economic opportunity in the broadest sense constituted the single most important motivating factor for emigrants from all countries to all destinations throughout the period. Most emigrants left the Old World in the expectation of improving their economic circumstances, whether this meant settling permanently overseas or making sufficient money to return home as wealthy "ex-colonials" or absentee landlords. Among the upper ranks of emigrants, the decision to seek new economic opportunities in America represented something of a calculated risk; they could transform their economic standing (and hence their social status) from "middling" to perhaps comfortable, well-off, or even better.

The economic condition of the majority of emigrants who departed as bound laborers was far different. Whether tramping the highways of southern England en route to London or hiking the roads of western France to the Atlantic seaboard, servants formed part of a broad stream of poor, young, and displaced persons who sought work and shelter in the major towns, cities, and ports. The same imperatives that encouraged people to migrate within the country influenced the decision to take ship for the colonies. Low levels of profit and productivity from an unskilled and underemployed work force, the dominance of the agricultural sector, which tied the great bulk of workers to backbreaking labor on the land, primitive technology, poor communications, segmented and underdeveloped markets, and vulnerability to adverse weather conditions, seasonal changes, and disease were the major causes of the endemic poverty that characterized early modern Europe. Poverty, in turn, was a major contributor to long-distance mobility.[34]

England provides the clearest example of the link between poverty and emigration. Its population rose from about three million in 1550 to four million by 1600 and over five million in 1650. The increase would have been most obvious in the sprawling suburbs and slums of the major cities, but in the countryside, particularly wood-pasture and forest areas, rapid demographic growth led to land shortages, growing social polarization, and migration. Contemporaries were alarmed by the specter of a burgeoning army of "masterless men"—vagrants, the idle and dissolute—infesting the highways and swarming into towns and villages, bringing disease and disorder in their wake. Harvest failure and dearth, recurrent between the 1590s and 1640s, brought widespread misery as well as sporadic food and enclosure riots throughout central and southern England. By midcentury, the third world of the poor had risen, in some regions, to startling proportions. Little wonder the period from 1630 to 1660, "probably among the most terrible years through which the country ever passed," witnessed the climax of English emigration to America.[35]

The perception of poverty, of course, varied a great deal. James Horn suggests that early Virginia attracted numerous impoverished gentry and younger sons seeking fame and fortune in an English version of the *conquista*. Others sought the tobacco coast as a refuge from debtors or in the hope of recouping losses sustained in trade and speculation at home. A number of the emigrants who left Trujillo for New Spain in the 1570s were in serious financial difficulties, "living on or below the threshold of poverty." They depended on financial assistance from family, patrons, or employers to make the move to America. In most cases, however, free emigrants were influenced by both push and pull factors in making the decision to settle in America. Perceived poverty at home offered a negative counterpoint to the prospect of better opportunities overseas. Letters from Spanish emigrants in the New World to relatives and acquaintances at home frequently referred to the "misery" of life in Castile, while portraying the economic possibilities of the Indies in positive but realistic terms. Free emigrants can be described in terms of "betterment migration," where movement is not solely a consequence of necessity but is encouraged "by the hope of social and economic improvement."[36] Favorable reports about the Delaware valley were circulating in southwestern Germany from the early eighteenth century and undoubtedly contributed to the attraction of America for German-speaking emigrants.

Most free emigrants were attracted to the colonies by the prospect of profit and wealth, but there were many variations on this theme. In the first phases of colonization, the possibility of plundering indigenous peoples and amassing great fortunes attracted a rather heterogeneous group who chiefly aimed to get rich quick and return home. The same principle applies to the development of plantation colonies, particularly the West Indies. Planters and merchants frequently moved to America for a few years, or long enough to realize a handsome profit, and then left.[37]

Even from the outset, however, there were those who emigrated with no clear intention of returning home. Economic security, the chance to set up a farm or small plantation, religious toleration, and "quiet" government all contributed the evolution of permanent settlements where profit was merely one factor among many conditioning the move to America. Emigrants who settled in the northern and middle colonies of British America, French Canada, and, in time, most of Spanish America generally belonged to this latter category of settlers. Pennsylvania, for example, was not only a "good poor man's country" but also had a reputation for broad-based religious toleration that attracted Anabaptists, Baptists, and Moravians from Germany besides large numbers of Quakers and Independents from England. Neighboring Maryland was a refuge for Catholics and also welcomed Puritans and other sects from Virginia. Virginia Anderson has recently emphasized that Puritans who emigrated to the Bible Commonwealth of New England were not influenced simply by religious zeal and the prospect of erecting a godly community; they hoped to prosper and live in at least modest comfort. There was no contradiction, as Calvin taught, between serving God and prospering in one's chosen trade.[38]

Moving to the New World

Two major factors that shaped the process of moving to the colonies, to a greater or lesser extent, can be identified: the state and private organization. Governments played a crucial role in sanctioning conquest and settlement, encouraging people to emigrate, and regulating the trade in servants or passage of free settlers. The degree of involvement of the state depended on a number of considerations: how far central government desired or was obliged to concern itself with the development of its colonies, the role played by autonomous agencies such as trading companies, merchants, and planters, and the general social economic background against which emigration took place. Perhaps the single most important determinant, however, was simply the relative attractiveness of any given destination. Colonies that appeared to offer few opportunities could not generate self-sustaining movements, and the state might attempt to intervene. French settlement in Canada provides a good example of the lengths to which some governments would go to promote colonization. Choquette shows that in the absence of self-sustained mass emigration, the French government was forced to encourage and finance settlement, not only in the initial stages but down to the end of the regime in 1763. Much of the recruitment, military and civilian, was supervised by the Ministere de la Marine. Naval officials organized the enlistment of soldiers and, whenever possible, skilled workers. Other agencies—the Compagnie des Indes Occidentales, hospitals, the church, prisons, and Ferme Generale—contributed civilian recruits in the form of indentured servants, filles du roi, and convicts. Government intervention was less evident in the settlement of the French Antilles, where market forces played a major role in attracting colonists throughout the seventeenth century. In the following century, however, the government promoted the continuing emigration of poor indentured servants against the wishes of planters and merchants. Ministers believed that it was essential to maintain a significant "white" presence on the islands to guard against slave revolt and invasion by the British or Dutch.[39] Frequently, the interests of the State were at variance with those of colonists.

In other countries, state involvement took different forms. The legislation that evolved to regulate emigration to Spanish America to some extent reflected the ideology associated with the establishment of the Inquisition, conquest of the last Muslim kingdom of Granada, and expulsion of the Jews from Spain in the late fifteenth century: the aspiration to create a uniform and devoutly Christian *communitas*. In Spain, royal legislation and authority functioned not to encourage emigration but to prevent the departure to the New World of persons classed as "undesirable": Jews, Moriscos, Gypsies. Almost alone among European colonizers, the Spanish crown did not conceive of its American possessions as a potential dumping ground for those condemned as troublemakers and criminals. Yet the legislation regulating emigration was far from monolithic in its effects. Discretionary enforcement of many provisions (such as restrictions on the emigration of married men departing without their wives) suggests that the crown and its officials were not so much concerned with preserving the purity of society in the New World as with collecting the fees and bonds associated with emigration and maintaining a general supervisory authority over the movement. Political expediency and financial benefits to the State were more important than following the strict letter of the law or some utopian ideal of society in Spanish America.

Apart from sanctioning colonization and regulating the trade in servants, the British government took little interest in emigration during most of the colonial period. Settlement was left entirely to private interests: trading companies, merchants, and planters. Only in the sphere of convict transportation, and to a limited extent, attracting foreign settlers, did the government develop a policy of actively encouraging and financing emigration, but even here the organization of the trade was left to the mercantile community. Not until the eve of the American Revolution was there any official concern about the hemorrhage of manpower from Britain.[40]

A number of similarities stand out in the pattern of privately organized emigration. First was the importance of family, kin, and friendship connections. Early modern Spanish emigration frequently was a collective undertaking in which family and kinship groups and networks incorporated the opportunities offered by the New World into their overall strategies for enhancing or preserving family stability and fortunes on both sides of the Atlantic. Involvement in and orientation toward the Indies within certain families resulted in the appearance of cycles and traditions of emigration in which people followed their relatives to America, sometimes after many years and often over more than one generation.[41] The relatively small size and coherence of the cities in Extremadura studied by Altman fostered the maintenance of communications and connections across the Atlantic, which, in turn, encouraged people to consider emigrating to join compatriots who would be in a position to help them get established in America. Similar mechanisms operated in Germany where, according to Wokeck, emigration became "*self-generating* as successful immigrants first reported favorably and invited and then supported relatives, friends and former neighbors in settling in America." Free English emigrants to the Chesapeake, as Horn shows, were frequently encouraged to emigrate and were helped in the colonies by relatives and acquaintances. In all three societies—Spanish, German, and British—kinship and friendship were vital to maintaining links between the Old World and the New.[42]

The distinction between emigrants who had kin, friends, and contacts in America and those who did not constituted a crucial difference between settlers and had a significant bearing on their fortunes in the colonies. Most emigrants—the poor, indentured servants, soldiers, unmarried girls—lacked not only money but also *human capital*. They had no one to help them adjust to life in the New World, no one to protect them if necessary; no family, friends, or patrons. Given the high levels of illiteracy among the lower classes, it is doubtful that they were able to keep in touch with relatives at home. In a sense, they had either abandoned or had been abandoned by their families. The social world of the poor was, at least initially, very constricted and provides a stark contrast to the expansive, transatlantic community enjoyed by some richer members of colonial society.

In the absence of family and friends, organization of the mass movement of the poor to America was undertaken by merchants, mariners, and planters. Operating largely independently, and responding to the ebb and flow of colonial trade, mercantile interests in London, Rotterdam, and the French Atlantic ports financed the transportation of hundreds of thousands of settlers; this form of emigration was a *market-driven* phenomenon. While this may be obvious, it is nevertheless worth stressing because without the lure of profits and a sufficiently high return on capital invested, there could have been no major shift of European population to the New World. Neither strategic considerations nor the desire to propagate Catholicism or Protestantism among newly discovered indigenous peoples would have generated the enormous volume of emigration that was one of the key characteristics of the period. Historians have therefore rightly emphasized the role of merchants in providing the essential link between Europe and America. They financed the cost of the emigrants' passage, arranged transportation, and supervised the sale of servants in the colonies. Throughout Europe, those sections of the trading community with transatlantic interests were responsible for the direction and regulation of emigration on a massive scale in response to the labor demands of the colonies.[43]

The great variety of motives for emigrating to the New World—poverty and despair, the hope of quick wealth, commercial benefits, setting up a smallholding, the search for religious toleration, or the effort to establish a godly community far from the oppressions and corrupting influence of ancien regimes in Europe—and the different social contexts from which emigrants were drawn underlines the diversity of migrant streams that converged on America across three centuries. Such differences were reflected in the method or means by which emigrants were able to undertake the move across the Atlantic and the attitude toward emigration displayed by European governments. The ways by which people heard about prospects overseas, the encouragement of family, friends, patrons, and the state, were powerful influences on the individuals' decision to emigrate and helped shape the form and direction of the movement.

Equally clear from this brief consideration of four European countries in the early modern period is that there were important similarities in patterns of emigration. First, the majority of men and women arrived in America under some form of labor contract. Plantation societies' voracious demands for a constant supply of cheap labor were met initially by recruiting Europe's underemployed, poor, and unwanted before switching to African and, to a lesser extent, Indian slaves. For unfree emigrants, moving to the New World represented a desperate lottery: a few winners achieved wealth and social prominence; the great bulk of losers went to an early grave or exchanged destitution in Europe for poverty and obscurity in America. Second, despite the high risks, emigration tended to be self-generating. If there were significant numbers of reluctant emigrants in the form of convicts or political prisoners, nevertheless by far the great majority of settlers took ship voluntarily, attracted by better prospects in the New World. Emigration was stimulated and maintained by market forces. Third, the critical distinction between free and unfree emigrants (and those of intermediate standing), in terms of opportunities and social developments, had an enormous impact on the evolution of colonial society. In some cases, such as the British West Indies, tiny planter elites dominated the political and economic lives of a mass of servants and slaves; in others, where unfree laborers were relatively few, the social gradient among Europeans was less steep. The use of indigenous and African labor in Spanish and Portuguese America resulted in the formation of societies based on a hierarchy of race and class in which Europeans occupied the upper ranks, while social distinctions within European society were modified to some extent by the new opportunities and exigencies of the new context. The proportion of free to unfree emigrants and the potential for bound laborers to become full members of their respective societies following their term of servitude are issues worthy of further comparative analysis.

A major conclusion that emerges from this volume is that studies of the peopling of America and subsequent development of colonial societies cannot be divorced from the European contexts from which emigrants were drawn. Europe and America in the early modern period are best conceived in terms of numerous and overlapping transatlantic societies—Spanish, Portuguese, British, and French, to name only the most prominent—intimately linked by ties of commerce, politics, kinship, and personal association. An understanding of the factors that encouraged people to emigrate, the means by which they were able to move to America, their motives for leaving their home countries, their hopes and expectations in the New World can only be achieved by detailed consideration of the *specific* backgrounds from which they came. If colonial societies resulted from the meeting of the Old World with the New, historians must abandon traditional national perspectives that have artificially set Europe apart from America and the experiences of one colonizing nation from those of others. Instead, we must focus on the rich and complex interrelationships that bound European nations to their colonies and, in some sense, to one another in terms of historical experience. These perduring transatlantic ties, with all their implications for currents and crosscurrents of influence and change in both Old World and New, formed the basis for the "making of America."

Notes

1. Syntheses embracing Pan-American social developments within a transatlantic framework are rare. Historians and historical geographers have tended to focus on particular national entities: British America, Spanish America, and French Canada, for example. See, however, D. W. Meinig, *The Shaping of America: A Geographical Perspective on 500 Years of History.* Vol. 1, *Atlantic America, 1492–1800* (New Haven and London, 1986), esp. Pt. 1; James R. Gibson, ed., *European Settlement and Development in North America: Essays on Geographical Change in Honour and Memory of Andrew Hill Clark* (Folkestone, Kent, 1978); R. Colebrook Harris, "The Simplification of Europe Overseas," *Association of American Geographers, Annals* 67 (1977). For an interpretive account, see Louis Hartz, *The Founding of New Societies: Studies in the History of the United States, Latin America, South Africa, Canada, and Australia* (New York, 1964).

2. For studies of emigration from Europe to the New World, mainly in a national context, see Peter Boyd-Bowman, *Patterns of Spanish Emigration to the New World (1493–1580)* (Buffalo, 1973); Magnus Morner, "Spanish Migration to the New World Prior to 1810: A Report on the State of Research," in Fredi Chiappelli, ed., *First Images of America* (Berkeley and Los Angeles, 1976), vol. 2; Gabriel Debien, *Les Engagés pour les Antilles (1634–1715)* (Paris, 1952); Marc Gaucher, Marc Delafosse, and Gabriel Debien, "Les Engagés pour le Canada au 18e Siècle," *Revue d'Histoire de l'Amérique Française* 13–14 (1959–1961); Henry A. Gemery, "Emigration from the British Isles to the New World, 1630–1700: Inferences from Colonial Populations," *Research in Economic History* 5 (1980): 179–231; and "Markets for Migrants: English Indentured Servitude and Emigration in the Seventeenth and Eighteenth Centuries," in P. C. Emmer, ed., *Colonialism and Migration: Indentured Labour Before and After Slavery* (Dordrecht, 1986), 33–54; Russell R. Menard, "British Migration to the Chesapeake Colonies in the Seventeenth Century," in Lois Green Carr, Philip D. Morgan, and Jean B. Russo, eds., *Colonial Chesapeake Society* (Chapel Hill, 1988), 99–132; Bernard Bailyn, *Voyagers to the West: A Passage in the Peopling of America on the Eve of the Revolution* (New York, 1986); R. J. Dickson, *Ulster*

Emigration to Colonial America, 1718–1775 (Antrim, 1976); Audrey Lockhart, *Some Aspects of Emigration from Ireland to the North American Colonies between 1660 and 1775* (New York, 1976); Walter Knittle, *The Early Eighteenth-Century Palatine Emigration: A British Government Redemptioner Project to Manufacture Naval Stores* (Philadelphia, 1936); Marianne Wokeck, "The Flow and the Composition of German Immigration to Philadelphia, 1727–1775," *Pennsylvania Magazine of History and Biography* 105 (1981): 249–278; Ian C. C. Graham, *Colonists from Scotland: Emigration to North America, 1707–1783* (Ithaca, 1956).

3. This figure and those offered in table 1.1 are necessarily tentative since few reliable estimates exist for the period. They are intended only to give an impression of the relative magnitude and timing of emigration from Europe, and thus no great weight should be attached to any one figure.

4. Philip D. Curtin estimates that nearly 10 million slaves were transported to the New World from the sixteenth to the late nineteenth century; *The Atlantic Slave Trade: A Census* (Madison, 1969), table 39, 137. Approximately 50 million people emigrated from Europe to the United States in the nineteenth and twentieth centuries, while the impact of immigration was even greater in parts of modern Latin America. In Argentina, for example, one-third of the population in 1914 was foreign born; John Higham, *Send These to Me: Immigrants in Urban America* (Baltimore and London, rev. ed. 1984), chap. 1.

5. Bailyn, *Voyagers to the West*, 24–26; Gemery, "Markets for Migrants," 35–40; Altman, Choquette, Horn, and Wokeck, this volume.

6. Bailyn, *Voyagers to the West*, 24.

7. Jack P. Greene, *Pursuits of Happiness: The Social Development of Early Modern British Colonies and the Formation of American Culture* (Chapel Hill and London, 1988), 7–8; Gemery, "Markets for Migrants," table II, 40.

8. The most extensive work on the regional origins of sixteenth-century Spanish emigrants has been done by Peter Boyd-Bowman in a series of articles, several of which appear in *Patterns of Spanish Emigration*. For the period 1493–1519, which Boyd-Bowman calls the "Antillean period" because of the settlement of the islands, he found that 30 percent of emigrants came from the provinces of Seville and Huelva alone: "More than one colonist in every three was an Andalusian, one in every five was from the province of Seville, and one in every six claimed the city of Seville as his home town" (5). In one decade (1509–1519), two-thirds of the 308 women counted were from Andalusia, over half from Seville

itself (8). In the next period, 1520–1539, Andalusia's share decreased to 32 percent (from nearly 40 percent), whereas Extremadura's share increased slightly, from 14.1 percent to 16.6 percent (17). Well over half the women, however, still were from Andalusia in this period (26). In the next period Boyd-Bowman studied (1540–1559), Andalusia's share increased to just over 36 percent (44) and again to over 37 percent in the years 1560–1579 (72).

9. See William Douglass and Jon Bilbao, *Amerikanuak: Basques in the New World* (Reno, 1975), 81.

10. Gemery, "Markets for Migrants," 34–40; Bailyn, *Voyagers to the West*, 24–26.

11. Bailyn, *Voyagers to the West*, Pts. II and V; Meinig, *Atlantic America*, Pt. 2. John J. McCusker and Russell R. Menard, *The Economy of British America, 1607–1789* (Chapel Hill, 1985), chap. 10. See also the migration studies mentioned above, n. 2.

12. See, for example, Eric Williams, *Capitalism and Slavery* (New York, 1966); Evsey D. Domer, "The Causes of Slavery and Serfdom: A Hypothesis," *Journal of Economic History* 30 (1970): 18–32; Carville Earle, "A Staple Interpretation of Slavery and Free Labor," *Geographical Review* 68 (1978): 51–65; H. A. Gemery and J. S. Hogendorn, eds., *The Uncommon Market: Essays in the Economic History of the Atlantic Slave Trade* (New York, 1979); Richard S. Dunn, "Servants and Slaves: The Recruitment and Employment of Labor," in Jack P. Greene and J. R. Pole, eds., *Colonial British America: Essays in the New History of the Early Modern Era* (Baltimore and London, 1984), 157–194; and *Sugar and Slaves: The Rise of the Planter Class in the English West Indies, 1624–1713* (London, 1973), chap. 2; Edmund S. Morgan, *American Slavery, American Freedom: The Ordeal of Colonial Virginia* (New York, 1975); Russell R. Menard, "From Servants to Slaves: The Transformation of the Chesapeake Labor System," *Southern Studies* 16 (1977): 355–390; David W. Galenson, "White Servitude and the Growth of Black Slavery in Colonial America," *Journal of Economic History* 61 (1981): 39–47; Vera Rubin and Arthur Tuden, eds., *Comparative Perspectives on Slavery in New World Plantation Societies*, Annals of the New York Academy of Sciences, vol. 292 (New York, 1977).

13. Gary B. Nash, *Red, White and Black: The Peoples of Early America* (Englewood Cliffs, N.J., 2d ed., 1982); Ronald H. Chilcote, ed., *Protest and Resistance in Angola and Brazil* (Berkeley and Los Angeles, 1972); Fredrick P. Bowser, *The African Slave in Colonial Peru, 1524–1650* (Stanford, 1975); James Lockhart, *Spanish Peru, 1532–1560* (Madison, 1968); Colin A. Palmer, *Slaves of the White God: Blacks in*

Mexico, 1570–1650 (Cambridge, Mass., 1976); Gad Hueman, ed., *Out of the House of Bondage: Runaways, Resistance, and Marronage in Africa and the New World* (London, 1986).

14. Ida Altman, "A New World in the Old: Local Society and Spanish Emigration to the Indies," chap. 2; Leslie Choquette, "Recruitment of French Emigrants to Canada, 1600–1760,'' chap. 5; Pieter Jacobs, "Legal and Illegal Emigration from Seville, 1550–1650," chap. 3; all in this volume.

15. For example, A. Roger Ekirch, *Bound for America: The Transportation of British Convicts to the Colonies, 1718–1760* (Oxford, 1987). Darrett B. Rutman and Anita H. Rutman, *A Place in Time: Middlesex County, Virginia, 1650–1750* (New York, 1984), 1: 71; Gemery, "Markets for Migrants," 33, 40.

16. Williams, *Capitalism and Slavery*, 19.

17. See the bibliographies in Abbot E. Smith, *Colonists in Bondage: White Servitude and Convict Labor in America, 1607–1776* (Chapel Hill, 1947); and David W. Galenson, *White Servitude in Colonial America: An Economic Analysis* (Cambridge, 1981).

18. Galenson, *White Servitude*, 12–13.

19. Richard Ligon, *A True and Exact History of the Island of Barbados* (London, 1673), 43–44; Edmund S. Morgan, *American Slavery, American Freedom: The Ordeal of Colonial Virginia* (New York, 1975), 128.

20. Sir Josiah Child, *A New Discourse of Trade* (London, 1693), 170.

21. For a discussion of this literature, see Gemery, "Markets for Migrants," 33–54.

22. Galenson, *White Servitude*, chaps. 3 and 4; and "'Middling People' or 'Common Sort'? The Social Origins of Some Early Americans Reexamined," *William and Mary Quarterly*, 3d ser., 35 (1978): 499–524; David Souden, "'Rogues, Whores and Vagabonds'? Indentured Servant Emigrants to North America, and the Case of Mid-Seventeenth-Century Bristol," *Social History* 3 (1978): 23–41; Anthony Salerno, "The Social Background of Seventeenth-Century Emigration to America," *Journal of British Studies* 10 (1979–80): 31–52; James Horn, "Servant Emigration to the Chesapeake in the Seventeenth Century," In Thad W. Tate and David L. Ammerman, eds., *The Chesapeake in the Seventeenth Century: Essays on Anglo-American Society* (Chapel Hill, 1979), 51–95.

23. Galenson, *White Servitude*, chap. 2.

24. Lorena S. Walsh, "Servitude and Opportunity in Charles County, Maryland, 1658–1705," in A. C. Land, Lois Green Carr, and Edward C. Papenfuse, eds., *Law, Society, and Politics in Early Maryland* (Baltimore,

1977), 112, 113; Morgan, *American Slavery, American Freedom*, 216; Bailyn, *Voyagers to the West*, chap. 5; Galenson, *White Servitude*, chaps. 3 and 4.

25. Galenson, *White Servitude*, 23–26; Horn, "Servant Emigration," 62–65.

26. "A Character of the Province of Maryland, by George Alsop, 1666," in C. C. Hall, ed., *Narratives of Early Maryland, 1633–1684* (New York, 1910), 358; Horn, "Servant Emigration," table 2.

27. Bailyn, *Voyagers to the West*, 26.

28. Quoted by Gemery, "Markets for Migrants," 45.

29. Horn, "Servant Emigration," 66–74; and "Moving on in the New World: Migration and Out-Migration in the Seventeenth-Century Chesapeake," in Peter Clark and David Souden, eds., *Migration and Society in Early Modern England* (London, 1987), 172–212; Souden, "'Rogues, Whores and Vagabonds'?," 28–32; J. Wareing, "Migration to London and Transatlantic Emigration of Indentured Servants, 1683–1775," *Journal of Historical Geography* 7 (1981): 356–378.

30. Christian Huetz de Lemps, "Indentured Servants Bound for the French Antilles in the Seventeenth and Eighteenth Centuries," chap. 6, this volume; Galenson, *White Servitude*, 31.

31. Huetz de Lemps, "Indentured Servants"; Choquette, "Recruitment of French Emigrants," chap. 5, this volume.

32. Marianne Wokeck, "Harnessing the Lure of the 'Best Poor Man's Country': The Dynamics of German-Speaking Immigration to British North America, 1683–1783," chap. 7, this vol.; Sharon V. Salinger, *"To Serve Well and Faithfully": Labor and Indentured Servants in Pennsylvania, 1682–1800* (Cambridge, 1987), chaps. 1–4.

33. James Lockhart's *Spanish Peru* remains the best single study of the careers, patterns of association, enterprises, and activities of Spaniards in the New World during the formative period of Spanish American society. For a more general discussion, see James Lockhart and Stuart B. Schwartz, *Early Latin America: A History of Colonial Spanish America and Brazil* (Cambridge, 1983).

34. For an overview of European economic developments, see Jan de Vries, *The Economy of Europe in an Age of Crisis, 1600–1750* (Cambridge, 1976); Carlo M. Cipolla, ed., *The Sixteenth and Seventeenth Centuries*, in Fontana's History of Europe Series (Hassocks, Sussex, 1977), chaps. 1–2, 4; Pierre Leon, *Economies et Sociétés Pre-Industrielles*, T. 12, *1650–1780* (Paris, 1970), Pt. 1; William Doyle, *The Old European Order, 1660–1800* (Oxford, 1978), chap. 1. See also, Peter Clark, ed., *The European Crisis of the 1590s* (London, 1985).

35. L. A. Clarkson, *The Pre-Industrial Economy in England, 1500–*

1750 (London, 1971), chaps. 1, 7; E. A. Wrigley and R. S. Schofield, *The Population History of England, 1541–1871: A Reconstruction* (Cambridge, 1981); Anthony Fletcher and John Stevenson, eds., *Order and Disorder in Early Modern England* (Cambridge, 1985), Intro.; A. L. Beier, *Masterless Men: The Vagrancy Problem in England, 1560–1640* (London, 1985), chaps. 2–3; and *The Problem of the Poor in Tudor and Early Stuart England* (1983); David Underdown, *Revel, Riot and Rebellion: Popular Politics and Culture in England, 1603–1660* (Oxford, 1985), chaps. 1–4; Joan Thirsk, ed., *The Agrarian History of England and Wales*, vol. iv, *1500–1640* (Cambridge, 1967), 621.

36. James Horn, "'To Parts Beyond the Seas': Free Emigration to the Chesapeake in the Seventeenth Century," and Ida Altman, "A New World in the Old," chaps. 4 and 2, this volume; Peter Clark, "The Migrant in Kentish Towns, 1580–1640," in Peter Clark and Paul Slack, eds., *Crisis and Order in English Towns, 1500–1700* (London, 1972), 137.

37. Horn, "'To Parts Beyond the Seas,'" and "Moving on in the New World," 193–194; Ida Altman, *Emigrants and Society: Extremadura and Spanish America in the Sixteenth Century* (Los Angeles, 1989), chap. 7; Huetz de Lemps, "Indentured Servants"; Dunn, *Sugar and Slaves*, 101–103, 142–143, 161–163, 200–201, 213–222.

38. Wokeck, "Harnessing the Lure of the 'Best Poor Man's Country'"; David W. Jordan, "'The Miracle of This Age': Maryland's Experiment in Religious Toleration, 1649–1689," *The Historian* 47 (1985): 338–359; Virginia D. Anderson, "Migrants and Motives: Religion and the Settlement of New England, 1630–1640," *New England Quarterly* 58 (1985): 339–383.

39. Choquette, "Recruitments of French Emigrants"; Huetz de Lemps, "Indentured Servants." See, also, Jacobs, "Legal and Illegal Emigration."

40. Smith, *Colonists in Bondage*, chaps. 1, 2, 4–9; Bailyn, *Voyagers to the West*, chap. 2; Knittle, *The Early Eighteenth-Century Palatine Emigration*.

41. Altman, *Emigrants and Society*, chap. 4; and "Emigrants and Society: An Approach to the Background of Colonial Spanish America," *Comparative Studies in Society and History* 30 (1988): 170–190.

42. Wokeck, "Harnessing the Lure of the 'Best Poor Man's Country'"; Horn, "'To Parts Beyond the Seas'"; Altman, "New World in Old." See also, David Cressy, *Coming Over: Migration and Communication between England and New England in the Seventeenth Century* (Cambridge, 1987), esp. chap. 11.

43. Galenson, *White Servitude*, 10–15, 97–102, 117–168; Salinger, "To Serve Well and Faithfully," chap. 1; Wokeck, "Harnessing the Lure

of the 'Best Poor Man's Country,'"; David Souden, "English Indentured Servants and the Transatlantic Colonial Economy," in Shula Marks and Peter Richardson, eds., *International Labour Migration: Historical Perspectives* (London, 1984), 19–33, 235–238; Gemery, "Markets for Migrants," 45–49.

Two

A New World in the Old: Local Society and Spanish Emigration to the Indies

Ida Altman

The relationship between a society and a colonizing enterprise can be analyzed by looking at a variety of factors that collectively define and sustain it. These include institutions of state and church, economic networks and undertakings, and the ideological framework (sometimes a post hoc construction) that provides the justification for the conquest and exploitation of other peoples, as well as more elusive considerations of cultural and social transference and change from metropolitan to colonial society. Central to the colonizing enterprise is the movement of people, who in their lives and careers create concrete and often enduring ties between sending and receiving societies. The study of early Spanish America generally has emphasized the impact of the relationship between metropolis and colony on the formation of societies in America while paying less attention to the Spanish origins and background of institutions and socioeconomic patterns or to the continuities that characterized long-term development in the Hispanic world as a whole. Consideration of the lives and activities of a group of emigrants to Spanish America in the sixteenth century who are defined by their common ties to a particular place—and hence, in many senses, to each other—provides the means not only to trace or test the continuity or transformation of patterns in the

New World setting but also to approach the question of change and impact on society in Spain itself.

To discuss the consequences of the opening of the New World and emigration on Spain, we must take into account both the broad context of Spanish historical development and the more narrowly defined milieu of local society that experienced most directly the effects of emigration and return migration. The movement to the Indies took place in the midst of demographic, political, economic, and even social changes that affected in some degree nearly every aspect of life in the Iberian kingdom of Castile. By the turn of the century, a new standard of religious homogeneity and orthodoxy had supplanted the pluralistic *convivencia* of Christian, Muslim, and Jewish kingdoms and communities of the Middle Ages. Populations in urban areas especially began to increase rapidly after the epidemics and famines of the first decade or two of the sixteenth century, with many towns and cities nearly (or more than) doubling in size.[1] Ferdinand and Isabella's drive to assert royal power over elements of the late medieval polity and society which had gained considerable independence during the period of royal weakness in the fifteenth century resulted in the creation, strengthening, or consolidation of a number of institutions (the Inquisition, the unification of the *hermandades* or rural militias, the royal council). The monarchs also succeeded in establishing more effective control over municipalities (at least those directly under the crown) and the unruly military orders, which had jurisdiction over huge areas, particularly in the southwest, from the time of the reconquest. The extension of royal control in the late fifteenth century made the regularization and standardization of tax collection feasible. During the sixteenth century, the municipalities increasingly acted as agents of royal government, overseeing the assessment and collection of ordinary taxes and supplying recruits for the frequent military levies ordered by the crown.

The period also brought economic change and expansion. The remarkable growth of Seville, linked to the opening of the New World and the rise of the Atlantic economy, as a center for commerce, industry, and commercial agriculture was probably the single most spectacular result of the economic shifts and trends of the late fifteenth and sixteenth centuries. There are indications, however, that most of these developments predated or perhaps coincided with the beginnings of the New World venture and that internal and external changes fueled each other. Seville was a major port city, with a thriving international community of merchants and financiers, long before 1492. Likewise, the financial nexus that linked the trade fair of Medina del Campo and the wool trade of the north with Seville in the south was long-standing. The Mesta, the association that represented the transhumant sheep raisers, was once considered to have been the favored Castilian economic institution well into the sixteenth century; but during the sixteenth century, transhumant stock raising was losing ground to commercial agriculture (vines and olives) and local stock raising in parts of the southwest and south (Extremadura and Andalusia).[2] Demographic trends—immigration from France, the shift of population from center to periphery and from rural to urban areas, the expulsion of the unconverted Jews in 1492—no doubt affected the pace and nature of economic change, but we still know little about the specific relationship of demographic trends or political events to economic developments or, in a sense, social change.

What was the significance for Castile of the opening of the New World in this period? The impact of the Indies was multifaceted, variable, and complex in its effects over time and place, complicated in that some aspects of society and economy were touched directly and decisively while others were virtually unaffected. But assessing the impact is problematic. The long-term debate over the price rise of the sixteenth century, for example, suggests the difficulty of reaching firm conclusions even regarding those questions that seem to lend themselves most readily to quantification.[3] It is more difficult yet to pin down amorphous and qualitative questions of social change and cultural and intellectual perceptions or expectations.

In some respects, emigration is an aspect of the European response which appears well suited to quantitative analysis. For the past two decades we have known quite a bit about the geographic origins and distribution of emigrants and the demography of the movement (numbers of women and families, age distribution).[4] Yet the volume of illegal emigration and the gaps in the sixteenth-century passenger lists (of "legal" emigrants) limit the extent to which we can produce numbers and statistics that fully define and quantify the phenomenon.[5] Gauging the overall demographic impact on Castile of the out-migration is even more elusive. Common sense alone suggests that the rapid population growth of the sixteenth century more than compensated for the departure of relatively small numbers of emigrants (usually estimated at roughly 250,000 to 300,000 for the first century, out of a Castilian population of perhaps seven million); in fact, the most recent demographic work for the period virtually ignores emigration as a factor affecting population.[6]

Clearly, quantitative methods can yield only a partial understanding of the impact of the Indies enterprise on Castilian society. The study of emigration need not be limited to such approaches, however. The examination of the lives, activities, and decisions of emigrants and their families and fellow townspeople provides insight into the functioning and structure of local society and how that society responded to or was affected by the participation of people in the settlement of America. Analyzing patterns of emigration in relation to the milieu that nurtured and facilitated it reveals the adaptability and fluidity that in many senses characterized Spanish society. This flexibility made it possible for many people to respond to the opening of the New World by going there permanently or temporarily, often accompanied or followed by family members, while it simultaneously worked to preserve, rather than threaten, the stability of socioeconomic structures and relations at home.

Here I discuss the relationship between emigration to America and local society in two neighboring cities in northeastern Extremadura, a region in southwestern Spain, paying particular attention to the development of cycles and networks of emigration that shaped the movement from this area and reflected the impact of the maintenance of ties between emigrants and people at home. Cáceres and Trujillo were fairly small cities, with populations of somewhere between 6,000 and 9,000 in the sixteenth century,[7] lying within a well-defined geographic subregion. The economy was mainly pastoral. Hog breeding and the cultivation of vines and olive trees supplemented sheep raising as the region's major commercial activities. Textile manufacture was of some importance in Cáceres especially, although the industry primarily supplied relatively low-quality cloth for the local market. Sheep raising actually encompassed two distinct sectors: the enterprises of local stock raisers (predominantly but not exclusively the local nobility) and the pasturage rented out to transhumant stock raisers of Castile or León who annually brought their herds to the south for winter grazing. Here again, as the largest private holders of land, the nobility dominated the rental of pastures.

Cáceres and Trujillo were much alike in a number of ways. Reconquered within years of each other in the thirteenth century, they remained (with only brief exceptions) under royal jurisdiction. Each controlled a large district that included towns, villages, and hamlets of varying size and wealth (although Trujillo's district was larger and more populous) and owned extensive properties (*propios*) consisting of grazing lands, olive groves, and the like. Their city councils were similarly constituted, with membership limited to the *hidalgo* (privileged) group and effectively monopolized by the principal families of the local nobility, and both cities had sizable religious establishments with several parishes as well as a number of convents and monasteries. The cities even resembled each other in their physical development and structure. Long before the sixteenth century, both had expanded well beyond their old enclosed nuclei, with the large and irregular main plazas lying outside and below the walls, although the walled centers of both remained the strongholds of the traditional nobility. Both cities experienced a great boom in private and public construction in the late fifteenth and sixteenth centuries, so that the buildings reflected the styles of that period.

At the same time, the cities were quite separate and distinct. Their districts were contiguous, and certainly there was some contact, movement, and intermarriage (especially at the level of the nobility) between the two; but their most important economic, political, and institutional ties linked them to the major centers of trade and capital (Segovia, Burgos, Medina del Campo, or Seville), higher learning (Salamanca, Alcalá), or government (the royal court, the high court of appeals in Granada) outside the region rather than to each other. Furthermore, despite the basic homogeneity of the region in which the cities lay and the similarity of their institutions and socioeconomic structures, people identified strongly with their specific place of origin and were much aware of their city's or town's history, which underscored and strengthened the sense of separateness and independence.

In the sixteenth century, Extremadura was a sparsely populated region, rather isolated and provincial despite the major routes of travel and communication that traversed the area and linked the cities to Toledo, Madrid, Salamanca, and Seville. The region had held relatively little attraction for the succession of conquerors and colonizers (Romans, Visigoths, Muslims) that over the centuries held sway in the Iberian peninsula, and it never existed as an independent kingdom or state. With the final reconquest of the region's key towns in the thirteenth century, Extremadura was simply incorporated into the crown of Castile. Nevertheless, although ranking well behind Andalusia as a source of emigrants in the sixteenth century, Extremadura as a whole played an active and important part in the movement to America almost from the beginning. The participation of *extremeños* overall was high in relation to the region's population; most notably, Extremadura contributed a seemingly disproportionate percentage of the active leadership in the early period of exploration, conquest, and settlement.

The second governor of Hispaniola, the first focus for Spanish efforts in the Caribbean, was Frey Nicolás de Ovando. Credited with consolidating royal authority on the island, Ovando was from a noble family of Cáceres.[8] The conqueror of Mexico, Hernando Cortés, came from Medellín, and Francisco Pizarro, conqueror of Peru, was from Trujillo, as was his relative Francisco de Orellana, explorer of the Amazon. Other prominent extremeños in the New World included Hernando de Soto, Diego de Almagro, and Pedro de Alvarado. These men stimulated interest in and emigration to the Indies from their hometowns and regions not only by their example but also through direct recruitment. Ovando, who departed Spain in 1502, was accompanied by a contingent of some 2,500 which included Francisco Pizarro and other extremeños, although apparently none of Ovando's own relatives.[9] The likely impact of Ovando's governorship on emigration from his hometown can be judged by comparing the known figures for emigration from Cáceres and its neighbor, Trujillo, in the early sixteenth century. Although for the century as a whole, emigration from Trujillo was more than double that from Cáceres (921 known emigrants compared to 410),[10] up until 1520, cacereño emigrants were nearly twice as numerous.

The real flood tide of emigration, from Extremadura as from elsewhere, followed the conquests of Mexico and Peru and the opening of those mainland areas to settlement in the 1520s and 1530s. At this point, the leadership role of extremeños in the Indies proved crucial not only in fomenting further emigration from the Cáceres-Trujillo region but in determining its focus and direction for decades to come. When Pizarro returned to Spain in 1529 to secure the royal *capitulaciones* (charters) for the conquest of Peru, he visited Trujillo and recruited his four half-brothers and a number of other men from his hometown and surrounding areas (including Cáceres) for the undertaking.[11] Early on, then, people from Trujillo especially but to a great extent from Cáceres as well forged significant connections with events and people in Peru. In the sixteenth century, Peru was the heavily favored destination, with nearly half the Trujillo emigrants and a third of the cacereños going there directly. Since many people moved on from their initial destination (especially in the early years), probably well over half the emigrants from the region as a whole ended up in Peru at some time. Not surprisingly, people in sixteenth-century Extremadura tended overwhelmingly to identify Peru with the Indies enterprise itself, sometimes making "Peru" synonymous with the Indies and almost invariably referring to returnees as "peruleros," not "indianos."[12]

What has been said so far about emigration from Cáceres and Trujillo—the discrepancy in overall volume of emigration, the strong connection to Peru—would suggest that the movements from the two cities, while remaining essentially separate, both converged and diverged. In the broadest sense, emigration from both places fell well within the parameters of what is generally known about sixteenth-century Castilian emigration. The movement as a whole was characterized by the predominance of private over public initiative and organization, the presence of increasing numbers of women and children over time, and the participation of a range of socioeconomic and occupational groups that constituted the middle sectors of Castilian society (only the very wealthy and very poor hardly participated). Other important aspects of the movement between Spain and the Americas included the maintenance of connections between people at home and in the Indies and among emigrants from the same locality who settled in the New World; the formation of networks that conveyed people to the same destinations as relatives or fellow townspeople who had preceded them, fostering cycles in which families might send one or more emigrants each generation; and the movement of temporary and permanent returnees back to their hometowns.[13]

Cacereño and trujillano emigrants conformed to these patterns, but close study of the two cities reveals some differences. While these were often differences of emphasis rather than kind, consideration of local variations sheds light on the question of impact. Specific circumstances shaped emigration from a given locality, while at the same time the nature of the movement away from and back to a place itself might affect local society, buttressing or modifying socioeconomic and political structures and patterns and perhaps, in turn, influencing emigration. The early participation of hidalgos in the movement from Cáceres is a good case in point, since it seems to have had a lasting influence on the composition of the emigrant group over time. Nearly 22 percent of the cacereño emigrants were hidalgos, while for Trujillo, the figure was closer to 14 percent. Not surprisingly—although the relationship to the composition of the emigrant group was not necessarily direct—nearly two-thirds of the twenty-six permanent returnees to Cáceres were hidalgos, while perhaps no more than one-third of the sixty-two trujillanos who went home belonged to that class.[14]

In many cases, emigration to the Indies was as much a collective, family enterprise as an individual undertaking, even if only one or two individuals actually made the move. Position in the family could work to determine who would leave home and who would stay. The younger sons in noble families who expected to receive only a limited inheritance often chose emigration as an alternative to careers in the military, church, or other professions, and a decline in family fortunes could mean the emigration of several siblings. The departure of entire families seeking opportunities in the New World became more common over time; fifty-six families left Trujillo in the sixteenth century, accounting for 27 percent of the emigrant group in that period. Thirteen families, with fifty-six people (or about 14 percent of the total emigrant group) left Cáceres.

Family also played a role in the move itself. Family members at home or in the Indies often provided assistance in the form of loans or donations to finance the journey. People already in America not only sent their relatives at home money and sometimes detailed instructions for making the rather complicated preparations for the journey but often returned to collect family members themselves or sent friends or agents to do so. A man named Alvaro Rodríguez Chacón left Trujillo around 1550 to settle in Mexico City, where he became a merchant; in 1574, he returned to Trujillo to get the children he had left behind. The next year he went back to Mexico with an entourage that included his three unmarried sons, his married daughter with her husband and four children, and his daughter's brother-in-law, wife, and children as well as several criados (servants).[15] Departing emigrants also turned to relatives to take charge of their property and affairs at home in their absence and placed young chidren in their care.

Emigrants followed their relatives to the same destinations, where they could hope for assistance in establishing themselves. The strength of this attraction was substantial. Francisco González de Castro left Trujillo in 1540 and settled in Santa Marta. Over the next almost forty years, three of his brothers (one married with three children), two nephews, and a first cousin with his wife and children (who eventually returned to Spain) went to live in Santa Marta or elsewhere in New Granada.[16] Alonso Guerra of Cáceres, who received an encomienda (grant of Indian labor and tribute) from Francisco Pizarro in Peru in 1537, eventually attracted six members of his immediate family—five sons and a brother—to Peru.[17]

Thus, the emigration and successful career of one individual could set in motion events that might affect a family for years. Licenciado Diego González Altamirano of Trujillo first went to Peru to serve on the audiencia (high court) of Lima in 1551, when he was around thirty years old; his wife, Doña Leonor de Torres of Granada, was ten years younger. Their eldest son, Francisco, was born in Lima and probably one or two of their other children as well. The same year they went, Licenciado Altamirano's brother, Juan Velázquez, also left for Peru. He had made an agreement with the alleged brother and sister of Alonso de Toro, a trujillano who had been murdered in Peru, that he would collect Toro's estate and bring charges against the guilty parties in the murder. Velázquez was to keep one-third of what he recovered. In 1559 or 1560, Licenciado Altamirano and his family returned to Trujillo, where he had a house on the plaza and a number of properties. In 1569, he left Trujillo again, probably accompanied by his oldest son, to take the post of criminal magistrate (alcalde de crimen) of the audiencia of Lima. His wife later joined him in Peru with their other four children. The family returned again to Trujillo by 1577, although one daughter stayed in Lima where she had entered a convent. Licenciado Altamirano died in Trujillo in 1579.[18]

The family's involvement in Peru did not end there. Pedro de Valencia, the son of Licenciado Altamirano and Juan de Velázquez's sister, Juana González de Torres, was in Peru by 1567, and in the 1570s, two of Valencia's sisters were also.[19] Licenciado Altamirano's son, Licenciado Don Blas Altamirano de Torres, subsequently went back to Peru and served as criminal magistrate and later as judge on the Lima audiencia in the seventeenth century; his oldest brother, Don Francisco, who inherited the family entail in Trujillo, also possibly went back to Peru at some point.[20] Family size, resources, experiences, and connections, then, frequently provided the impetus and means for emigration as well as determined the specific form it would take.

The brief discussion of the families of Francisco González de Castro, Alonso Guerra, and Licenciado Altamirano suggests that careful examination of the choices and activities of emigrants, of the timing and objectives of their moves, and of the connections that bound them to other emigrants can reveal a great deal about the formation and operation of networks that shaped and facilitated emigration to the New World. At the same time, these choices and patterns reflect aspects of local socioeconomic structures and relations that, in turn, could affect the nature of the movement. It has been suggested that family position and relations were of great importance in determining who might emigrate, how, and where. At the same time, however, individuals and families participated in other and broader social networks that hinged on more distant ties of kinship and acquaintance and patron-client relations which frequently acted to supplement and extend the ties of close familial relationships. The information available on a large group of emigrants who left Trujillo for New Spain (Mexico) in the period 1568–1580 brings into focus how these varying ties of relationship, patronage, and acquaintance could intersect and bolster one another and, in turn, facilitate emigration.

Within the sixteenth century movement from Trujillo to the Indies as a whole, this group that went to Mexico was unusual chiefly for its size and direction. Starting with the departure from Trujillo in 1568 of Gonzalo de las Casas, son of a cousin and close associate of Cortés named Francisco de las Casas who had been in Cuba, Mexico, and Honduras and acquired an encomienda in Oaxaca in New Spain,[21] at least 114 individuals from Trujillo left for New Spain. Many of them were accompanied by spouses, servants, or apprentices who were not from Trujillo or whose origin cannot be established with certainty (the wife of stonecutter and architect Francisco Becerra, for example, was from the town of Garciaz in Trujillo's district). This figure is also conservative in that in cases where the number of children in a family was not listed, they have been counted as two, although of course there could have been more (hence, a unit of parents and children is counted as four people, unless otherwise known). This group constituted more than half the total number (207) of trujillanos who chose New Spain as their initial destination during the sixteenth century.

While neither the overall socioeconomic composition of the group nor the existence of a number of familial and other ties among the emigrants was atypical, the notable concentration and coherence of the group endowed it with a somewhat distinctive character; it offers a kind of distillation of many of the patterns that characterized the larger movement as a whole. And although emigration from the area of Cáceres and Trujillo in the sixteenth century was hardly a mass phenomenon, the movement from Trujillo in that decade was substantial enough to have been quite noticeable to people at home. In fact, the 1570s marked an all-time high for emigration from Trujillo; a total of 209 individuals departed, including 79 to Peru. This was followed by a near-record low number (35) of departures in the 1580s. It should also be noted that while the 1570s witnessed the second highest level of departures from Cáceres (64 in that decade, compared to 100 in the 1530s), emigration from Cáceres also dropped to nearly nothing in the 1580s (3 known emigrants). The coherence and size of the Trujillo group that went to New Spain in the 1570s suggest, therefore, that people were making careful and considered decisions about when to go, with whom, and where.

Probably the two most notable aspects of the socioeconomic and demographic composition of the group were its strongly familial character and the presence of a large number of adult men already established in their occupations. Only seven of the adult men failed to specify any trade or profession, although three were listed as criados, one of them a carpenter. Gonzalo de las Casas was an encomendero (holder of an encomienda) by virtue of his father's death and his succession to the grant. Francisco Becerra, the master stonecutter who emigrated in 1573, was accompanied or soon was followed by two of his former apprentices, now stonecutters in their own right.[22] In 1574, another master stonecutter, Diego de Nodera, applied for a license to emigrate to New Spain with his wife, an apprentice, and a criada. He too had known and worked with Becerra in Trujillo. Nodera's father, a master in the same trade, had lived many years in Mexico, apparently dying sometime before 1574. The younger Nodera, twenty-three years old in 1574, might have been refused a license to emigrate, although it is not known why.[23] The group also included three blacksmiths, two shoemakers, a tailor, three carpenters (including an uncle and nephew) and an apprentice carpenter, a barber, and three priests. Alvaro Rodríguez Chacón, mentioned before as returning to Mexico with a number of family members in the 1570s, was a merchant.

The strong showing of trades and professions and the familial character of the group together suggest that most of the male emigrants were relocating with their families in the expectation of settling down to work at an occupation in which they were already trained and working. The group included fourteen families consisting of two parents and at least one child; eight families of one parent and children; and two married couples with no children. The notion that most of these emigrants had a fairly clear idea of the situation awaiting them is strengthened by the fact that a number of them were joining relatives already in New Spain. In 1574, Catalina de Cuevas took her four sons, two daughters, and a servant to join her husband, Juan de Contreras. Isabel García traveled with her three daughters, brother, and servant to join her husband in 1577.²⁴ In 1578, sisters Isabel García la Castra and Isabel García la Cuaca took their five children to join their half-brother, Francisco García, who had left Trujillo ten or twelve years earlier and every year sent them money and other things.²⁵

There were other such cases. Alonso Blanco took his three daughters and son to join his cousin, Martín Blanco, a priest from Cabeza del Buey whom Alonso Blanco actually had assisted financially several years before when he decided to leave Spain for Mexico.²⁶ In 1577, Juan Ramiro followed his brother, Alonso Ramiro, to Mexico, two years after the latter went there. Alonso Ramiro and his wife, Inés García, had gone to Mexico with their three sons, and Ramiro had set up a tailor's shop in Puebla de los Angeles with his cousin, Alonso Morales. Morales wrote to Juan Ramiro in 1576 urging him to leave Castile and "take yourself out of that wretchedness," adding that in New Spain work paid well and food was cheap. He also suggested that Ramiro should bring along his (Morales's) brother, Pedro.²⁷ Finally, Alonso González, a priest, went to Mexico in 1576 and almost immediately sent back for his sister, Juana González, her husband, Juan Rubio, and their five children.²⁸

Yet other connections bound many of the emigrants. In addition to the nuclear family units mentioned, several individuals made the journey with siblings or other relatives. Juana González traveled in the party of her brother-in-law, Francisco Jiménez, a shoemaker who took his wife and daughters to New Spain; and María González accompanied her sister, Inés González, and her husband and daughter.²⁹ The priest Hernando de Cuevas took his sister, Ana González de Cuevas, to New Spain in 1574.³⁰ Brothers Juan de Plasencia, a carpenter, and Bartolomé Rodríguez both went to New Spain in 1576 but as criados of different men. They jointly presented testimony in support of their application to emigrate to the local authorities in Trujillo, so we might surmise that they had decided to make the journey before securing positions with their respective employers, neither of whom was from Trujillo.³¹ Similarly, the priest Bachiller Alvar García Calderón took as his servant a twenty-four-year-old native of Jaraicejo (a town with close ties to Trujillo but not in its jurisdiction) named Francisco Díaz in 1577. Díaz was the nephew of Isabel García of

Trujillo, who took her daughters to Mexico to join her husband in the same year.[32] Here again one might guess that Díaz's decision to emigrate hinged primarily on his aunt's departure, whereas his employment as the priest's criado provided him with the means to make the move at the same time that she did. It has already been observed that Alvaro Rodríguez Chacón was responsible not only for the emigration of his own children and grandchildren but also for that of the brother and family of his son-in-law.

Like those of kinship, the ties of patronage and acquaintance provided structure for the group and, in some instances, doubtless stimulated the decision to move. The role played by encomendero Gonzalo de las Casas (who already had lived for some time in Mexico) was crucial. Las Casas might have persuaded Becerra, who had worked on his house in Trujillo, to leave Trujillo for the New World. Once reestablished in Mexico, Las Casas apparently sent home asking for specialists in architecture and construction to come work on the monastery being built in Yanhuitlán.[33] The connections between Becerra and the other stonecutters who emigrated in the 1570s have been discussed. Las Casas also served as the guarantor for Andrés Hernández, a carpenter who left Trujillo for New Spain in 1580 with his wife, children, an apprentice, and his nephew, Alonso Sánchez, a carpenter.[34] Doubtless Las Casas acted as a focus of attraction for emigrants from Trujillo and as a pivotal figure within the trujillano community in New Spain. Alonso González, who went to Mexico City in 1576, the year of his arrival sent a letter back to his sister and brother-in-law in Trujillo with one of Las Casas's criados who was returning to Spain.[35] Well-established and influential men like Las Casas and Alvaro Rodríguez Chacón were responsible for recruiting a substantial number of emigrants, just as more modest individuals like Alonso Ramiro and Alonso González sought to convince their close relatives to join them in New Spain.

In terms of socioeconomic composition, the large number of artisans and servants among the emigrants underscores the group's essentially plebeian nature. Although there were hidalgos among these emigrants, with the exception of Las Casas and his three sons (one of whom was probably illegitimate), most of the hidalgos appear to have been fairly marginal. The predominance of commoners in this particular group was not unusual but instead reflected quite closely the composition of the sixteenth-century emigrant group from Trujillo as a whole. Fourteen, or 12 percent, of the 114 individuals in the group claimed hidalguía, very close to the proportion of hidalgos identified among the total group of 921 emigrants who left Trujillo in the sixteenth century. The proportion of hidalgos among Cáceres's emigrants was higher. The early and prominent participation in the Indies enterprise of members of some of Cáceres's leading noble families set a precedent that continued to affect the composition of the cacereño emigrant group throughout the sixteenth century. While certainly some of Trujillo's important families were well represented in the Indies (especially, of course, in Peru), their participation seems to have begun later than that of the cacereño nobles and never reached the same levels. Trujillo's emigrants were mainly working-class men and women, endowing the movement from that city with a more strongly plebeian character.

Not only were most of the people in the 1570s group to New Spain commoners but a number of them were experiencing real financial problems. Juan Rubio, brother-in-law of priest Alonso González, in petitioning to go to New Spain in 1578 with his wife and five children to join González, stated that they lived in great ("*grandísima*") poverty. A tavern keeper named Hernán González testified that he had known Rubio and his family for fifteen years and that they were very poor. They made their living by reselling his wine, while the older children helped out by delivering firewood. The family was hard put to find the money for the passage. Alonso González had been in Mexico for such a short time when he sent for them in March 1576 that he could not afford to send any money. He did arrange, however, for them to collect a debt of 42 ducados owed to him for the sale of his "piece of house" and urged them to "leave that miserable country" ("*ruin tierra*"). Juan Rubio estimated that all his belongings might be worth 60 ducados, and he planned to sell his "part of a house."[36] In another case, Lorenzo del Puerto, who stated, "I am a shoemaker by trade and poor person," petitioned to take his wife and daughter to New Spain in 1577. Witnesses claimed that without the necessary capital to invest in his business, Puerto was losing his assets day by day; "he dies of hunger," one said.[37] Sisters Isabel García la Castra and Isabel García la Cuaca, who were single and "poor," asked for a license to go to Mexico in 1578 with their five children to join their half-brother who "is rich." Witnesses testified that the sisters were so poor that if they did not set up a tavern or inn or employ themselves in some disreputable fasion, "they will not be able to support themselves because they are already too old to serve anyone."[38]

Even allowing for a possible tendency to exaggerate the severity of economic circumstances, one can hardly avoid the conclusion that a number of these emigrants were experiencing real hardship in Trujillo and living either on or below the threshold of poverty. In such cases, the financial assistance of relatives, patrons, or employers obviously would be crucial to making the move to America. Juan de Belvis received a license to go to Mexico with his wife and children in December 1570, but he had to renew it in 1576. He had been unable to leave before "for having been poor and with little health."[39] Fabián Hernández applied for and received a license to take his family to New Spain in 1578 but was unable to go within the designated period "for reason of being with much need and labor." He might have gone later, in 1588.[40] Certainly, the cost of passage could deter people of meager means from making the journey. By 1580, the price of passage from Spain to Veracruz (New Spain) or Nombre de Dios (Panama) had risen to between 18 and 22 ducados. The cost of provisions increased expenses another 35 to 50 percent; so by 1580, the total cost of the journey per adult passenger was between 30 and 40 ducados. Purchase of cabin space would mean an additional expense.[41]

In the large group of emigrants who went to New Spain in the 1570s, we have seen a variety of relationships, socioeconomic statuses, and specific circumstances that shaped and influenced individual or family decisions. Viewed collectively, however, these individualized circumstances and decisions suggest underlying similarities that gave coherence to the phenomenon. The most important of these hinged on the motivation and means to emigrate. Studies of emigration often raise the question of the relative strength and importance of "push" and "pull" factors—those circumstances in the home society, on the one hand, that impel certain individuals or groups outward and those elements in the receiving society, on the other, that work to attract settlers. Among the emigrants discussed here, clearly the most basic and important motivation for leaving Trujillo in the 1570s was perceived economic opportunity. The chance to improve the economic opportunities and well-being of oneself and one's family seems to have played a key role in the decisions made by these emigrants, from the poorest to the wealthiest. Alvaro Rodríguez Chacón stated while he was back in Spain that the sole purpose of his visit was to take his children back with him to Mexico "because [they] are poor and without means." His son-in-law Cristóbal Hernández Tripa's brother, Hernán González, said that Cristóbal Hernández would take him and his family because "he has the means and possibility to benefit and help us... with his estate."[42]

We have seen that letters from relatives who preceded these emigrants to New Spain emphasized the theme of improved economic opportunities, generally in realistic terms. Priest Alonso González wrote to his sister and brother-in-law from Mexico that "although this [country] is not what it was," by working hard one still could earn a decent living.[43] Even encomendero Gonzalo de las Casas probably made an essentially pragmatic determination based on his economic possibilities on both sides of the Atlantic when he decided to take his three sons to Mexico. Las Casas's family in Trujillo seems to have been quite well off, if not, perhaps, truly wealthy. In the 1520s, Gonzalo's father, Francisco de las Casas, owned rural and urban properties estimated to be worth 9,000 or 10,000 ducados, and Gonzalo succeeded to the entail created by his parents, which included a house on Trujillo's plaza, on the death of his older brother.[44] Gonzalo's properties in Trujillo were sufficiently ample to enable him to marry all three of his daughters into prominent local families. But by the 1560s, he might have judged that his real wealth and economic future lay in Mexico where his father had been an early encomendero involved in gold mining, not in Trujillo; so he took his sons there.

In almost any case where one attempts to weigh the relative importance of push and pull factors in the decision to move, the evidence for the primacy of one or the other usually is inconclusive; rather, it appears that a complex and dynamic interaction normally occurred between the two. Where there existed a deterioration (real, perceived, or potential) of economic circumstances at home, coupled with the possibility of establishing oneself successfully in the Indies, emigration could become an attractive option. Thus, the search for opportunity might take the form of emigration to America when an individual perceived some realistic means of achieving his or her objectives and expectations there. Frequently, the connection with relatives, patrons, or acquaintances who were planning to make the same move or had already done so offered precisely such means. The other notable similarity that characterized the emigrant group (and not only that of the 1570s) was therefore the existence of connections of relationship and patronage, networks that, in turn, reinforced and made viable the quest for opportunity.

On a larger scale, the development and maintenance of such networks that connected people in Trujillo and Cáceres with emigrants in the Indies and returnees who came back to reestablish themselves in Spain proved central to the movement to the New World and provided opportunities on both sides of the Atlantic to individuals and families whose possibilities otherwise might have been limited. The careers of three members of a hidalgo family of Cáceres—Sancho de Figueroa, Antonio de Figueroa, and Francisco de Avila—show the sustained impact involvement in the Indies could have on one family. All three men were active in Guatemala and Honduras. Sancho and Antonio de Figueroa probably went to America together or around the same time, in the 1520s; both were encomenderos in San Salvador (Guatemala) in the 1540s, although Antonio died by 1549.[45] Francisco de Avila must have followed his brothers and joined them in San Salvador; presumably, he was there when he sold his part of their father's estate to Sancho de Figueroa for 800 pesos de oro.[46] Sancho de Figueroa and Francisco de Avila both returned to Cáceres, the former in the 1540s, the latter perhaps as late as 1570. Possibly Avila did not do as well in the Indies as did his brother Sancho, which might account in part for his long delay in returning. But Sancho de Figueroa, who had no legitimate children, made Avila his universal heir, as did their fourth brother, the vicar Juan de Figueroa, who had remained in Cáceres.[47] After his return, Avila was thus quite well off.

Relatively little is known about the careers and experiences of the brothers in the New World. Sancho de Figueroa's 1549 will and the two inventories of his estate made after his death (which occurred within two years of his return to Spain) show that by the time he returned to Cáceres, he had become a man of some substance.⁴⁸ Whatever wealth he had accumulated must have resulted primarily from his activities in the Indies. A family in which three out of four brothers emigrated surely was not very well off, and their sister, doña Isabel de Figueroa, seems to have made only a modest marriage.⁴⁹ We do have some information on Sancho de Figueroa's economic involvements in Guatemala. He compiled a *probanza*, or testimonial, there in 1537, claiming that he had been a conquistador and received an encomienda from Pedro de Alvarado.⁵⁰ A longtime resident of San Salvador, he owned four stores on the city's main plaza which he promised to leave to a chaplain "to make certain visits to Indian villages." In his will, however, Figueroa arranged for his executors in Guatemala to transfer the stores to the local *cofradía* (confraternity) of Our Lady of the Conception, which he said lacked any other property. Before he left San Salvador, Figueroa signed a notarized statement to the effect that he would return to live in the city.⁵¹ Yet while he retained some ties with San Salvador, his marriage and other activities undertaken after his return to Cáceres suggest that he intended the move back to Spain to be permanent.

One of the executors of Figueroa's will in San Salvador was Francisco de Cabezas, probably his business partner. Figueroa brought 800 ducados belonging to Cabezas with him to Spain, and Cabezas later sent more money to Seville. Figueroa, in turn, sent him ten black slaves and "other things" and requested that Cabezas send "500 pesos of gold from my estate," so evidently he still had an income and property in the Indies. The inventory of Figueroa's estate included records of accounts he had with Cabezas and Cabezas's power of attorney. Figueroa also brought from the Indies sums of money sent by other emigrants there to people in Spain.⁵²

In 1548, after his return from Guatemala, Figueroa married doña Francisca de Ulloa, the daughter of Hernando de Ulloa and Catalina de la Rocha, who brought a sizable dowry to the marriage and the guarantee of half the goods of her father's estate after his death.⁵³ Figueroa died the following year, and his widow, doña Francisca, remarried soon thereafter; she died by 1557. The rather complicated settlement of Figueroa's estate in the late 1550s therefore fell to doña Francisca's second husband, Alonso de Ribera, as the guardian of their children, and Juan de Figueroa, who was administering the estate left by his brother Sancho.

Doña Francisca's brother, Alvaro de Ulloa, prepared an inventory of Figueroa's properties in 1549, and a second was made in 1552.[54] These inventories show that Figueroa's properties and assets were fairly diversified and that he had made a number of investments immediately after returning to Cáceres, spending, for example, well over 2,000 ducados just on the purchase of *censos al quitar* (annuities) in 1548 and 1549. Figueroa was not a large stock raiser, although with his brothers he owned part of a pasture (*dehesa*) called the Arenal, where he grazed a herd of 640 sheep (including rams and six dogs) purchased at the time of his marriage. Although he owned relatively little pastureland and only modest herds, Figueroa did hold a good deal of agricultural property, including grain fields and a vineyard, an orchard, and an olive grove, and hence derived a significant portion of his income from agriculture. Sales from the produce of his estates in 1551 came to around 360 ducados. Unfortunately, the inventories did not include an assessment of the value of the real property he held in lands and houses or the censos he purchased before his marriage, since these items did not represent joint property and therefore were not part of the settlement made between Figueroa's brother and doña Francisca's second husband. Figueroa's household had included six slaves—two women and four men—two of whom died soon after he did. Two of the remaining slaves were sold as part of the final settlement of property.

Sancho de Figueroa made his brother, Francisco de Avila, his heir; if Avila failed to return from the Indies, the estate would go to Sancho's sister's daughter, doña Isabel de Figueroa. Sancho had an illegitimate daughter named Francisca de Figueroa, who was to enter the convent of Garrovillas (a town to the west of Cáceres), where she would have a female slave (from his household) and an income of 6,000 maravedís annually. He donated a dress to each of the two daughters of his cousin, Inés Gutiérrez, who were in the same convent, and left money for dowries for another cousin's daughter and the daughter of a man who lived in Torremocha (a village near Cáceres) to enter the convent of Garrovillas. His nephew, Francisco de Ovando, received a horse with a saddle and bridle, a sword, and a "very good coat of arms."

Figueroa also willed several items to his wife, all of which, of course, she would inherit in addition to her portion of the assets generated during their marriage (the *bienes multiplicados*) and the properties that belonged to her from her dowry and inheritance. She received part of the estate of Cervera (she had inherited half the estate from her father), which Figueroa had bought from her brother, three cows, and all the household furnishings. She also could keep one of the female slaves. Sancho also willed to her a piece of gold jewelry. The final settlement of property did require doña Francisca to give up certain items, however, including the silver Figueroa brought back from the Indies, a sword with a silver hilt, and some printed books and other writings.

By the time Sancho de Figueroa's brother, Francisco de Avila, returned to Cáceres, probably around 1570–71, all his siblings had died, and he became heir to the properties of his brother, Juan de Figueroa (which included some censos and vineyards near the town of Casar), as well as Sancho de Figueroa's estate, which had been administered by Juan de Figueroa, who also acted as the guardian of his niece and nephew (his sister's children, orphans by 1551).[55] Avila married doña María de Paredes in 1573, but the couple had no children before Avila's death in 1583. His wife remarried the following year. According to a local historian of Cáceres, Avila founded an entail and willed the establishment of the convent of San Pedro in his house in the parish of San Juan (one of the parishes outside the walled center of the city); construction began in 1609.[56]

Because of the varied nature of their circumstances and objectives, probably no returnee from the Indies could be called typical; but Sancho de Figueroa and Francisco de Avila in many ways exemplified the aspirations—and limitations—of many emigrants who returned to reestablish themselves at home. Sancho de Figueroa, absent for more than twenty years, returned to Cáceres a much wealthier man than he had left it, married a noble heiress, acquired rents, properties, and slaves, and placed his illegitimate daughter and other female relatives in a convent. Like many other returnees, he maintained some connections and business dealings with people he had known in the Indies. His rise to the upper ranks of cacereño society was cut short by his untimely death, and his failure—like that of Francisco de Avila many years later—to father any legitimate children prevented him from establishing a prominent family line linked to an entailed estate. Francisco de Avila stayed away from Cáceres much longer than did his brother, and his activities after returning suggested less ambition and energy than those of Sancho de Figueroa. Yet he inherited all his brothers' properties, married into a noble family, and might have founded a new convent, fulfilling an aspiration, common to many hidalgos, of creating an *obra pía* (good work, or charity) that would reflect the donor's piety, wealth, and generosity. It appears that ultimately mortality, rather than lack of means or ambition, frustrated the aspirations of these brothers.

Furthermore, again reflecting patterns characteristic of many returnees to Cáceres and Trujillo, the relatives of these brothers by blood and marriage maintained and cultivated connections with other local people involved in the Indies. Alonso de Ribera, the second husband of doña Francisco de Ulloa (Sancho de Figueroa's widow), by his first marriage was the father of two sons who went to the Indies—Rodrigo de Chaves, who returned, and Juan Pantoja de Ribera, who remained in Honduras where he had mines and cacao groves.[57] Alonso de Ribera's daughter, doña María de Ribera, married Juan Cortés, a native of Trujillo, close friend and ally of Hernando Pizarro, and returnee from Peru who had participated in the division of Inca emperor Atahuallpa's treasure at Cajamarca. Juan Cortés acquired a seat on Trujillo's city council after his return. Their daughter, doña Catalina Cortés, married a cacereño nobleman, Diego de Ulloa, and their son, don Gaspar Cortés, married doña Juana de Sotomayor, the daughter of Sancho de Vargas and doña Beatriz Solano; Vargas went to Chile as a royal captain in 1581.[58]

There were also other ties with people who were involved in the Indies. Doña Francisca de Ulloa's daughter by her second husband, doña Catalina de Ribera, inherited an entail created for her by her father (he had also established an entail for his oldest son by his first marriage, Alvaro de Ribera) and married Pedro Rol de Ovando. Pedro Rol had a brother and several cousins who went to the Indies, and two of his siblings married children of the very successful returnee to Cáceres, Francisco de Godoy; Godoy, in fact, was married to Pedro Rol's first cousin, doña Leonor de Ulloa.[59] Sancho de Figueroa's nephew, Francisco de Ovando, also had connections with a cacereño emigrant in the Indies; in the 1550s, he sold rents in a pasture to Juan Cano in Mexico (through Cano's brother, Pedro) for a total of nearly 600 ducados.[60] Cano, an associate of Cortés, became a wealthy encomendero by virtue of his marriage to doña Isabel Moctezuma, daughter of the Aztec emperor and former mistress of Cortés. Juan Cano accumulated substantial properties in and around Cáceres and Aldea del Cano (the town in Cáceres's district where Figueroa's nephew owned a house and lands), as well as in Mexico, before eventually returning to Spain, where he died in Seville in the 1560s.[61]

The connections between families like the Figueroas, Riberas, and Ovandos of Cáceres, while perhaps not as direct and striking as those forged between some of the wealthy and powerful returnee families of Trujillo (which intermarried extensively), nonetheless clearly indicate that involvement in the Indies through family members who emigrated and returned became a factor taken into account in arranging marriages, buying and selling properties, and conducting other transactions. Like the ties of acquaintance and patronage, the common experience of the Indies (even if often indirect) broadened social networks, complementing and sometimes reinforcing the ties of family and kinship. In addition to the economic ramifications of participation in the Indies enterprise, the "American connection" seems to have become something of a social convention and focus of identification that fostered close association among these families, perhaps imbuing them with a sense of distinctiveness in local society.[62]

Discussion of emigration from Cáceres and Trujillo underscores the importance of considering the question of the impact of the New World on the Old in the context of local society rather than at the broader regional or national level. The activities, relationships, loyalties, and expectations of the great majority of people were centered on and shaped by their place of origin and residence. Individuals who left their hometowns for elsewhere in Spain or Europe or emigrated to America often maintained active ties with home; emigrants who returned to Spain from the Indies usually went back to their hometowns. Hence, in the local context, we might expect to find some of the best evidence for the significance of the Indies to Spanish society. Information on emigration from Cáceres and Trujillo suggests that the impact varied from place to place in terms of the importance, size, and composition of the movement to America and the consequences of participation in the Indies enterprise on society at home. These variations are of much interest in terms of both defining the movement as a whole and understanding its relationship to local society. Ultimately, they point not to fragmentation but rather to the underlying coherence of the phenomenon.

The collective, familial aspect of the movement accounted in large part for its social coherence. We have seen that assuring and improving the welfare and possibilities of family members, whether in Spain or in America, was a major concern and priority of many emigrants, regardless of their socioeconomic background or status. Family fortunes, position, and strategy played a crucial role in emigration from beginning to end, and cycles and networks of emigration based on family and ties of patronage and common origin linked cities like Cáceres and Trujillo to people and places in the New World. The sense of familiarity that resulted from these multiple and enduring connections, in turn, encouraged continuing emigration. From the point of view of many people in Cáceres and Trujillo, the Indies were not an isolated and remote enclave of the royal domain but represented a significant extension of the arena in which they could function to pursue opportunity and advancement for themselves, their families, and their compatriots.

Notes

1. See Vicente Pérez Moreda, "El crecimiento demográfico español en el siglo XVI," in *Jerónimo Zurita: Su época y su escuela* (Zaragoza, 1986); and Annie Molinié-Bertrand, *Au siècle d'or: L'Espagne et ses hommes: La population du royaume de Castille au XVIe siècle* (Paris, 1985). Molinié-Bertrand calculates that Burgos grew 192 percent, to 20,000 inhabitants, in the period from 1528 to 1561 (135); Córdoba's *vecinos* (citizens) increased from 5,845 to 11,600 (1530 and 1571 censuses), excluding in the latter figure 2,307 moriscos counted individually (280). Rates of growth were far from uniform in Castile's towns and cities, however.

2. See David E. Vassberg, *Land and Society in Golden Age Castile* (Cambridge, 1984), 79–83.

3. See J. H. Elliott, *The Old World and the New* (Cambridge, 1970), 60–72.

4. See Peter Boyd-Bowman, *Indice geobiográfico de cuarenta mil pobladores españoles de América en el siglo XVI*, 2 vols. (Bogota, 1964; Mexico, 1968). Boyd-Bowman has published a number of articles in which he analyzes his data on sixteenth-century emigration; several were reprinted in his *Patterns of Spanish Emigration to the New World* (Buffalo, 1973).

5. Auke Pieter Jacobs discusses the gaps in the passenger lists and the problems of estimating illegal emigrants in "Pasajeros y polizones: Algunas observaciones sobre la emigración española a las Indias durante el siglo XVI," *Revista de Indias* 172 (1983): 439–479.

6. See Pérez Moreda, "Crecimiento demográfico," 65–66, and Molinié-Bertrand, *Au siècle d'or*. Molinié-Bertrand estimates, for example, that the population of the *partido* (district) of Trujillo grew 39.2 percent in the years 1528–1561, the first period of significant overseas emigration (185–186).

7. Calculations of the cities' populations in the sixteenth century vary a great deal according to the source, and further variations result from the use of different multipliers (usually 4.5 or 5.0); see Pérez Moreda, "Crecimiento demográfico," 62–64, for discussion of coefficients. He suggests that 4.0 may be preferable to 4.5. For population figures for Cáceres and Trujillo, see Jean-Paul LeFlem, "Cáceres, Plasencia y Trujillo en la segunda mitad del siglo XVI (1557–1596)," *Cuadernos de Historia de España* 45–46 (1967); Angel Rodríguez Sánchez, *Cáceres: Población y comportamientos demográficos en el siglo XVI* (Cáceres, 1977), 53; *Historia de Extremadura*, 9 vols. (Badajoz, 1983), 3: 486; Annie Molinié-Bertrand, "Contributions a l'étude de la société rurale dans la province de Trujillo au XVIe siècle," *Melanges offerts a Charles Aubrun*, 2 vols. (Paris, 1972), 2: 128. While the exact figures cannot be established, it is clear that at mid-century the cities had between 6,000 and 9,000 inhabitants and that Trujillo was somewhat larger than Cáceres.

8. For Frey Nicolás de Ovando, see Ursula Lamb's *Frey Nicolás de Ovando: Gobernador de Indias (1501–1509)* (Madrid, 1956); and Troy Floyd, *The Columbus Dynasty in the Caribbean, 1492–1526* (Albuquerque, 1973), 51–54. For the Ovando family, see Ida Altman, "Spanish Hidalgos and America: The Ovandos of Cáceres," *The Americas* 43:3 (January 1987); 323–344.

9. Members of the Ovando family did become active in the Indies later in the sixteenth century; see Altman, "Spanish Hidalgos."

10. The term "emigrants" is used here to refer to individuals who

intended to leave Spain; it is not always possible to determine if a person who planned to emigrate actually did so. The figures are based on a number of sources. The most important published ones are Boyd-Bowman, *Indice geobiográfico*, and the *Catálogo de pasajeros a Indias durante los siglos XVI, XVII y XVIII*, 5 vols. (Seville, 1940–1946, 1980). Additional emigrants were identified in the Archivo General de Indias (AGI), Archivo Histórico Provincial de Cáceres (AHPC), Archivo Municipal de Trujillo (AMT), and the Archivo del Conde de Canilleros (ACC) in Cáceres.

11. See James Lockhart, *The Men of Cajamarca: A Social and Biographical Study of the First Conquerors of Peru* (Austin, 1972), 135–137, for a biography of Francisco Pizarro.

12. Although "indiano" is the more familiar term, I have found only one example of its use in sixteenth-century Trujillo, in 1549; see AGI Justicia 1176, no. 2, ramo 8, testimony of Juan de la Jara.

13. James Lockhart discusses these patterns in his article, "Letters and People to Spain," in Fredi Chiappelli, ed., *First Images of America*, 2 vols. (Los Angeles, 1976), 2: 783–796.

14. These figures include only those people whose hidalguía can be established clearly from the documentation; ambiguous cases were not counted. Cáceres may have had a somewhat higher percentage of hidalgos in its population than Trujillo. Julio Fernández Nieva, *Historia de Extremadura*, 3: 550, estimates that hidalgos formed 15 percent of Cáceres's population in the late sixteenth century and 12.6 percent of Trujillo's. Marie-Claude Gerbet, in *La noblesse dans la royaume de Castille: Étude sur ses structures sociales en Estrémadure (1454–1516)*, 151–152, estimates that 17 percent of the adult males in Cáceres were nobles in the late fifteenth century.

15. AGI Indif. General 2054, 2055, 2056; AGI Contratación 5222; *Catálogo* 5, nos. 3507, 3843.

16. AGI Indif. General 2083, 2087; AGI Contratación 5227; *Catálogo* 3, nos. 1210, 2481, 2509 and 5, no. 1381.

17. AGI Patronato 106, ramo 7; Boyd-Bowman, *Indice* 2, no. 2744; AGI Contratación 2723, no. 2. Alonso Guerra is mentioned as being in the Indies in the 1532 will of Juan de la Huerta of Cáceres (AHPC Pedro de Grajos 3923).

18. See AGI Contratación 5217A for the first trip (1551) and *Catálogo* 5, nos. 1826 and 2887 for the 1569 trip. AGI Contratación 5221 gives ages of family members. Lic. Altamirano's will and many other documents pertaining to the family are in AMT Pedro de Carmona B-1-27. For Velázquez's agreement with Juan de Toro and Marina de Ruiz, see AMT García de Sanabria A-1-1. Juan de Velázquez probably was a minor

in 1551, since his father Francisco González was also a party to the agreement.

19. See AGI Indif. General 2084 (*información* of Diego de Velázquez, vecino of Jaraicejo, longtime retainer of Hernando Pizarro), for Pedro de Valencia. For his sisters, doña María de Valencia and doña Isabel de Altamirano, see AMT Pedro de Carmona B-1-23.

20. Vicente Navarro del Castillo, *La epopeya de la raza extremeña en Indias* (Mérida, 1978), 399, says that Francisco Altamirano de Torres was corregidor of La Paz at some time. Navarro also states (431) that Fray Diego de Torres de Altamirano, bishop of Cartagena in 1617, belonged to the family, but I have found no other reference to a son named Diego.

21. For Gonzalo de las Casas, see *Catálogo*, vol. 4, no. 897. In 1568, he took with him his sons don Francisco and don Andrés (his sons by doña Leonor de Vargas) and Pedro Suárez (his son by Ana de Aguilar). For Francisco de las Casas, see Boyd-Bowman, *Indice* 2, no. 3124, AGI Justicia 117, no. 1, and Justicia 1144, no. 3.

22. For Becerra's apprentices, Alonso Pablos and Martín Casillas, see Navarro del Castillo, *La epopeya*, 391, 415. Alonso Pablos, like Becerra, was the son of a master stonecutter.

23. For Diego de Nodera and his father, see AGI Indif. General 2056. See also Carmelo Solís Rodríguez, "El arquitecto Francisco Becerra: Su etapa extemeña," *Revista de Estudios Extremeños* 29 (1973): 304, 382.

24. For Catalina de Cuevas, see *Catálogo* 5, no. 3583; for Isabel García, see *Catálogo* 5, no. 4339.

25. AGI Indif. General 2059.

26. Ibid.

27. For Alonso Ramiro, tailor, see *Catálogo* 5, no. 3819, AGI Contratación 5222, Indif. General 2055, and Enrique Otte, "Cartas privadas de Puebla del siglo XVI," *Jahrbuch für Geschichte von Staat, Wirtschaft und Gesellschaft Lateinamerikas* 3 (1966): 56–58.

28. AGI Indif. General 2059.

29. See *Catálogo*, no. 3067, for Francisco Jiménez and his family. In a petition of 1574, Jiménez asked to take two "doncellas"—his sister and his wife's sister, as well as his wife, two daughters, and a "criado de su oficio" (see AGI Indif. General 2055); but his sister was not listed with the group in the catalog entry, so it is not known if she went. For María González, see *Catálogo* 5, no. 4376.

30. See *Catálogo* 5, nos. 3595, 3821. For Cuevas's properties and affairs in Trujillo, see AMT Pedro de Carmona A-1-9, and Bartolomé Díaz 1580 (unnumbered).

31. In 1576, Juan de Plasencia was twenty-five years old; see AGI

Contratación 5224. For his brother, Bartolomé Rodríguez, twenty-two years old, see *Catálogo* 5, no. 4168.
  32. See AGI Contratación 5226.
  33. See Solís Rodríguez, "Francisco Becerra," 336.
  34. Navarro del Castillo, *La epopeya*, 401; AGI Indif. General 2060.
  35. AGI Indif. General 2059.
  36. Ibid.
  37. AGI Indif. General 2058; see also *Catálogo* 5, no. 4314.
  38. AGI Indif. General 2059.
  39. AGI Indif. General 2057.
  40. AGI Indif. General 2059.
  41. See Nicholas L. Scrattish, "New Perspectives on Castilian Migration to the Audiencias of Mexico and Lima, 1540–1580" (Ph.D. dissertation, University of California, San Diego, 1976), 120–121.
  42. AGI Indif. General 2054, 2056.
  43. AGI Indif. General 2059.
  44. AGI Justicia 1144, no. 3; for the entail, see Federico Acedo Trigo, "Linajes de Trujillo" (MS, AMT), Loaysa, 184.
  45. Navarro del Castillo, *La epopeya*, 154; Boyd-Bowman, *Indice* 2, no. 2730A; AHPC Pedro de Grajos 3924.
  46. AHPC Pedro de Grajos 3924. A record of the transaction was included in the 1549 inventory of Sancho de Figueroa's estate.
  47. AHPC Pedro de Grajos 3924, 3926.
  48. Sancho de Figueroa's will is in AHPC Pedro de Grajos 3924; the inventories are in AHPC Pedro de Grajos 3924 and Diego Pacheco 4100.
  49. The inventory of the estate of doña Isabel's husband, Alvaro de Ovando, who died in 1547, is also in AHPC Pedro de Grajos 3924.
  50. See Salvador Rodríguez Becerra, *Encomienda y conquista: Los inicios de la colonización de Guatemala* (Sevilla, 1977), 44, 97.
  51. AHPC Pedro de Grajos 3924.
  52. AHPC Pedro de Grajos 3924.
  53. Ibid. Doña Francisca's dowry included half of her father's estate at La Cervera, consisting of a house, farmlands, barley fields, and corrals; half of a vineyard and half of his pastures in Pozo Morisco; one-third of an oven; and half of whatever had belonged to doña Francisca's deceased mother. Doña Francisca had only one sibling, her brother, Alvaro de Ulloa, and obviously their father made a simple division of his estate between the two children.
  54. AHPC Pedro de Grajos 3924, Diego Pacheco 4100.
  55. See ACC Hernando de Ovando, leg. 4, no. 39, for the division of property made in 1551 between Francisco de Ovando and doña Isabel de Figureroa, the children of Alvaro de Ovando and doña Isabel de

Figueroa. Francisco de Ovando received the "tercio y quinto" ("third and fifth"), or larger portion, of his father's estate, including 99 fanegadas of land and a main house in the town of Aldea del Cano, in Cáceres's district.

56. For Avila's activities after his return, see AHPC Pedro González 3828, 3829. For the entail, see Publio Hurtado, *Ayuntamiento y familias cacerenses* (Cáceres, 1919), 148. I could not find Avila's will or any other records substantiating Hurtado's statement regarding the entail; Hurtado's information is often confusing and unreliable.

57. See Archivo del Monasterio de Guadalupe, Fondo Barrantes MS B/3, fol. 270, for Juan Pantoja de Ribera and AHPC Diego Pacheco 4100. For Rodrigo de Chaves, see Boyd-Bowman, *Indice 2*, no. 2723, and AHPC Diego Pacheco 4100.

58. For Juan Cortés, see Lockhart, *Men of Cajamarca*, 295–296; for doña Catalina Cortés, see AMT Pedro de Carmona, B-1-23; for don Gaspar Cortés and Sancho de Vargas, see Acedo, "Linajes," Vargas, 48a43, a68.

59. For this branch of the Ovando family, see Altman, "Spanish Hidalgos," 335–343. For Alonso de Ribera's entail, see ACC Mayorazgo de Ribera, leg. 1, no. 16.

60. ACC Hernando de Ovando, leg. 4, no. 39.

61. For Juan Cano, see Francisco de Icaza, *Conquistadores y pobladores de Nueva España* (Mexico, 1923), 1: 31; Miguel Muñoz de San Pedro, *Doña Isabel de Moctezuma, la novia de Extremadura* (Madrid, 1965), 28, 31, 33; and Charles Gibson, *The Aztecs under Spanish Rule* (Stanford, 1964), 424–426.

62. For a discussion of returnees, their activities and associations, see chap. 7, "Return Migration," in Ida Altman, *Emigrants and Society: Extremadura and Spanish America in the Sixteenth Century* (Berkeley, Los Angeles, and Oxford, 1989).

Three

Legal and Illegal Emigration from Seville, 1550–1650

Auke Pieter Jacobs

Almost from the start, commerce between Spain and the New World concentrated in the port of Seville, and it was there that emigrants gathered to arrange their voyage to America. The legal procedures to control that emigration were developed in the first half of the sixteenth century and would survive until the first half of the eighteenth century without any significant modifications except those arising from the increasing slowness of the Habsburg bureaucracy. These procedures reflected the general composition of the migration movement, which by around 1550 included people intending to settle in the Indies, short-term migrants, second-time or reemigrants, and those who did not fulfill the legal requirements. The House of Trade (Casa de la Contratación) not only regulated emigration but also oversaw commerce to the Indies.[1]

Here I consider the complicated and sometimes protracted bureaucratic procedures and legal requirements that regulated emigration and how this administrative framework, together with the financial exigencies of undertaking the journey from their homes in Spain to the New World, helped determine the range of choices available to potential emigrants and to some extent shaped the composition of the emigrant group in the late sixteenth and early seventeenth centuries. The expense and unwieldiness of the legal process of emigration have led some to assume that many emigrants chose to circumvent legal requirements and emigrate illegally.

Cumbersome though the bureaucratic process was, however, it did provide at least a partially effective means of regulating departures from Seville, particularly since legal procedures were reinforced by inspections of ships about to depart. Thus, evading the authorities was not easy. Resorting to illegal means might have been attractive to individuals who for some reason wanted to avoid coming to the attention of the authorities; but illegal methods (obtaining fraudulent documents, embarking without documents) did not always mean a significant savings on the cost of the journey and in fact could increase expenses considerably. It was far more effective and economical to emigrate illegally by enlisting as a soldier or seaman on one of the ships of the fleet and then deserting in the Indies, and the evidence suggests that this was a common practice. The very nature of this form of illegal emigration skewed the composition of the illegal emigrant group, since it was available only to the men. Hence, to understand the possibilities for individuals considering departing from Spain for the Indies, we must take into account a number of interrelated considerations—the bureaucratic process, the ways of evading or subverting the legal requirements, the relative costs of the various means of obtaining the desired objective of embarkation, and the financial, legal, occupational, and gender status and constraints that affected and defined each individual who intended to emigrate.

In terms of legal procedures, the most heavily controlled group consisted of people going to the Indies for the first time.[2] In theory, control of the procedures was shared by royal and local authorities, but an emigrant's name had to appear on a royal license granted by the Council of the Indies and signed by the king himself.[3] Having obtained a license (or inclusion in a license), the emigrant had to apply for a proof of purity of blood (*información de limpieza de sangre*) in his birthplace.[4] All emigrants, except members of households, royal officials, and members of religious orders, needed individual informaciones.[5] Individuals who returned to the Indies after having spent some time in Spain were exempt from presenting the deposition on purity of blood because they were supposed to have done so when they left Spain for the first time. Emigrants had to present these documents in the House of Trade to the royal officials who verified their authenticity. When the license and proof of purity of blood were approved, the emigrant received written permission to embark.

Legal Procedures

Application for a royal license had to be presented at the Council of the Indies in Madrid (during the years 1601–1606, the court was in Valladolid) accompanied by a declaration in which the emigrant explained his reasons for wanting to leave for a specific viceroyalty or province of the Indies. The most frequently used argument was poverty and the existence of relatives overseas who would be willing to help them. Emigrants sometimes mentioned that those relatives had sent them money or other forms of assistance to finance the voyage.[6] This declaration referred not only to the applicant himself but also to his relatives and servants (listed with their names, ages, and physical characteristics). All these data would appear in the royal license, if granted. This statement, which was not necessarily drawn up in the emigrant's place of origin, was confirmed by two or three witnesses.

Approval of the application in the Council of the Indies usually took between two and three months if the applicant did not appear personally at court but left the presentation to a relative or deputy. With the reign of Philip III and reorganization of the Council of the Indies, the delay could extend to more than four months.[7] Whereas his father had limited his attention only to doubtful cases, Philip III wanted to be consulted personally on every application. To avoid passengers' missing the fleet as a result of this administrative delay, another document, the certificate, was introduced. This document was drawn up by one of the two secretaries for the two viceroyalties (Peru and New Spain) declaring that the license had been conceded but still awaited the royal signature. If the emigrant presented a certificate, he had to guarantee delivery of the royal license within a period of from one to two months under penalty of between 50 and 200 ducados,[8] depending on the number of persons included in the certificate. The emigrant and those included in the certificate in some cases left without a license because it still had not arrived from court. From August 28, 1584, on, the validity of the license was limited to two years from the date of issue in an attempt to circumvent an increase in forgeries and sales of licenses.[9]

After receiving a license, the emigrant had to apply for a proof of purity of blood in his birthplace. Unlike the license, this document usually pertained to the individual only, except when households emigrated as units and when parents and children were all born in the same place. If spouses were born in different places, each had to apply for a separate proof of purity of blood with the children included in the información of the parent whose place of origin they shared. Should the children be born elsewhere, they needed a separate información.

An emigrant presented the application at the city hall of his birthplace (or of the city that had jurisdiction over his village). He declared that he had obtained a royal license or that he was included in one and that an additional deposition of purity of blood was needed to obtain a license to embark. This declaration was followed by testimony taken in the form of a questionnaire that examined witnesses regarding the emigrant's marital status, age, and physical characteristics. The testimony also concerned whether any of the emigrant's antecedents to the second degree had been condemned by the Inquisition or was a converted Jew or Muslim and whether emigration was a means of escaping trial or evading debts owed to the royal treasury.

When the list of questions was approved by the *corregidor* (royal official), his lieutenant, or the *alcalde mayor* (chief magistrate), a notary was assigned to hear the testimonies of the witnesses. Although officially the presence of one of these authorities was required, in most cases the actual taking of testimony was left in the hands of the notary. The applicant had to find witnesses, who normally were older people of the village or town. Relatives could not serve in this capacity. The minimal number of witnesses was usually six, but when the información was drawn up in the House of Trade for natives of Seville, the number never exceeded three. After the testimonies of the witnesses had been obtained, the document was returned for approval to the city hall. Three notaries had to confirm the authenticity of the handwriting, signature, and seal of the notary who had drawn up the deposition. Sevillian natives only needed the approval of the royal officials if the declaration was prepared in the House of Trade.

When the emigrant and any companions presented themselves at the House of Trade in Seville with the royal license and other required documents, a scribe wrote a petition to the royal officials requesting a license to embark. With these petitions added to their documents, emigrants presented themselves in the office of the secretary, where the license and deposition of purity of blood were checked. The most frequent omissions (lack of information about age, physical characteristics, or marital status) could be corrected by obtaining declarations from witnesses from their places of birth who were living in Seville or by guaranteeing delivery of the missing information within a certain period of time determined by the distance between Seville and the emigrant's birthplace. Failure to present this additional information within the specified period meant a fine of between 50 and 200 ducados.[10]

Once the documents were approved, the names of the emigrant and any companions were written down in the passenger registry, including place of birth, destination in America, master of the ship on which they would make the voyage, and the date the documents were presented. The deposition of purity of blood was not returned to the emigrant but remained in the House of Trade, along with a copy of the royal license and decision of the royal officials to grant the emigrant the license to embark. On the reverse of the royal license, the shipmaster to whom the emigrant was assigned was ordered to concede a place on board.

The difference between licenses and informaciones can be seen by comparing the number of emigrants and the number of documents they presented for the years 1614 and 1615, as seen in tables 3.1 and 3.2. The figures show clearly that licenses often pertained to more than one person. Traveling with a license of one's own was more the exception than the rule. Tables 3.1 and 3.2 also show that real control over emigration to the Indies lay in the hands of the local authorities, while royal government generally limited itself to issuing a collective document (the license) that was valid only with additional local information about all the persons mentioned.[11] The number of informaciones was lower than the number of emigrants because of the emigration of households, royal officials, and members of religious orders. The latter, however, had to present a license from their prelates with the royal license. In 1615, the number of informaciones was somewhat low-

TABLE 3.1. *Number of Legal Emigrants and Returnees, 1614–15*

	1614		1615	
	M	F	M	F
Emigrants	329	153	581	227
Passengers[a]	24	—	17	—
Reemigrants	214	17	230	24
Total	567	170	828	251

Source: AGI Contratación 5.336–5.349.
[a] Passengers are those who had permission to stay for only a limited period in America.

TABLE 3.2. *Number of Documents Presented at the House of Trade, 1614–15*

Emigrants and Passengers		
Depositions of purity of blood	370	419
Royal licenses	99	128
Certificates	35	12
Reemigrants		
Royal licenses	74	142
Certificates	29	9

Source: AGI Contratación 5.336–5.349.

er because of the departure of the viceroy of Peru, the Prince of Esquilache, with 159 servants in his retinue who did not need depositions of purity of blood. A simple declaration by the viceroy that they did not belong to one of the excluded groups was sufficient. People going back to the Indies had to present two witnesses at the House of Trade to testify that they were really the persons included in the license. The tables show that reemigrants were more likely to be traveling alone than were emigrants who went for the first time.

Taking a more detailed look at the composition of the legal emigrant group, we see that for both years, royal officials and members of religious orders accounted for more than half of the legal emigrants (table 3.3). The fact that these two groups were most numerous is not surprising as they were the most likely to know about and feel constrained to follow all the legal procedures for emigration.

TABLE 3.3. *Composition of the Legal Emigrant Group, 1614–15*

Occupation/Year	1614	1615
Royal officials	25	20
Relatives	40	37
Servants (male)	92	173
Servants (female)	28	83
Children of servants	11	2
Total 1	196	315
Members of religious orders	36	85
Relatives	—	—
Servants (male)	34	39
Servants (female)	1	2
Children of servants	2	—
Total 2	73	126
Totals 1 and 2	269	441
Others	237	384
Total	506	825

Source: AGI Contratación 5.336–5.349.

Costs of Emigration

Expenses for the regular legal emigrant included fees for the notaries who drew up the required documents, travel from the emigrant's hometown to Seville, the stay in Seville awaiting departure of the fleet, and passage, accommodations, and provisions on the ship. The notaries usually charged per written page. Although no information has been found on the actual prices of the required documents, notarial charges apparently did not constitute a substantial part of the emigrant's costs. If the emigrant no longer lived in his birthplace but decided to present himself there, costs could rise significantly. Most emigrants, however, authorized a relative or acquaintance to present the deposition in their name.[12] The House of Trade charged an administrative fee for the presentation of the documents and the license to embark.[13]

Indication of the average travel time between the point of origin and Seville can be deduced from the date of the deposition on purity of blood and the date the documents were presented in

TABLE 3.4. *Lowest Number of Days Spent between the Different Regions and Seville in 1605*

Region	Number of Days	Approximate Distance to Seville (miles)
Asturias	79	500
Basque Provinces	73	530
Galicia	62	600
León	52	420
Segovia	48	350
Salamanca	38	300
Jaén	33	155
Madrid	30	340
Valladolid	28	375
Cáceres	23	170
Granada	21	155
Córdoba	4	90

Source: AGI Contratación 5.282–5.292.

Seville, if we assume that the emigrant left his hometown immediately for Seville. The final date of the deposition approximates the date of departure in most cases because application for the proof of purity of blood was tantamount to a public declaration of intention to emigrate. Such a declaration could cause a sharp drop in the price that an emigrant would have obtained for his personal belongings under normal circumstances. This supposition is confirmed by a letter of June 1619 from Cristóbal del Casar, sent from Vera Cruz in New Spain to his brother-in-law, Juan Martínez Gallego, a resident of Cazalla de la Sierra and native of Guadalcanal (both in the modern province of Seville). In this letter, Cristóbal del Casar, after explaining to his brother-in-law how to handle affairs in Seville, warned him to keep the reason for the sale of his property in Guadalcanal (emigration to the Indies) a secret; otherwise, he would not be paid a reasonable price. "And if they ask why you want to sell it, tell them that you are going to live in Cazalla de la Sierra," his wife's hometown.[14]

The figures in table 3.4 suggest an average rate of six to twelve miles a day, a reasonable speed for travelers on foot. If an emigrant traveled on horseback, the daily mileage rose greatly. For example, the steward of the marquis del Valle, Antonio García de la Parra, left Valladolid on May 26, 1605, and arrived, traveling via

Toledo, at Tosina (a village 22 miles from Seville) on June 5, 1605. It took him thirteen days to travel about 400 miles.[15] In that same year, Juan de Morón, his wife, four children (the eldest a six-year-old boy), and a servant left Ariza, a village on the border of the provinces of Zaragoza and Soria, on May 14, 1605, and arrived in Ciudad Real on May 23, covering a distance of about 250 miles in ten days.[16] Daily distances improved during the spring season.

The costs of overland travel through Spain are difficult to estimate. Most travelers took only their clothes and presumably slept wherever they could find shelter.[17] In some cities, the poor traveler could find a bed for free in a municipal hostel.[18] Members of religious orders who went at the expense of the royal treasury were reimbursed 2 reales (68 maravedís) a day for their travel expenses.[19] This reimbursement probably was minimal. If we use this figure to calculate travel expenses, the trip to Seville from the northern provinces would cost about 150 reales (5,100 maravedís).

After the royal officials assigned the emigrant to a ship, he contacted the shipmaster or owner himself to make the arrangements for the voyage. A contract fixed the type of accommodation, number of packing cases for personal belongings and weapons, manner of payment, and daily rations of water, salt, and firewood that the shipmaster would provide. A typical emigrant traveled in a cabin (*rancho*), while the more affluent could obtain a chamber of 110 to 132 inches in length for about 100 to 120 ducados. Victuals did not mean any additional freight fare unless the passenger wished to debark with whatever remained, in which case he had to pay the full freight fare. Emigrants paid at least half their costs in Seville and the balance within a week to thirty days of arrival in the Indies.[20] Those who had a special royal license permitting them to travel on the galleons of the armada that accompanied the fleets—usually royal offiicials and members of religious orders and their retinues—had to pay a fixed price of 20 ducados for the *avería* (convoy tax) in addition to the cost of accommodations and victuals.[21]

Provisions for the voyage were purchased in Sanlúcar de Barrameda just before departure. The passengers' diet differed little from that of the soldiers and seamen aboard.[22] In 1599, Gil Verdugo de Avila and his servant bought for their trip to New Spain 300 pounds of biscuit, 96 pints of wine, 48 pints of vinegar, 200

TABLE 3.5. *Expenses Claimed by Salvador Hernández and Two Companions for Their Voyage to Tierra Firme, 1603*

Weight/Measure	Victuals	Price (in maravedís)
250 pounds	biscuit	5,100
120 pints	wine	2,788
48 pints	olive oil	748
72 pints	vinegar	170
288 pints	water	612
4 pieces	dried ham	3,400
4 pieces	saddle	510
6 pieces	cheese	544
?	dried cod and sturgeon	3,400
?	chickpeas, rice, condiments, etc.	612
1	cooking pot (copper)	
Total expenses, victuals		17,884
Travel expenses (two adults, 27 ducats each; child, 200 reales)		26,928
Transport from Sanlúcar de Barrameda to the ship		1,496
Total travel expenses		28,424
Total expenses		46,308

Source: AGI Contratación 755, no. 11.

pounds of olive oil, 48 pints of capers, 2 dried hams, 150 pounds of raisins, and 50 pounds of almonds.[23] In 1603, after Salvador Hernández and his two companions, Juan Gutiérrez (a ten-year-old boy) and Diego Hernández, decided to leave the ship of master Lupercio de la Cruz, their victuals were dumped into the sea. Subsequently, he prepared a claim for indemnification that included a detailed account of his travel expenses (see table 3.5).

Victuals accounted for nearly 40 percent of the expenses of Salvador Hernández and his companions for their voyage from Sanlúcar de Barrameda to Tierra Firme. Most passengers took more provisions with them than necessary because of the uncertain duration of the voyage, which normally lasted two months but could take up to half a year or more. But leftovers often were substantial because of the frequent seasickness of passengers. For the shipowners, they constituted lucrative extra earnings. After one voyage, Gaspar Vera de Maldonado, owner of the ship *Nuestra Señora del Rosario*, declared he had sold these leftovers for 150,000 maravedís.[24]

Added to the above expenses were those incurred during the wait in Seville before the fleet's departure. In quite a few cases, passengers declared that they could not afford to wait for the fleet that would sail them "directly" to the destination mentioned in the royal license. Requests to leave on the first fleet to depart were usually granted because otherwise emigrants were forced to consume in Seville the provisions purchased for the voyage. Nevertheless, the waiting period in Seville probably averaged two to three months.

A comparison between these travel expenses and the known wages of some occupations in Castile and Andalusia suggests that savings from wages alone would not suffice to finance emigration.[25] Emigrants who went on their own account either needed to sell their properties or depended on remittances sent by relatives overseas.

Finally, we can make some observations about the emigration of servants, a classification that could include a wide range of occupations. Emigration as a servant did not necessarily mean lower travel expenses, but it had the advantage of assuring a job on arrival in America, especially if the servant formed part of the entourage that would assist a royal official. With the exception of judicial posts and those financed directly by the royal treasury, public offices were sold in the Indies as well as in Spain.[26] The officials who bought their offices could remunerate themselves not only through the exercise of their new positions in the Indies but also by selling places for servants while still in Spain, a well-known proceeding in Seville, as will be seen. It is doubtful, however, that these sales to servants were sufficient to meet the expenses of obtaining office. Few officials paid the avería for themselves and their retinue in Seville but rather agreed to pay it in the Indies where credit was more readily available. Some servants even paid their own avería.

Illegal Emigration

We have seen that travel expenses were substantial and beyond the economic means of most potential emigrants. In some cases, illegal emigration could offer a solution to the economic problem. The main sources of information on illegal emigration are trial records concerning cases that were discovered. These records reveal a good deal about the different ways that emigrants attempted to avoid or mislead the authorities. The cases never indicate why some emigrants tried to circumvent the legal procedure, except where such actions resulted from genuine ignorance of the law or simpleness of mind.[27] As a result, it is impossible to guess to what extent membership in one of the groups excluded from emigrating underlay efforts to avoid the legal process. Inquisitorial documents from the Indies do not indicate that emigration of undesirables reached impressive figures, although it must be borne in mind that the Inquisition in America never reached the levels of penetration achieved in the peninsula. It is also quite possible that after arriving in the Indies, people in the undesirable categories altered their behavior or identity so as to escape any possible future prosecution.[28] In any case, the geographic expanse of America perhaps made it relatively easy for such individuals to go unnoticed. The increase in the number of Inquisition trials at the end of the sixteenth century resulted from the immigration of Portuguese Jews and foreigners suspected of Lutheranism.[29] The audiencia of the House of Trade was more interested in capturing illegal emigrants and forgers or vendors of official documents than in the underlying reasons for such activities.

Emigrants seeking to evade the authorities could choose among various options. The most expensive of these was obtaining false papers. Others tried to arrange with a shipmaster to travel without any papers at all, while some stowed away on the ships, later to appear at sea. The majority enlisted as soldiers or seamen.

Two types of fraud existed: first, forging an official document and attempting to present it as authentic; and, second, use of an authentic document by a person other than the one named in it. In the first case, forging the deposition of purity of blood was unnecessary, but in the second case, it was necessary because name and physical characteristics had to coincide.[30] In both cases, the initial contact between the forger or the salesman of official documents and the emigrant was made by an intermediary. The favored sites for such transactions were the House of Trade itself and the plaza of San Francisco, where notaries and scribes conducted business. Normally the intermediaries were commercial agents who acted as middlemen between tradesmen and merchants, or between merchants and shipowners, and hence had extensive contacts in Seville's commercial and maritime community. Acting as intermediaries between scribes and emigrants could bring these agents lucrative profits.

The most interesting case was the discovery of eleven false licenses dated between November 24 and December 23, 1604, in Valladolid. A total of forty-nine persons were implicated, only two of whom were Sevillians.[31] The intermediary was Gonzalo de los Reyes, a twenty-six-year-old native of Seville, who described his profession as commercial agent. He found his clients mainly in the House of Trade and mediated between them and Juan Bautista, a scribe who once had worked in the office of a lawyer of the audiencia of Seville. Bautista held office in the plaza of San Francisco and had asked Los Reyes to send him passengers who needed licenses to travel to the Indies because he had two or three to sell. A certain Agustín Gutiérrez was the first to use the services of Los Reyes. His name did not appear on any of the licenses, so Bautista suggested that Gutiérrez give him his personal data so he could send an application to court. About a month later, Los Reyes accompanied Gutiérrez to Bautista's office to get the license. Bautista charged 34 ducados (12,716 maravedís) for the license. When Gutiérrez complained about the price, Bautista argued that it included permission to take two servants; these places could be sold for 20 ducados each. Gutiérrez paid the 34 ducados. With the mediation of Los Reyes, he eventually sold the two places for servants to Rodrigo de Sotomayor of Seville and a low-ranking nobleman named Francisco Machado of Puebla del Príncipe in the province of Ciudad Real for 17 ducados each. The "servants" each paid 6 reales to Reyes for his services.

Some time later, Los Reyes met with María Pérez, wife of Miguel Sánchez, a baker who had come from Talavera de Badajoz in Extremadura nearly a year before. She was looking for a passenger holding a license permitting him to take a married servant with him. Among the licenses Juan Bautista kept in his office was one for a Miguel Hernández, his wife, and a maidservant. Before leaving Talavera de Badajoz, they had drawn up their deposition of purity of blood, which they handed over to Bautista to alter the names. The physical characteristics of Miguel Sánchez coincided with those of Miguel Hernández in the license. Miguel Sánchez/

Hernández paid 24 ducados (9,976 maravedís) for this transaction, while Los Reyes listed a woman named Luisa de Treceño as the servant.

In another case, the mediation of Los Reyes between the squire Don Juan or Don Pedro Osorio and the servant Juan de Chaves failed because the squire disappeared after receiving first 4,080 maravedís for accepting Chaves as a servant and later an additional 2,720 maravedís for victuals. Chaves threatened to lodge a complaint against Gonzalo de los Reyes who, to avoid judicial complications, introduced him to Juan Bautista. Within two months another license was created for Chaves, his niece, and a servant for the price of 1,700 maravedís. Bautista sold the places for the niece and the servant separately. Chaves spent a total of 8,500 maravedís just to get his documents "in order."[32]

The use of false documents sometimes resulted from bureaucratic inflexibility. When Juan Martín, a candle maker from Cartaya in the province of Huelva, left Seville in March 1608 to apply for a license for himself, his wife, and his daughters in Madrid, Isabel de Piña, a mulatto, asked him to include in his application a request for a servant so that she could leave with him. When Martín returned, he reported that the Council of the Indies had denied the request, but he promised to seek another solution. While presenting his documents at the House of Trade, Juan Martín met three emigrants from Toledo who lived in Triana. He went to their lodgings to ask if they could help him. There he met the guitar player Pedro de Ramos, who told him, after hearing that Isabel de Piña could pay 10,200 maravedís for the license, that he had friends at court who could help her. Two weeks later, Isabel received her own license. Isabel de Piña and Juan Martín were both arrested after they had already embarked. In the meantime, Pedro de Ramos had left Seville. Isabel de Piña was absolved, while Juan Martín had to postpone emigrating because he was condemned to one year's exile from Seville. Pedro de Ramos was condemned in absentia to the galley for ten years.[33]

In the case of the sale of authentic documents, we may imagine that lost or stolen licenses circulated in Seville; there exist, however, very few references to their loss or robbery.[34] Licenses were sometimes stolen because they had been left behind with luggage at hostels, but they apparently were not the main objective of such thefts. Fake applications might have been presented, although there is no documentary evidence for such a practice. Another possibility may explain the circulation of authentic licenses. Some passengers who came to Seville with licenses and depositions of purity of blood might not have left as individual emigrants but rather as servants. Since they then would not need their licenses, they could sell them if they wished. On May 27, 1603, Ana de Acosta from Seville was registered in the House of Trade as an individual passenger for Santo Domingo. Twenty days later, another Ana de Acosta, with exactly the same personal data, was registered as servant of the corregidor of the Andes del Cuzco, Don Pedro de Guzmán.[35] Sales of authentic licenses were made on the street and, in most cases, through intermediaries. Prices were similar to those for false licenses, although forging the deposition of purity of blood meant an additional expense.[36]

Travel expenses for illegal emigrants were not necessarily higher than normal if the emigrant was named in the license and the license included places for one or two servants that could be sold. In most cases, however, the forger would try to sell each place separately.

Although the majority of emigrants did not have their own licenses, there was also a group that was not included in a license and did not have proof of purity of blood. These emigrants must be distinguished from stowaways because the shipmaster or another member of the crew consented to their presence on board the ship for a consideration. These cases are more numerous than those of stowaways but normally did not involve more than twenty persons. The prices charged by the crew were higher than the fares for legal emigrants, although sometimes food was included.

An interesting case was the passage of undocumented emigrants on the merchant ship *San Buenaventura* of master Juan de Brizuela, which arrived in 1617 at the city of Asunción on Isla Margarita. Juan de Brizuela was accused of transporting eighteen emigrants without documents—fifteen men and three women, among them a Frenchman and an English seaman—along with eight legal emigrants. These eighteen emigrants had already boarded the ship in Cádiz before the final inspection took place. Brizuela ordered the illegal emigrants to leave the ship and hide on shore. The night after the inspection they reboarded the ship.

On reaching the harbor of Asunción, five miles from the city, the illegal passengers were sent to shore with the order to hide themselves in the forest until the following day when the inspection had been completed. The shipmaster was denounced by two of the legal emigrants, and the case was handed over to the House of Trade in Seville; but the documents do not reveal if Brizuela was sent as a prisoner to Seville.[37] Such was the fate of Francisco Pérez Granillo in 1605. He was suspected of having transported to Santo Domingo thirty-four emigrants without documents in his *patache* (a small boat that accompanied the galleons). In his defense, he argued that these passengers came from the other ships of the fleet and were placed on his ship at the island of Guadeloupe because it sailed empty.[38]

Even if such emigrants managed to hide during the final inspection of the ships, they easily fell victim to extortion. In 1616, this is what happened to Esteban de Bonifacio when he was asked by the royal scribe of the armada and fleet of Tierra Firme, Cristóbal Chamorro, in the harbor of Puerto Velo if he had a license. Bonifacio answered that he did not have one because he had traveled as a servant of merchant Jacome Quesada and that he would return to Spain in the same fleet. Chamorro replied that it would be a pity to denounce him to the captain-general of the armada, but he could overlook the infraction for a consideration of 150 reales (5,100 maravedís). A little later Chamorro's son arrived to collect the money. In the same port, Chamorro also extorted 10,200 maravedís from Agustina de Tamayo, half the price she still owed a seaman for having arranged her clandestine voyage.[39] Prices for such passages could be high. Antonio de Acosta and Diego de Figueroa (both from Fregenal de la Sierra in the province of Badajoz) paid 800 reales to travel to Campeche in New Spain but were discovered by inspector Gaspar de Vargas on the ship of master Juan de Navarro in June 1605.[40]

It would be difficult to establish a reasonable estimate of the volume of emigration of passengers without documents because of the fragmentary nature of the records. Sometimes there remains only the accusation by a public prosecutor, such as the one lodged against Alonso Pabón for having transported three women without documents to New Spain.[41] Some cases were not prosecuted for lack of proof. Infantry captain Pedro de Esquivel was accused by the scribe for the food rations of the galleon *San Gregorio* (of the armada of captain-general Luis Fernández de Córdoba that returned from Tierra Firme in 1605) of having transported forty-two emigrants without documents; but Esquivel was never prosecuted.[42]

Passengers who hid themselves in the hold of the ships, later to appear at sea, were not the most welcome guests aboard because the shipmaster would be suspected of transporting illegal emigrants while receiving no economic compensation for his risk. Stowaways survived thanks to the mercy of other passengers or simply by robbing food. In some cases, they might perform tasks such as cleaning the ship. In 1608, the shipmaster of the galleon *San Marcos*, Cristóbal del Real, found in one of the chambers of the galleon a fourteen-year-old boy hidden by some Dominican friars. Two of these friars were his brothers whom he had assisted in bringing luggage on board. He stayed overnight on the ship, meaning to leave in the morning; but when he awoke, the ship was already at sea. He was condemned to two years on the galleys based in Cartagena which defended the coast of Tierra Firme, but he managed to escape. The bondsman responsible for delivering him to the prison of Cartegena had to take his place until the boy was recaptured.[43] A similar incident occurred in the same year on the merchant ship *San Salvador* of master Pedro Romero. Two men, a blacksmith and a field laborer, seventeen and twenty years old, appeared when the ship was heading for the Gulf of Las Damas.[44] Stowing away was usually the act of an individual, and the cases never reached numbers of any real importance.

Soldiers and Seamen

The most significant group of undocumented emigrants were the soldiers and seamen who left their ships with the purpose of remaining in the Indies. Soldiers sailed on the galleons that accompanied the merchant fleets to protect them against pirates or, in time of war, against enemy attacks. The levy of soldiers for the armada took place in the regions around Seville. A captain of infantry needed a royal *cédula* (order) allowing him to recruit soldiers in specifically named villages and cities. Normally, the captain was sent to his native district to stimulate enlistment through his local influence. He had to present himself to the local authorities with the cédula before he could obtain permission to raise a military banner and beat the drums in front of the city hall officially announcing the levy of soldiers. The soldiers had to be older than fifteen years and younger than fifty, healthy, and, if possible, single. In times of crisis, these rules were hardly respected and, instead of relying on volunteers, men might even be forced to enlist.[45] After being accepted, the recruits received their first pay, for which reason a considerable number of them deserted en route to Seville. To reduce the number of deserters, the levies for the armada of the Indies were concentrated in the regions nearest Seville such as Andalusia, Extremadura, and New Castile.[46]

The armadas were financed by the avería, a form of insurance that the merchants who participated in the fleet paid for protection of merchant ships and their cargoes. The avería was based on the value of the cargo, which determined the percentage each merchant had to pay. Part of the avería could be paid in the Indies if a guarantee was made in Seville.[47] The system for collecting the avería made it nearly impossible to give to the captain in advance the money needed for the levy of soldiers. He had to obtain credit not only for the initial salary payment but also for clothes and food during the trip to Seville.[48] The desertion of soldiers before reaching Seville or in the city itself made it possible for the captain to offset his expenses by substituting for the defectors passengers disguised as soldiers.

To avoid desertion in the various ports of the Indies, the captains-general of the fleets of Tierra Firme, for example, were obliged to post coast guards a little north of Puerto Velo and to rent houses that could serve as hospitals for the sick. The most trustworthy under-officers were assigned to guard these hospitals.[49]

Such measures had little or no effect, mainly because of the open opposition of local officials, who considered their authority compromised. In the first quarter of the seventeenth century, the absenteeism of soldiers and seamen was significant, reaching about 20 percent of the total crew of the galleons.[50] In 1606, captain-general Gerónimo de Portugal y Córdoba announced that every soldier or seaman leaving the galleons without a license was condemned to death.[51] Another measure adopted to control deser-

TABLE 3.6. *Fluctuations in Number of Soldiers of the Admiral's Galleon of the Fleet to Tierra Firme, 1601–02*

Date of Control	Place of Control				
	Cádiz	Cartagena	Puerto Velo	La Habana	Sanlúcar de Barrameda
19.3.1601	107				
8.6.1601		108			
24.6.1601		82			
29.6.1601			80		
3.8.1601			72		
22.8.1601		81			
31.8.1601		90			
20.9.1601				90	
24.10.1601				90	
10.11.1601				88	
26.11.1601				87	
12.12.1601				87	
26.12.1601				86	
13.1.1602				81	
29.1.1602				84	
10.2.1602				87	
27.2.1602				76	
16.4.1602					76

Source: AGI Contratación 67A, no. 1, ramo 2.

tion was regular inspections of galleons in the ports of Spain and in the Indies on arrival and departure (see tables 3.6 and 3.7).

Fluctuations in the number of soldiers and seamen were partly due to real illnesses or deaths; absenteeism among soldiers, however, seems to have been more definitive than among seamen. Seamen were more easily replaced because presumably a transient maritime community existed in most ports of the Indies. Every fleet included merchant ships that went to the Indies with the intention that they would be destroyed and used for parts to repair other ships. Consequently, the seamen on such ships had to find another ship to return to Spain. Because the lists of seamen on these ships are incomplete, however, it is difficult to ascertain how many of them remained in America and how many returned on other ships.

Crew members regularly feigned illness and subsequently

TABLE 3.7. *Fluctuations in Number of Seamen of the Admiral's Galleon of the Fleet to Tierra Firme, 1601–02*

Date of Control	Place of Control				
	Cádiz	Cartagena	Puerto Velo	La Habana	Sanlúcar de Barrameda
19.3.1601	78				
8.6.1601		65			
24.6.1601		64			
29.6.1601			64		
3.8.1601			70		
22.8.1601		74			
31.8.1601		70			
20.9.1601				71	
24.10.1601				78	
10.11.1601				78	
26.11.1601				78	
12.12.1601				78	
26.12.1601				79	
13.1.1602				78	
29.1.1602				78	
10.2.1602				78	
27.2.1602				76	
16.4.1602					76

Source: AGI Contratación 67A, no. 1, ramo 2.

escaped from hospitals.[52] Others tried to reach the coast by swimming out at night to canoes waiting to bring them to shore.[53] Some obtained licenses to disembark to wash their clothes and then made good their escape.[54]

The desertion of soldiers generally was more a calculated act than an impulsive adventure. The manner of recruiting soldiers in the vicinity of Seville resulted in the enlistment of a number of first-time soldiers who were escaping unemployment. Juan Gómez, a velvet weaver from Málaga who had enlisted as a soldier for the first time, was apprehended when he attempted to escape from the galleon *Nuestra Señora del Rosario* in Cartagena on May 18, 1613, along with Pedro Suárez, a fellow soldier. Although Gómez denied that he had received any outside help, the captain-general also examined Hernán Pérez, soldier of the garrison of Cartagena, who had visited the galleon to buy some gunpowder and cables. Pérez declared that he had been invited to have supper with the soldiers, one of whom asked what the possibilities were like for carriers. Pérez answered that there were none in or around Cartagena.[55] This is the only example found of a soldier inquiring about possible opportunities in his original occupation; but we might suppose that visitors on ships in the ports of the Indies often heard such questions. Favorable answers could have motivated escape attempts.

In 1614, 201 soldiers and seamen fled from the galleons in New Spain and 259 from the galleons in Tierra Firme. In 1615, there were 163 absentees from the galleons of New Spain (there are no figures for the 1615 galleons of Tierra Firme).[56] The number of soldiers and seamen who deserted from the galleons reached a total of 460 persons in 1614, considerably more than the 353 legal male emigrants of the same year. Absenteeism of soldiers and seamen became the most important way of avoiding the bureaucratic procedures regulating emigration. The shortage of seamen and professional soldiers allowed emigrants to disguise themselves as such. Unemployed craftsmen could travel to America to find out if the New World offered better possibilities than their homeland. This form of illegal emigration was, of course, only available to men.

Conclusion

Spaniards who wanted to emigrate to the Indies had to solve the problem of how to survive during a journey that could last, from the time they left their hometowns, at least half a year, during which time most would have no regular income. Emigrants could choose among various options. Many people left Spain in connection with their occupation or profession. This group included royal officials, members of religious orders, and their servants. Soldiers and seamen were supposed to limit their activities to the voyage itself but sometimes chose to remain in America and thus become part of the immigrant population. With the exception of royal officials, this group that went to the Indies as a result of their occupations had the lowest expenses. Members of religious orders normally went at the expense of the royal treasury. Most servants paid for the voyage by working for a specified period of time for their masters after arriving in the Indies. Relatively few soldiers and seamen actually were disguised passengers who bribed their way on board.

Emigrants who lacked an occupation that could help defray the costs of the journey faced substantial travel expenses that could be met only through their own means or by assistance from relatives overseas. A serious problem of legal emigrants who went on their own account was the need to hide the real reason for the sale of their properties, because otherwise the proceeds would be too low to meet their expenses. In contrast, emigrants who left without any documents had to keep secret both their departure from Seville and their arrival in the Indies, and usually their travel expenses were higher than those of their legal counterparts. Without any doubt, the most expensive way to emigrate was that chosen by individuals who tried to mislead royal officials in Seville with false documents or the improper use of authentic documents. Although we cannot be sure about the number of emigrants who went without any documents, relatively few used forged or altered papers. Emigration to the Indies seems to have been beyond the means of most early-seventeenth-century Spaniards.

The legal procedures to control Spanish emigration to the Indies did not have the proposed effects. We may estimate that about 50 percent of the annual movement to the Indies consisted of emigrants who had not fulfilled these procedures. The high percentage of illegal emigrants reduced the overall proportion of female emigrants as the illegal movement was predominantly male. During 1614 and 1615, for example, about 30 percent of the legal emigrants were women, but overall their representation in the emigrant group was probably half that figure. Finally, the frequent complaints by royal officials in the Indies about the arrival of emigrants not holding licenses does not mean that all of them were illegal emigrants since, as seen, traveling with a license of one's own was more exception than rule.

Acknowledgments

I would like to thank Hugo de Schepper, Bart Hageraats, and Karin Paardenkeeper for their comments on the chapter and the Unger van Brero Foundation for the grant that made possible the main part of the research.

Notes

1. The Casa de la Contratación de las Indias was founded in 1503 to control the commerce between Spain and the Indies. By January 8, 1504, it had taken over the regulation of emigration from the royal officials in Cádiz. *Colección de documentos inéditos relativos al descubrimiento, conquista y organización de las antiguas posesiones españolas de América y Oceanía* (Madrid, 1864), 31: 212–213.

2. The distinction between settlers and short-term emigrants is hard to establish because there are few indications in the documents about how long the latter planned to remain in the Indies, except in the case of married emigrants who left without taking their wives. They obtained permission to be absent for three years, if their wives agreed. To assure their return they had to post a bond. It waas also to extend the stay if they obtained royal permission and their wives agreed again. The cases of short-term emigrants, however, are few (see table 3.1).

3. The Council of the Indies was founded on August 1, 1524, to advise the crown on all matters concerning government of the Indies. See also Ernst Schäffer, *El Consejo Real y Supremo de las Indias: Su historia, organización y labor administrativo hasta la terminación de la Casa de los Austrias*, 2 vols. (Seville, 1935–1947), 1: 80.

4. Discussion of the origins of the requirement to prove purity of blood would exceed the limits of this study. Any male passenger who went for the first time to the Indies had to prove that since 1552 (women since 1554), he was not a descendant to the second degree of converted Jews or Muslims or of any person condemned by the Inquisition. The main objective was to avoid the presence in the Indies of anyone whose sincerity about the Catholic faith was suspect. See, for instance, the excellent study of A. A. Sicroff, *Los estatutos de limpieza de sangre: Controversias entre los siglos XV y XVII* (Madrid, 1985), and Antonio Domínguez Ortiz, *Los judeoconversos en España y América* (Madrid, 1971).

5. The requirement of purity of blood to the second degree was already established by a royal cédula of September 24, 1501, for anyone who wanted to hold public office. Members of religious orders had to prove their purity of blood when entering the order. Domínguez Ortiz, *Los judeoconversos*, 80.

6. All documents cited have been found in the Archive of the Indies in Seville (AGI). Of interest for this study were the sections, Contratación, Escribanía, and Justicia. Numbers indicate, respectively, the *legajo* (bundle), ramo, and individual number of the document. Numbers in parentheses indicate the number of an individual deposition of purity of

blood: AGI Contratación 5321 (11). Antonio Rodríguez wrote to his wife, Inés de Orduña, from Mexico on March 4, 1611, that he had sent a certain amount of flax so that she could finance the voyage by selling it in Seville.

7. In 1600, the Council of the Indies was reformed by introducing the Chamber of the Indies as a superior board. In 1604, four secretaries were added. In 1609, the number of secretaries was reduced to two. At the same time, the Chamber of the Indies was abolished and would not return until 1644. See J. Ots Capdequi, *El estado español en las Indias* (Mexico, 1965), 63–65.

8. The coinage and monetary equivalents are as follows: a ducado was worth 11 reales or 374 maravedís; the real was a silver coin worth 34 maravedís; the maravedí was the smallest unit of money of account.

9. *Recopilación de leyes de los reynos de las Indias*, facs. ed. (Madrid, 1973), Bk. IX, title 26, law VI, fol. 2v.

10. In 1614, there were 42 depositions of purity of blood with omissions. The guarantees presented 21 additional depositions. In twenty cases, we do not know if the guarantor delivered the required additions, and in one case, the emigrant was not permitted to leave.

11. Verification of lineal descent of emigrants was delegated to the local civil authorities. On the walls of parish churches and cathedrals hung the *sanbenitos* in memory of the persons condemned by the Inquisition. The examination of witnesses, mostly older people, was most effective in bringing to light a possible condemnation in the descent of a potential emigrant.

12. E. Lorenzo Sanz, *Comercio de España con América en la época de Felipe II*, 2 vols. (Valladolid, 1979–80), 1: 35–36.

13. AGI Justicia 945, fols. 160–161. The administrative fee for emigrants in the House of Trade in the mid-sixteenth century was 17 maravedís.

14. AGI Contratación 5365 (23).

15. AGI Contratación 5270, ramo 1 (27).

16. AGI Contratación 5282 (19).

17. AGI Contratación 5260A (58). Juan Rodríguez de Llano left the village of Cangas in Asturias on May 20, 1599, to travel, via Salamanca and Madrid, to Seville. His trip took place in the midst of the plague that affected Spain from 1596 to 1602. To avoid contagion by travelers, everybody who entered a city or village had to declare that he came from a disease-free region. In the declaration of Juan Rodríguez de Llano, the notary also described the clothes he would wear during his voyage, but there was no description of any luggage.

18. Linda Martz, *Poverty and Welfare in Habsburg Spain: The Example of Toledo* (Cambridge, 1983), 149–150.
19. AGI Contratación 5301, ramo 1 (20).
20. Contracts can be found, for instance, in AGI Contratación 72, ramo 2, no. 1; 150, no. 11; 5281 (97).
21. Guillermo Céspedes del Castillo, "La avería en el comercio de las Indias," *Anuario de Estudios Americanos* 2 (1945): 515–698. L. Zumalacarregui, "Contribución al estudio de la avería en el siglo XVI y principios del XVII," *Anales de Economía* 4 (1945): 383–424. Unlike the supposition of these two authors, we have found emigrants paying the avería only when they traveled on the galleons. There is no documentary evidence that passengers on merchant ships had to do the same.
22. Earl J. Hamilton, "Paga y alimentación en las flotas de Indias (1503–1660)," in *El florecimiento del capitalismo* (Madrid, 1984), 103–123; see also, Carla R. Phillips, *Six Galleons for the King of Spain: Imperial Defense in the Early Seventeenth Century* (Baltimore, 1986), 241–242.
23. AGI Contratación 5260B (24).
24. AGI Contratación 644, ramo 6, no. 3.
25. Earl J. Hamilton, *American Treasure and the Price Revolution in Spain, 1501–1650* (Cambridge, 1934), 400–402.
26. F. Tomás y Valiente, *La venta de oficios en Indias, 1492–1606* (Madrid, 1972); J. H. Parry, *The Sale of Public Office in the Indies under the Hapsburgs* (Berkeley, 1953).
27. H. J. Tanze, "El conocimiento del Derecho en la legislación de Indias," *Actas del III Congreso del Instituto Internacional del Derecho Indiano* (Madrid, 1973), 269–277. Although every Spaniard had to know the law, simpleness of mind was one of the few arguments considered valid to reduce punishment.
28. B. Escandell Bonet, "Una lectura psicosocial de los papeles del Santo Oficio de la Inquisición y sociedad peruanos en el siglo XVI," in J. Pérez Villanueva, ed., *Inquisición española: Nueva visión, nuevos horizontes* (Madrid, 1980), 437–467.
29. Richard E. Greenleaf, *Inquisición y sociedad en el México colonial* (Madrid, 1985); A. Toro, *Los judíos en Nueva España* (Mexico, 1982). See also the different articles in the excellent survey, J. Pérez Villanueva and B. Escandell Bonet, eds., *Historia de la Inquisición en España y América* (Madrid, 1984).
30. The cases were usually discovered by the differences between the physical characteristics mentioned in the documents and those of the emigrant.

31. Few Sevillians presented false documents because control was so easy. For the same reason, very few passengers tried to pass as Sevillians. When Francisco del Campo tried to do so, he presented a copy of his certificate of baptism. When the officials checked the parish register, it turned out to be false. AGI Contratación 84A, no. 9, year of 1617.

32. AGI Contratación 5283 (82) and 71B, no. 6.
33. AGI Contratación 74A, ramo 1, no. 3.
34. AGI Contratación 5282 (34); 5290 (97) and 5299, ramo 2 (22).
35. AGI Contratación 5277 (86) and 5277 (44). A similar case occurred in 1608, when Gerónimo de Castañeda from Toledo registered on 11 January in the House of Trade as servant of Juan López de Córdoba bound for Peru and on 22 January as an individual emigrant to Peru. AGI Contratación 5304 (3), 2 and 5307, ramo 1 (41).
36. In 1584, a false deposition of purity of blood was purchased for six ducados (2,250 maravedís). AGI Contratación 60B, ramo 2, no. 16.
37. AGI Contratación 599, no. 3.
38. AGI Contratación 72, no. 1.
39. AGI Contratación 83D, ramo 3, no. 1.
40. AGI Contratación 150, no. 11.
41. AGI Contratación 148, ramo 2, no. 5.
42. AGI Contratación 71B, ramo 3, no. 1.
43. AGI Contratación 74B, ramo 3, no. 2 (4).
44. AGI Contratación 74B, ramo 3, no. 2 (1).
45. J. Marchena Fernández, "Las levas de soldados a Indias en la Baja Andalucía, Siglo XVII," *Actas de las III Jornadas de Andalucía y América* (Sevilla, 1985), 93–117.
46. I. A. A. Thompson, *Guerra y decadencia: Gobierno y administración en la España de los Austrias, 1560–1620* (Barcelona, 1981), 135–146. See also Geoffrey Parker, *El ejército de Flandes y el Camino Español, 1567–1659* (Madrid, 1976), 61–87.
47. Céspedes del Castillo, "La avería en el comercio," 515–698.
48. Thompson, *Guerra y decadencia*, 135–146.
49. AGI Contratación 599, ramo 1, no. 2.
50. F. Serrano Mangas, "Armada y flotas de Plata, 1620–1648," Ph.D. dissertation (Seville, 1987), 426–433.
51. AGI Contratación 73B, ramo 2, no. 1.
52. AGI Contratación 75B, ramo 2, no. 2.
53. AGI Contratación 75B, ramo 3, no. 1.
54. AGI Contratación 74B, ramo 2, no. 1.
55. AGI Contratación 599, ramo 1, no. 2.
56. AGI Escribanía 967.

Four

"To Parts Beyond the Seas": Free Emigration to the Chesapeake in the Seventeenth Century

James Horn

Henry Fleet was born in 1600, eldest son of William Fleet, gentleman, of Chartham, Kent. At the age of twenty-one, he took ship to Virginia where he was captured by Anacostan Indians and held prisoner at Yowaccomoco on the Potomac River for five years. After his release, he returned to England but was soon back in America trading along the Chesapeake Bay as well as farther afield to New England. Now an experienced Indian interpreter and mariner, Fleet cashed in on the developing fur trade and became an agent for several wealthy London merchants in the 1630s. He helped establish Lord Baltimore's colony in Maryland in 1634 and owned land there for nearly twenty years before moving across the Potomac to Fleet's Bay in newly formed Lancaster County, Virginia, where he built a large estate in the early 1650s. One of the most important and respected members of the county, Fleet represented Lancaster in the colony's legislature and served as a justice of the peace until his death in 1661.[1]

Fleet led a long and adventurous life, but there is more to his story than this brief outline reveals. In the same year that he set sail for the Chesapeake, his kinsman, Sir Francis Wyatt from Boxley,

Kent, took up residence at Jamestown as the new governor of Virginia. Fleet's brothers, Edward, Reginold, and John, settled in Maryland in the 1630s and 1640s, and he was related by marriage to the Kentish families of Argall and Filmer. Captain Samuel Argall, a tough merchant-planter who arrived in 1612, was influential in the early affairs of the colony and served briefly as deputy-governor. Henry and Samuel Filmer, Fleet's nephews, settled in Virginia in the 1640s. Thus, from a small group of parishes a few miles apart in central Kent, the sons of a number of locally prominent gentry, linked by ties of marriage and kinship, emigrated to the Chesapeake Bay during the first four decades of colonization.[2]

The second point to note about Fleet's career is his London connections. His father was a shareholder in the Virginia Company and possibly already had contacts with colonial merchants before his son's voyage. Possibly Fleet courted them himself when he returned to London from captivity in 1627. In any event, the development of contacts with the capital's business community was vital to his trading activities in America. By the 1630s, London was the hub of colonial trade, providing capital, labor, and marketing outlets for a rapidly growing volume of goods shipped back from the Chesapeake, West Indies, and New England. Throughout the seventeenth century, London was a vital link between mercantile interests in English provinces and the American colonies.[3]

Another case study provides a somewhat different picture. The importance of kinship and contacts with the city are apparent in the career of Edward Bennett. He was born in Wivelscombe, Somerset, in 1578, the son of a tanner. After a good marriage, he developed connections with wealthy merchants in Wells and London through his wife's family. Evidently he profited from the expanding colonial trade of the early 1600s, since by the 1620s, he had established himself as a large merchant in London and owned a fleet of ships trafficking to Virginia and Newfoundland. His brothers, Robert and Richard, emigrated to Virginia in the 1620s, and Edward himself settled in Warrascoyack County (later Isle of Wight) for a short period before returning to London in 1629. But Bennett was not only motivated by profit; he was a man of strong religious principles and was at the heart of early Puritan migration to the Chesapeake. At the same time that the Plymouth separatists carved out a home for themselves in New England, Bennett and his followers created a sanctuary for Puritans in the south. The counties along the southern bank of the James River (fig. 4.1) became a stronghold of nonconformity for the rest of the century, and the Bennetts became one of the most powerful families in the colony. Edward continued to support Puritan settlement in Virginia during the 1630s and 1640s but never returned to America. He lived long enough, however, to see the creation of a godly republic in England and died sometime in the 1650s.[4]

The lives of men such as Fleet and Bennett, leading merchants of their day, are reasonably well documented. Less is known about the thousands of petty traders and poor to middling settlers who composed the majority of free emigrants to Virginia and Maryland in the seventeenth century. Charles Barcroft "left his trade in London and went to Virginia" in 1636 following the death of his brother who was his factor there. He left behind his wife, Elizabeth, who went to live with her parents in Whitechapel. Allegations were subsequently made that he was on bad terms with Elizabeth and that this was the major reason for his decision to leave England.[5] Agnes, wife of George Grace, a merchant of the City of London, deposed in the 1630s that her husband had lost a considerable amount of money trading in Holland and, unable to pay his debts, "went to Virginia where he now lives in a poor condition."[6] Thomas Constable of the Drapers Company was described simply as "a poor man" when he emigrated in 1618.[7] Thomas Thurston, a Quaker, was a cordwainer from Gloucestershire; William Kelloway, a husbandman from Portsmouth.[8]

These examples suggest the diversity of social backgrounds that characterized free emigration in this period. At the lower end of the social ladder, some settlers were barely distinguishable from the mass of laborers—indentured servants—who made up the great majority of emigrants. Small merchants, petty retailers, artisans, and men with perhaps a modest sum to invest in a tobacco plantation or small-scale merchandising made up the middle ranks of colonists, while at the top were big merchants, gentry, and government officials who formed the colonial elite. Puritans and royalists, gentlemen and paupers—all found passage across the Atlantic to Virginia and Maryland.

These case studies suggest, also, something of the diversity of

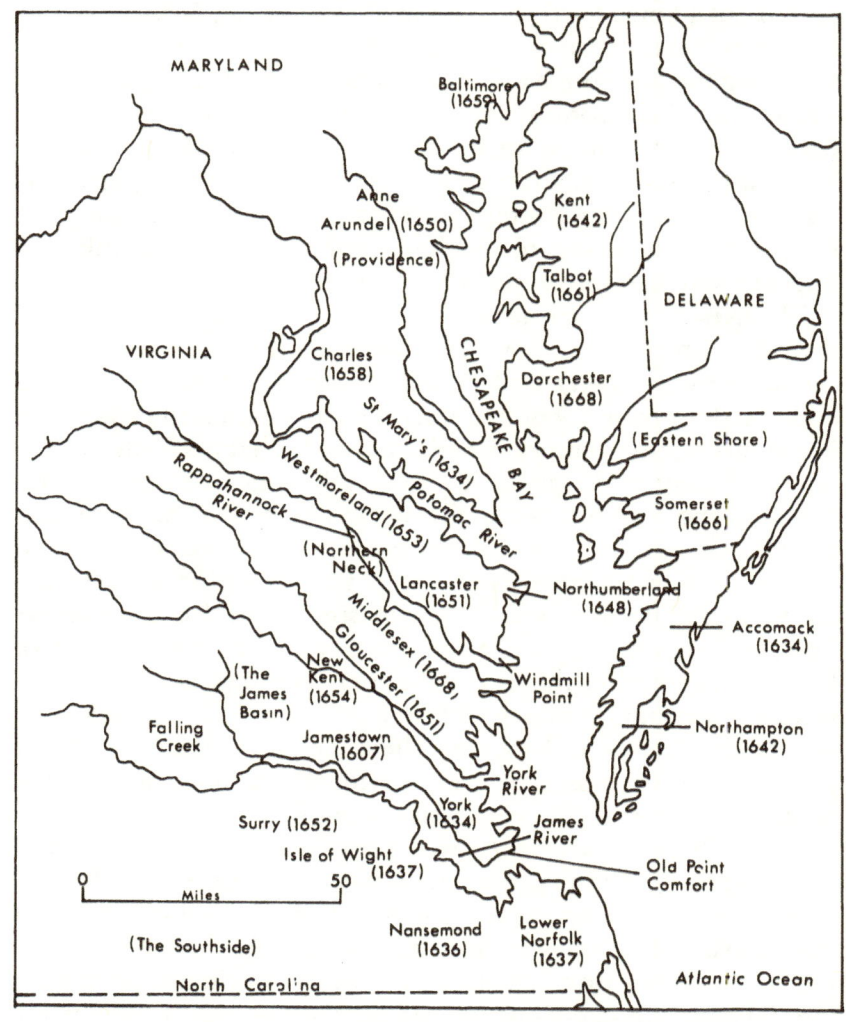

Fig. 4.1. The Chesapeake in the Seventeenth Century

reasons that prompted emigration. Making a living was the most common motive, but some emigrants looked to combine profit with faith and sought to create a haven for those whose religious convictions, whether Puritan, Quaker, or Catholic, encouraged them to leave home. Others had less lofty ideals and fled England because they were in debt or in trouble. Some intended to stay for good; others remained only a year or two before returning or moving elsewhere. Free emigration was not, therefore, a single, concentrated outpouring of people united by a common vision of a new start in America but rather a multilayered, multifaceted phenomenon comprising wave upon wave of colonists who found their way to the tobacco coast from very different backgrounds and for very different reasons.[9]

The aim here is to sketch an outline of the social and economic backgrounds of free emigrants and consider the major influences that guided and shaped emigration to Virginia and Maryland in the hundred years after the founding of Jamestown. Whereas recent research has explored the social origins and character of servant emigration, there has been little sustained analysis of free emigrants. In contrast to New England, where the great majority of settlers arrived as members of family groups unencumbered by long terms of service, most immigrants in the Chesapeake (and West Indies) arrived as servants who had contracted to serve as laborers for between four and seven years.[10] Along the tobacco coast, free settlers may have composed less than a quarter of all immigrants in the seventeenth century. But although a minority, their influence on the social, economic, political, and cultural development of the early Chesapeake has never been doubted. The problem has been practical rather than interpretive: sources for the study of the English backgrounds of servants are more plentiful than those for free emigrants. Few lists of free settlers have survived which allow a systematic analysis of their origins, and little evidence exists which throws light on why people chose to move to the Chesapeake.

Material used in this chapter has been pieced together from a wide range of primary and secondary sources, notably, genealogies, probate records, court records, and letters, to create biographies of just over six hundred free settlers.[11] Possibly, the origins of several hundred more will be uncovered in the future, but new evidence is unlikely to alter the fact that the origins of the vast majority will remain obscure. The key issue, then, is to what extent this sample is representative of free emigration as a whole. There is an obvious bias toward wealthy and high-status emigrants—middling groups and poorer settlers are less visible in the records, as are women, who make only a shadowy appearance—and more evidence has survived for some regions than others. Hence the dominance of London is in part a consequence of a greater volume of extant sources than elsewhere, particularly the records of central courts such as the High Court of Admiralty and Chancery. But sufficient material survives to reconstruct an outline of the social and regional origins of free settlers and the main impulses that governed emigration: the various forms that emigration took, the significance of family and kinship, and the continuing importance of transatlantic links. The first section describes who the emigrants were and where they came from. Part II considers motives for emigration. Part III discusses kinship ties, business connections, and the relationship between provincial and metropolitan commercial interests. The final section explores transatlantic links and return migration.

I

Over half a million people left England during the seventeenth century, approximately 377,000 of whom went to America, "a ratio of emigrants to domestic population almost twice that of Spain's."[12] Around 200,000 settled in the Caribbean, 120,000 went to the Chesapeake, and the remainder went to New England. Most settlers, therefore, emigrated to colonies that produced the major staples of colonial trade, tobacco and sugar. The peak period of emigration was from 1630 to 1660, but the Chesapeake attracted large numbers of colonists throughout the rest of the century.[13] Virginia and Maryland were immigrant societies, highly sensitive to the social composition of new arrivals and closely attuned to demographic and social changes in England. Change in the parent country could have a profound influence on colonial development, hence the importance of understanding the English context of New World emigration and the continuing connections that linked Anglo-American society throughout the seventeenth century.[14]

The vast majority of Chesapeake settlers, 70 to 85 percent, arrived as indentured servants—bound laborers who contracted to work in the tobacco fields for between four and seven years in return for their passage across the Atlantic and certain freedom dues after their term of service was completed.[15] A constant supply of cheap labor was essential to maintain the rapid expansion of Virginia's and Maryland's tobacco industry.[16] Tobacco was the key to the region's fortunes. Initially considered a luxury in Europe, it could be produced at low cost in the Chesapeake and sold at a handsome profit in London. From the early 1620s, when extensive cultivation began, tobacco governed the course of Chesapeake society and economy until the end of the colonial period.[17] "We have [no] trade at home and abroad," a contemporary commented, "but that of Tobacco. . . . [It] is our meat, drink, clothes, and monies."[18] The tobacco trade largely dictated the pace, magnitude, and character of immigration.[19]

There are no reliable sources from which to construct a robust estimate of the size of free emigration to the Chesapeake in the seventeenth century, but the figure probably lies somewhere between 18,000 and 36,000. Toward the lower end of the range is likely to be more accurate, possibly around 25,000.[20] What do we know about their social origins? Overall, free emigrants share a number of similarities with indentured servants. The majority were young, male, and single and came predominantly from the same parts of England, namely, London and the Southeast, the West Country and the Northeast. Factors that influenced unfree migration also influenced free migration: the propensity to move while young and unmarried, contacts with mercantile communities, and proximity to major ports. These considerations suggest that free emigration was not autonomous from the general forces that shaped the movement of people within England and abroad during this period.[21] But there are also obvious differences, notably, the higher social status of free emigrants, the possession of capital, and important business or kinship connections with colonial merchants, officials, and planters.

Table 4.1 shows the occupational backgrounds of free emi-

TABLE 4.1. *Status or Occupational Background of Male Emigrants to the Chesapeake, 1600–1699*

Status/Occupational Background	All Emigrants		London Emigrants		London % All Emigrants
	No.	%	No.	%	
Gentry	132	30.6	21	11.5	15.9
Professional	34	7.9	7	3.8	20.5
Merchants	119	27.6	52	28.6	43.7
Mariners	19	4.4	5	2.7	26.3
Food, drink, and supplies	38	8.8	34	18.7	89.5
Clothing and allied	41	9.5	32	17.6	78.0
Leather trades	7	1.6	4	2.2	57.1
Building and woodwork	15	3.5	14	7.7	93.3
Metalwork	9	2.1	7	3.8	77.7
Agriculture	14	3.2	6	3.3	42.9
Semiskilled and unskilled	3	0.7	—	—	—
Total	431	99.9	182	99.9	42.2

grants. Immediately striking is the high proportion claiming gentry origins. This is partly a reflection of the high visibility of gentry in the records, as has been explained, and the practice of scions of middle-class families to accord themselves gentry status in America.[22] However, sons of gentlemen and men of high rank were numerous in the early years of settlement. One of Virginia's first governors, Captain John Smith, complained of the multitude of "Masters" and "Gentlemen" sent to the colony who "could doe nothing but complaine, curse, and despaire." "One hundred good labourers," he remarked, were "better than a thousand such Gallants as were sent me."[23] Over half of the 105 men and boys who founded Jamestown in 1607 were described as gentlemen, while 33 of 120 men who arrived the following year were from gentry stock.[24] Some came from prominent families. George Percy, who sailed with the first expedition, was the eighth son of the earl of Northumberland. He was about twenty-six when he arrived in Virginia and had previously served as a soldier in the Netherlands. Three of the four West brothers, sons of Lord de la Warr, served as governors of the colony. George Sandys, treasurer of Virginia in the 1620s, was the son of the Archbishop of Canterbury and brother of Edwin, an influential member of the Virginia Company and important London merchant.[25]

The founders of Maryland in 1634 included a number of prominent Catholic gentry such as the Calverts, Thomas Cornwallis, and Jerome Hawley, all of whom invested heavily in the new colony. Lord Baltimore's vision was to erect "a New World aristocracy" who would control both land and political office. To ensure the development of a well-ordered society, it was considered vital to attract men of wealth and high status to oversee the transfer of English institutions to America, enforce the law, and provide governance. "By granting manorial privileges with large tracts [of land], the Calverts aimed to attract to Maryland the younger sons of England's landed gentry.... A hierarchical society based on land and rents duplicated the social system familiar to the lords Baltimore as English landowners and colonizers of Ireland."[26] The attempt failed. Baltimore's vision was destroyed during the 1640s by internal dissension and the growth of the tobacco industry, which led to a rapid rise in the fortunes of small and middling planters. The effort to promote a rigidly stratified society crumbled as new wealth led to the emergence of a "home-grown" elite who challenged the political power of Baltimore's aristocracy.[27] Similarly, in Virginia most of the important gentry who arrived in the first couple of decades rarely stayed more than a few years before returning home. Throughout the rest of the century, there was a steady, if small, flow of gentlemen to Virginia and Maryland, particularly younger sons, but there was no direct transfer of England's ruling classes to the tobacco coast.

In the absence of a nobilitas major, a Chesapeake elite emerged out of a fusion of minor or middling gentry and men from mercantile origins. There was frequently no clear distinction between them. It was commonplace for sons of provincial squires to take up trading and become, in Moll Flanders's words, "Gentleman-Tradesman."[28] Maurice Thompson, who became one of the greatest colonial merchants of his day, was born in 1604 to a Hertfordshire gentry family. His brother-in-law, William Tucker, was also a leading London merchant but styled himself "Esquire" in his will.[29] John Lewger and Captain William Blount of St. Mary's County, Maryland, were described as both merchants and esquires in the tax assessment of 1642. Giles Brent, Esq., and Mr. Richard Thompson, also of Maryland, were described as a "merchant-planter" and "planter-trader," respectively.[30]

The categories "Gentry" and "Merchants" in table 4.1 are therefore imprecise. By virtue of emigrating to the Chesapeake, most "gentry" became merchants and active managers of plantations. However, there was also a large group of emigrants, from the middling or lower echelons of England's trading community, who had no pretensions to gentry status.[31] America opened up bright new horizons for small merchants. Unlike the Levant and Far Eastern trades, dominated by mercantile monopolies and operating under "restricted corporately controlled conditions," American commerce was free to all comers. By 1640, 330 merchants from London alone were involved in the tobacco trade compared to 57 active Levant merchants. A great expansion of Chesapeake commerce occurred in midcentury with the rapid growth of the tobacco industry and the increasing involvement of merchants from English outports. Robert Brenner's study of the mercantile community of Civil War London reveals that most new men came from the "middle layers" of seventeenth-century society and were "almost to a man, born outside of London.... From their provincial homes, they sometimes moved directly into colonial entrepreneurship either via the City or through emigration to the colonies. Quite often, however, they spent the early part of their careers in a variety of other City occupations—as shopkeepers, domestic traders, sea captains, or smaller merchants—noncolonial trades."[32]

Since the tobacco trade involved the production of leaf as well as its marketing, many colonial merchants found themselves settling temporarily or permanently in the Chesapeake. Thomas Burbage and George Menefie, two important Virginia planter-merchants, led a quasi-amphibious existence crossing the Atlantic on numerous occasions to sell tobacco and procure goods for sale in the Chesapeake. They were as at home in the busy streets of the metropolis as the sparsely populated expanse of the Tidewater. George Faulkener deposed in the later 1650s that he had traded to Virginia for sixteen years and after the first voyage had lived in the colony for twelve months. He returned to London and then moved to nearby Deptford, Kent, where he had but a small estate, "having suffered great losses at sea."³³ William Ball, a London merchant, moved to the Rappahannock River in the 1650s, but it seems unlikely that he intended to stay for good since his wife and children remained in England; they did not join him until the 1660s.³⁴

Approximately 9 percent of emigrants came from food- and drink-processing occupations (table 4.1). There was often a close connection between merchants and men involved in the victualing trade: cheesemongers, grocers, brewers, fishmongers, and salters. William Harris and Thomas Deacon, London cheesemongers, formed partnerships with both Maurice Thompson and William Tucker in the late 1630s and settled briefly in Virginia around the same time.³⁵ Two other partners of Thompson were George Snelling, a brewer from Southwark, and William Pennoyer from Bristol who set himself up as a shopkeeper in London.³⁶ As noted, many merchants had themselves been involved in provisioning or shopkeeping before moving into colonial trade.

Other occupations mentioned in table 4.1 are largely unremarkable. Forty-one settlers had been involved in clothing or textile trades before taking ship for the Chesapeake. They included five haberdashers, three tailors, two point makers, two serge makers, a silk weaver, a cloth worker, and a linen draper. It is doubtful whether they expected to practice their crafts in Virginia or Maryland. Tailors could find employment, but there was little domestic cloth production until the end of the century. More probably, they had fallen on difficult times and converted their remaining funds into capital to finance setting up a modest tobacco plantation. A small proportion of emigrants (5.6%) were artisans, such as carpenters, joiners, masons, and blacksmiths. Plantation economy did not require numerous specialist trades, and wages were not high enough in the Chesapeake to attract skilled workers in large numbers while there was plenty of work in England. Neither did the tobacco coast hold much attraction for men from farming backgrounds. Whereas almost half the indentured servants who emigrated from Bristol in the seventeenth century were sons of farmers, farm laborers, or former smallholders, only 3 percent of free settlers had agricultural occupations. There is little evidence, therefore, of large-scale free emigration from the English countryside. Yeomen and husbandmen appear to have been reluctant to

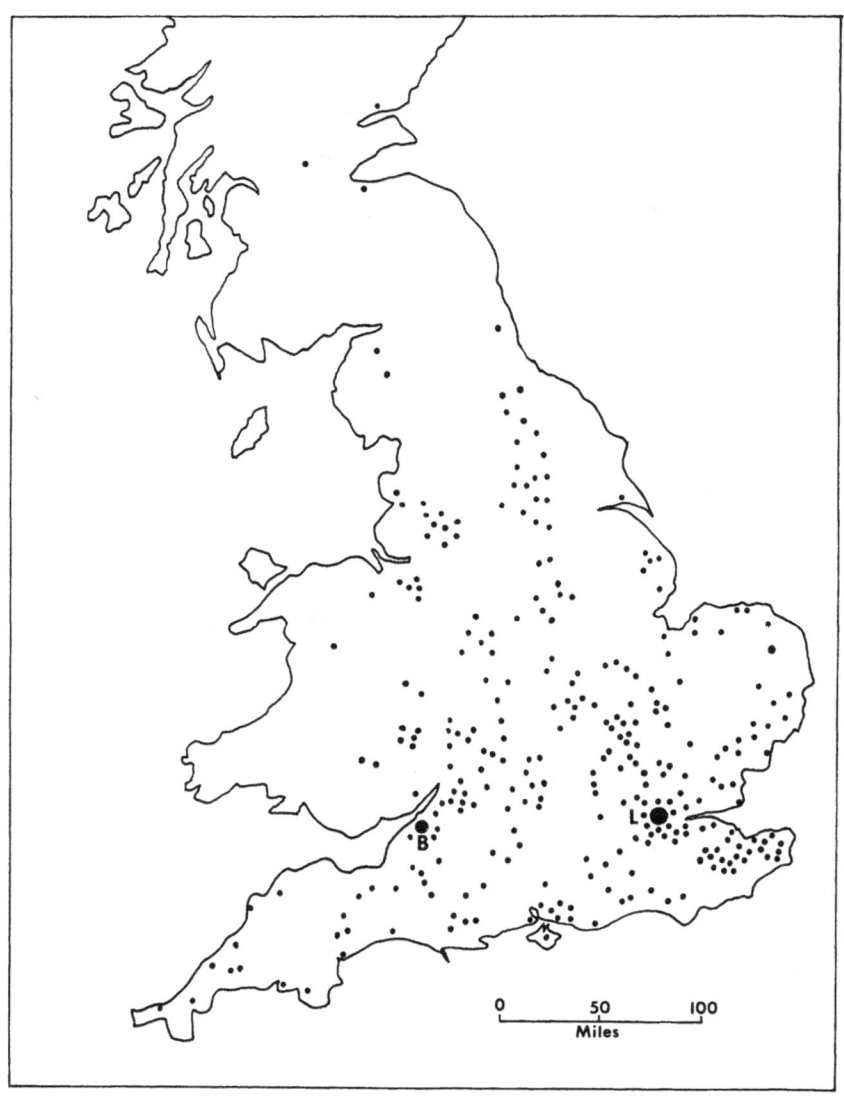

Fig. 4.2. Origins of Free Settlers to the Chesapeake in the Seventeenth Century

TABLE 4.2. *Regional Origins of Free Emigrants to the Chesapeake in the Seventeenth Century*

Regional Origins	N	%
London and Southeast	291	48.2
Central and Southern England	130	21.5
Southwest England	18	3.0
East Anglia	33	5.5
Central England	70	11.6
Wales	6	1.0
Northwest England	18	3.0
Northeast England	26	4.3
Scotland	3	0.5
Ireland	4	0.7
Foreign	5	0.8
Total	604	100.1

give up their holdings in England for Chesapeake plantations. Those who chose, or were forced, to leave the land may have been too poor to afford the cost of setting up a plantation of their own and consequently joined ranks of indentured servants.[37]

What parts of England did free emigrants come from? Figure 4.2 strongly suggests that the majority were from southern England. Nearly a third of the sample (32.6%) were from London and just under half from the metropolis and southeastern counties (table 4.2).[38] Another 20 percent came from a broad sweep of counties stretching from the Thames Valley to the Bristol Channel.[39] East Anglia, so prominent in Puritan migration to New England, contributed only 5.5 percent.[40] Farther north, apart from Yorkshire, which produced the most settlers after London, Gloucestershire, and Kent, few counties were represented by more than a handful of emigrants.[41] No community, except London and Bristol, regularly contributed large numbers of settlers throughout the century. Emigrants came from villages and towns scattered throughout England. Two regions were particularly important, however: the counties surrounding London and Bristol's hinterland, areas in proximity to the two major colonial ports where business connections between country and city were strongest.[42]

Like indentured servants, many emigrants (nearly 60%) had

lived in urban communities. Approximately 15 percent were from small market towns; 6 percent from larger towns of 5,000 people or more; 39 percent from the cities of London, Bristol, and Norwich; and the remainder (40%) from villages. If some market towns, like Thornbury and Dursley in Gloucestershire, hardly merit the description "urban," being little more than two or three streets surrounded by countryside, others, such as Ashford and Faversham in Kent, were much more substantial and boasted a couple of thousand inhabitants each. One must be cautious not to make too many distinctions between rural and urban life in preindustrial England. "Agriculture," as Peter Clark and Paul Slack point out, "pervaded the life of the market town."[43] But there were also significant differences between rural and urban environments. Larger towns exhibited a much wider range of occupations, higher population density, and greater extremes of wealth and poverty. Provincial capitals such as Canterbury, Winchester, and Norwich had important administrative and religious functions as well as being social and economic centers of their regions. The influx of people on market and court days provided valuable opportunities to pass on news and gossip or develop business relations. Many aspiring merchants doubtless made initial contacts in their own county town before moving to the great commercial centers of London and Bristol.[44]

Of emigrants from urban backgrounds, nearly two-thirds had lived in London or Bristol. By 1650, Bristol was England's second port after London. At the center of a broad communications network, the city was linked to the Midlands by the Severn Valley and with South Wales, Somerset, and the Southwest peninsula by coastal waterways. In the second half of the seventeenth century, Bristol "found an expanding role as a major participant in the Atlantic trade by engaging in the tobacco and sugar trades and in the Newfoundland fisheries and by interloping in the African slave trade." By 1700, nearly half the ships entering the port were engaged in American commerce. The city provided a wealth of experience and entrepreneurial skill, besides capital and marketing facilities for colonial products.[45]

Several emigrants from Bristol were from well-connected families. Miles and John Cary were the son and grandson, respectively, of John Cary (1583–1661), a wealthy merchant. Colonel Robert

Pitt was also from a prominent mercantile background and was grandson of Thomas Pitt (died 1613), a chamberlain of the city. Pitt and John Cary emigrated to the south side of the James River, Virginia, where a number of Gloucestershire families had established themselves. Edward Thruston, "chyrurgeon," was son of John (1606–1675), another Chamberlain. He, like Miles Cary, settled in Warwick County, Virginia. The fortunes of these Bristol men in America varied considerably. Colonel Pitt established a lucrative trade in servants and rose to high office in Virginia before dying in old age. Miles Cary was not so lucky. He was killed during an engagement with the Dutch in the James River in 1667. His nephew, John, returned to England in the 1670s and became a prosperous merchant in London. Edward Thruston also returned to England, settling first in London and then in Long Ashton, Somerset, where his family originated.[46]

Despite Bristol's growing importance, London maintained an unquestioned preeminence in colonial trade throughout the century. Simply in terms of size, London dwarfed all other English cities. Bristol's entire population could have fitted comfortably into one of the capital's suburbs. As Defoe noted, London was less one city than several joined together.[47] Its population rose from approximately 200,000 in 1600 to around 490,000 in 1700, by which time it was the largest city in Europe.[48] London's phenomenal growth, more rapid than any other European capital in the seventeenth century, was the result of three main factors: political centralization, a massive increase in trade and manufacturing, and upheavals in provincial economies. Above all, it "was the combination of the political and mercantile roles that made the metropolis tick. . . . London was almost unique in Europe in combining the role of capital city and great port."[49] As England emerged from the periphery of a predominantly intra-European trading system, London developed as one of the principal centers of worldwide commerce. The capital's huge share of the nation's trade cannot be overemphasized. Even allowing for Bristol's increasing involvement in the Atlantic trade, London engrossed between two-thirds and three-fourths of the country's exports and imports throughout the century.[50] Much of the growth in overseas trade came from the rising volume of reexports, mainly American and Eastern products, which constituted 38 percent of all London's exports by value in 1700. The development of the metropolis as an entrepôt for colonial goods was one of the key features of the late Stuart period.[51]

"With so much wealth and activity concentrated in London," Theodore Rabb has remarked, "it was natural for the metropolis to become an essential catalyst for the growing interest in overseas enterprises."[52] Nearly all the important trading ventures originated from there, and many of the new mercantile companies that sprang up in the late sixteenth and early seventeenth centuries were located in the city. London provided financial backing, political connections, commercial expertise, and an enormous population from which colonists were recruited. "The City was the crucible in which an empire was forged."[53]

One hundred ninety-seven emigrants gave their origin or place of residence as London. Their status and occupational backgrounds are given in table 4.1. Far fewer gentry (less than one-sixth) emigrated from the capital than the provinces; most gentry were from rural origins. In contrast, the majority of colonists involved in food and drink processing, provisioning, the cloth industry, and the building and woodworking trades came from the metropolis. To a certain extent, the figures reflect London's general occupational structure. Clothing trades, for example, comprised over a fifth of *all* occupations in the capital from the 1540s to 1700. The proportion of Londoners engaged in victualing and food processing rose from 10 percent in the first half of the century to 16 percent in the second half—a response to the increasing numbers of fashionable visitors to the capital during the "season" as well as to the rising demand of shipping. Merchants made up only 7 to 11 percent of all occupations, but this owes in part to the small number of merchants living in extramural parishes. If only the city within the walls, one of the wealthiest areas of London, is considered, the proportion rises to 20 percent.[54] Emigrants, therefore, came from a wide range of occupations found in the capital, with an emphasis, not surprisingly, on those trades connected with overseas commerce. They appear, also, to have come from an equally wide spectrum of society: from relatively humble backgrounds like Ralph Crake, a member of the Drapers Company, described as "a poor fellow" when he emigrated in 1628, to city plutocrats like Maurice Thompson and Edward Bennett.[55] The bulk of Londoners who set themselves up in the Chesapeake, however, were from the middling sections of the social ladder—petty merchants, shopkeepers, and traders—and a cut above indentured servants, who were drawn predominantly from the lower classes.[56]

To sum up, the majority of free emigrants were young to middle-aged males from southern and central England. Precise age at emigration is difficult to determine, but a small sample of 98 men (table 4.3) suggests that about 40 percent were under twenty-five and 57 percent were less than thirty. Free emigrants were typically older than indentured servants, a large proportion of whom left England while still in their teens or early twenties (table 4.3). Older age is a reflection of the higher status of free emigrants and the fact that they had usually established themselves in a trade before moving to the colonies. Whether or not they were married is also difficult to determine. What little evidence exists suggests most emigrants were single. Of 169 settlers, free and unfree, who left England for Virginia in 1635, only 7 (4.1%) were members of family groups. This compares with over half the New England emigrants who left in the same year.[57] Single men formed the largest group of free emigrants into Maryland between 1634 and 1681: 71 of a sample of 122 men were single, 49 were married, and 2 were widowers. Since these figures include immigrants from Virginia as well as those directly from England, the number of married men might well be inflated by the influx of families from the older colony who arrived in Maryland around midcentury.[58] Single men who settled in the Chesapeake probably married women servants or returned to England for a bride. The sex ratio among free emigrants (239.2) did not compensate for the imbalance between male and female indentured servants, which for most of the century was two or three men for every woman.[59]

Emigrants came from a broad range of occupations—sixty-eight trades are represented in table 4.1—but there was a clear preponderance of men from gentry and mercantile backgrounds. Gentlemen-tradesmen, merchants, mariners, shopkeepers, and provisioners comprised approximately four-fifths of the sample. Only a few colonists came from agricultural backgrounds. There was no wholesale transfer of England's agrarian classes to the tobacco coast. As far as free emigration is concerned, the Chesapeake was

TABLE 4.3. *Age of Free Settlers and Indentured Servants Who Emigrated to the Chesapeake, 1607–1707 (in percentages)*

Age Categories (years)	Free Settlers, Males 1607–1699 (N 98)	London Servants, 1635 Males (N 1740)	London Servants, 1635 Females (N 271)	London Servants, 1682–1686 Males (N 414)	London Servants, 1682–1686 Females (N 159)	Liverpool Servants, 1697–1707 Males (N 518)	Liverpool Servants, 1697–1707 Females (N 284)
Under 15	3.1	3.8	3.0	6.5	1.9	23.0	4.2
15–19	10.2	27.4	30.0	21.0	25.8	32.0	30.6
20–24	26.5	39.9	48.1	51.0	57.2	26.8	46.5
25–29	17.3	14.2	11.1	12.6	11.9	9.5	13.6
30–34	18.4	8.5	4.1	8.0	2.5	5.4	3.5
35–39	11.2	3.2	1.5	0.2	0.6	1.9	1.4
40–44	7.1	1.6	0.7	0.2	—	1.0	0.4
45 and over	6.1	1.4	1.5	0.5	—	0.4	—
Total	99.9	100.0	100.0	100.0	99.9	100.0	100.0

settled by merchants and traders, not by uprooted English farmers. Substantially more servants came from agricultural backgrounds than free settlers.[60] This characteristic is underlined by the large proportion of the latter from urban origins.

II

Motives for emigration were diverse. In the early years of colonization, some gentry were attracted by the prospect of easy wealth or military adventure; exploration and conquest were considered worthy pursuits for a gentleman. Hopes that North America would furnish the English with fabulous riches faded, however, in the face of hardships endured in the first years of settlement.[61] By 1612, it was clear that Virginia was no Mexico or Peru. "It was the spaniards good hap," lamented William Simmonds, "to happen in those parts where were infinite numbers of people, whoe had manured the ground with that providence that it afforded victuall at all times; and time had brought them to that perfection [that] they had the use of gold and silver. . . . But we chanced in a lande, even as God made it. Where we found only an idle, improvident, scattered people, ignorant of the knowledge of gold, or silver, or any commodities; and carelesse of anything but from hand to mouth . . . nothing to encourage us but what accidently wee found nature afforded."[62] Tobacco, not gold and silver, saved Virginia from collapse. Gentlemen of fortune would have to hang up their swords and take up the hoe if they expected to strike it rich.[63] As it became evident that the high risks involved in moving to the Chesapeake were not matched by quick wealth, the aristocracy lost interest in the New World.

If the tobacco coast failed to meet expectations of an El Dorado, and the English "*conquista*" proved very different from that of the Spanish, nevertheless possibilities of making a modest profit remained. A number of early arrivals may best be described as *hobereaux*, impoverished gentry who gambled on Virginia to recoup dwindling fortunes at home. Sir John Berkeley of Beverston, Gloucestershire, who emigrated to Virginia in 1620 to erect an ironworks, was described as "estranged from his friends and reduced to poverty." He died in the Indian massacre two years later. A near neighbor, George Thorpe, Esq., of Wanswell Court, Berkeley, "did secretlie flie out of England to Virginia" in 1620 to avoid creditors, as did his associate Arnold Oldisworth, Esq., who reputedly owed the Crown £6000 in 1631. Another Gloucestershire gentlemen, William Tracy of Hailes, was jailed for debt on the eve of his departure for the Berkeley plantation on the James River and had to be bailed out by friends.[64] Financial problems were not confined to the upper classes. The case of George Grace, a merchant of London, has already been mentioned. During the late 1620s or early 1630s, he shipped to Delft "a great quantity" of cloths, but owing to plague in the city, his servants were not able to sell his merchandise and exchanged the cloth for Bibles, "being the best bargain they could make." The Bibles, worth £300, were exported to London where they were seized, leaving Grace unable to pay his debts. He fled to Virginia where, according to his wife, "he now lives in a poor condition."[65] Throughout the century, Virginia and Maryland provided a distant refuge for immigrants fleeing from creditors.[66]

The Chesapeake also provided a sanctuary for religious refugees. Perry Miller exaggerates in proposing that religion "was the really energizing propulsion" in the founding of Virginia, but he is surely correct to suggest that it was an important instrumental stimulus for emigration.[67] Despite the pious exhortations of the Virginia Company, there was little sustained effort to bring the Protestant faith to indigenous peoples of the Chesapeake. Unlike Spanish and French colonies, settlement in English America was not followed by a vigorous attempt to convert Indians, and thus there was no large-scale movement of Anglican missionaries to the tobacco coast. In fact, until the early eighteenth century, there were insufficient ministers to serve the needs of English colonists let alone convert Indian peoples.[68] Rather than becoming a New World forum for a Protestant (Anglican) crusade, Virginia and Maryland attracted men and women whose religious beliefs were becoming marginalized in England—Puritans and Catholics—or proponents of new radical sects such as the Quakers.

From its inception, Maryland was intended as a haven for Catholics. By the early seventeenth century, despite modest growth, the Catholic community in England existed only as "a tiny and embattled minority."[69] Although there was no organized pogrom against Catholics, they were generally excluded from the highest offices in local and central government and lived under increasing surveillance by the church courts and quarter sessions.[70] Maryland provided a refuge from religious and civil disabilities suffered in England; in Lord Baltimore's colony, they could openly practice their religion and enjoy political patronage. During the first fifteen years of the colony's existence, Baltimore's most important supporters came from Catholic backgrounds. "Maryland," according to Russell Menard, "appealed primarily to the Roman Catholic younger sons of English gentry families, men who saw in the settlement on the Chesapeake an opportunity to serve their Church and make their mark in the world."[71] Five of the six major initial investors were Catholics. Thomas Cornwallis contributed the largest share. His motives for emigrating were varied, a combination of ambition, enterprise, and faith, but he confided to Lord Baltimore that "Securety of Contiens was the first Condition that I expected from this Government." He threatened to leave the colony rather than "consent to anything that may not stand with the Good Contiens of A Real Catholick."[72] There was no possibility, however, that Maryland would become an exclusively Catholic province; not enough Catholics emigrated from England, and, even if they had, an entirely Catholic colony was politically unacceptable to the English government. Nevertheless, down to the Glorious Revolution, Catholics were able to dominate the political life of Maryland in a way that would have been impossible in the parent country.[73] Baltimore may have been disappointed that more of his coreligionists chose not to settle in the Cheapeake, but sufficient numbers emigrated or were converted to maintain an important presence in the colony.[74]

On August 28, 1618, Thomas Locke of London wrote to William Trumbull in Brussells, "The last weeke there were some 100 or verie neere of Brownists shipped to Virginia, and shortlie there wilbe twice as many puritanes, god speede them well."[75] The scale of Puritan emigration to the Chesapeake was far smaller than that to New England but was nonetheless significant and deserves consideration. Separatist settlements in Virginia were guided by the same impulses that led the Pilgrims to Plymouth. Like the Pilgrims, early leaders of Virginia's Puritan movement, Edward Bennett, Christopher Lawne, and Francis Blackwell, were associated with the separatist church in the Netherlands before emigrating to America. Bennett probably moved to Holland in the first years of the seventeenth century, residing initially at Delft and then at Amsterdam where he became one of the elders of the Ancient Church. He may have begun shipping colonists to Virginia about the same time that Blackwell emigrated in 1618. By 1620, he was a wealthy merchant in London and one of the principal pillars of Puritan emigration to America. In 1622, he financed the establishment of a plantation at Warrascoyack and moved there himself four years later. When he returned to England in 1629, his nephew, Richard Bennett, assumed the leadership of Puritans in the colony. Christopher Lawne, from Blandford, Dorset, was born around 1580. As a young man he moved to Norwich and followed the trade of a buttonmaker; he possibly came into contact there with Dutch separatists fleeing from persecution in their own country. In 1610, or before, he emigrated to Amsterdam and became a prominent critic of the internal feuds between different branches of the separatist church. Eight or nine years later, he transported himself to Virginia and settled at Lawne's Creek on the south side of the James River a few miles downstream from Jamestown. Francis Blackwell was another elder of the Ancient Church in Amsterdam and was responsible for organizing the expedition of 1618 when approximately 180 Brownists took ship in the *William and Thomas*. He and 130 others died en route in one of the most terrible crossings of the century.[76]

There are no reliable figures for Puritan emigration, but its impact on Chesapeake society was considerable. By midcentury, there were large numbers of nonconformists in Isle of Wight, Nansemond, and Lower Norfolk counties. Mr. Thomas Harrison, a Puritan minister of Lower Norfolk County, was said to have 118 members in his church in 1648, which represented about a quarter of the adult population;[77] a formidable "schismaticall party, of whose intentions," the Assembly of the same year declared, "our native country of England hath had and yet hath too sad experience."[78] Several hundred Puritans migrated northward to Providence on the Severn River, Maryland, in the following year. At the same time, nonconformists from the Eastern Shore of Virginia began moving to Maryland. The Eastern Shore, like the area south of the James, was a stronghold of Puritanism. Notable among early settlers of Northampton County were William Stone, nephew of a wealthy London merchant, who became governor of Maryland in 1648 and who promoted the exodus of Puritans from Virginia, and Obedience Robins, born in Brackley, Northamptonshire, who was one of the colony's leading nonconformists.[79]

Quakerism arrived in America in the mid-1650s. George Fox, a founder of the movement, wrote in his diary in 1655 that "about this time several Friends went beyond the seas to declare the everlasting Truth of God."[80] Fifty-nine, nearly half of whom were women, migrated between 1656 and 1663 alone.[81] Most Quakers went to New England, but some missionaries, like Thomas Thurston, ended up in the Chesapeake after first proselytizing in Massachusetts.[82] Owing to a greater freedom of conscience in religion than elsewhere in the colonies, Maryland "was the scene of the first substantial convincements in Quakerism on the mainland of the New World."[83] In the absence of a strong Anglican church, Quakerism, like other nonconformist sects, flourished. Commenting on the religious complexion of restoration Maryland, Charles Lord Baltimore informed the Privy Council that "the greatest part of the inhabitants of that Province (three or four at least) do consist of Presbiterians, Independents, Anabaptists, and Quakers, those of the Church of England as well as those of the Romish being the fewest."[84]

Quaker links with Bristol may have been especially close. The West Country was an important center of Quakerism, and the Society of Friends in Bristol were in regular contact with Friends in Virginia from at least 1667.[85] Edward Beare of Bristol, "a maker of apparell," emigrated in 1673, while Jonathan Packer sought a "speedy effecting" of his request to marry in 1678 "being suddenly bound away to Virginia."[86] The movement was not all one way. William Bressie, a Quaker from Isle of Wight County, was described in 1672 as "now resident in Bristoll."[87] Quakerism evidently appealed to men and women of middling status, especially those involved in mercantile activities, skilled work of various kinds, and the clothing trade. Some 29 percent of Bristol Friends were involved in commerce or food and drink processing, and clothing trades accounted for another 40 percent.[88] Thus, the sorts of people associated with transatlantic commerce appear commonly to have been attracted by nonconformity. The main reason for emigrating remained primarily mercantile, but colonists like John Baynton, a Quaker who left Bristol in 1688, may have found Virginia more congenial to his religious views than English society.[89]

Nonconformists of another kind, political rather than religious, settled in the Chesapeake during the 1640s and 1650s as echoes of the civil wars and overthrow of the monarchy reached the colonies. Susana Chidley wrote to her uncle, John Ferrar, in October 1649 and reported that four ships were about to sail to Virginia "and abundance of quality go in them." She met with few people who did not know of some who were going, or resolved to go, to America.[90] According to Clarendon, Sir William Berkeley, a staunch royalist and governor of Virginia in the 1640s and early 1650s, "invited many gentlemen and others thither, as to a place of security which he could defend against any attempt, and where they might live plentifully, [and] many persons of condition, and good officers in the war, had transported themselves, with all the estate they had been able to preserve."[91] Sir Henry Chicheley, Sir Thomas Lunsford, and Sir Grey Skipwith were among the royalist sympathizers who left England after the execution of Charles I. Lunsford had been appointed lieutenant of the Tower of London in 1641 and fought for the king in both civil wars. He may have met Chicheley, a fellow officer, while imprisoned in the tower in 1648. Another cavalier emigré, Colonel Henry Norwood, describes meeting them both at Ralph Wormeley's plantation on the York River in 1650, where they passed an evening "feasting and carousing" with other royalist officers "lately come from England."[92] Chicheley later married Wormeley's widow and established an extensive estate in Middlesex County, Virginia. He served as a member of the House of Burgesses, councillor, and, on several occasions, as governor.[93]

The number of "cavaliers" who emigrated to Virginia during the 1640s and 1650s was not large. By far the great majority remained in England either in retirement or fomenting plots against Parliament and the Republic. Others fled to the continent.[94] But although Virginia did not become a royalist bastion as Berkeley hoped, a number of cavaliers established prominent families in the colony who dominated the political and economic life of their repective localities for the remainder of the century.[95] Numerically, royalists were insignificant, but in local as well as provincial politics they exercised an influence wholly disproportionate to their numbers.⁹⁶

III

A striking feature of free emigration to the Chesapeake is the importance of kinship connections. "Given that emigration... by and large was organized and carried out on an individual and private basis rather than through official recruitment and public sponsorship, it was the family that in many senses provided structure and coherence to the entire process."⁹⁷ Ida Altman's comment refers to sixteenth-century Spanish emigration to America, but the point is applicable to English settlement of Virginia and Maryland in the seventeenth century. As in the case of Spanish migration, the decision to move to America might be related to a range of familial considerations: an individual's position within the family (younger sons, for example), contacts with relatives in London or other major ports, and kinship connections in the Chesapeake.⁹⁸ While relatively few settlers emigrated in family groups, family and kinship were significant in influencing the decision to emigrate, facilitating the move and sometimes determining where individuals eventually settled.

The importance of family ties can be illustrated by a few examples. Henry Fleet's connections to the Wyatt, Filmer, and Argall families of Kent have been described already. The Filmers were also linked to the Horsmanden family of Lenham, as was St. Leger Codd who emigrated to Northumberland County in the 1670s and Maryland ten years later. Thomas Warren of Ripple, Kent, was related to the Gookin family of the same parish. Daniel Gookin arrived in Virginia in 1621. Did Warren hear about opportunities in the Chesapeake through his kinsman?⁹⁹ Kentish gentry were bound together by ties of blood as well as common interest. The tangled web of cousinage, such a distinctive feature of the Chesapeake squirearchy in the late seventeenth and early eighteenth centuries, was long predated in English shires.¹⁰⁰

A number of kin (usually brothers) emigrated together. William and George Fitzgeffrey, born in Bedfordshire, sailed for Virginia in 1623; Hugh and Justinian Yeo of Harton, Devon, settled on Virginia's Eastern Shore in the 1650s; and John and Lawrence

Washington moved to the Northern Neck in the mid-1660s.[101] Thomas Lygon arrived in Virginia with Sir William Berkeley in 1642 and settled in Henrico County. A branch of the family had experimented with tobacco production in England during the 1620s, and it is possible that Lygon's interest in the Chesapeake sprang from this ultimately unsuccessful venture. It is more likely, however, that he was taking advantage of his kinship with Governor Berkeley to secure an advantageous position in the colony.[102] Perhaps similar reasons induced George Sandys to emigrate with his kinsman, Governor Sir Francis Wyatt, in 1621.[103]

Some free settlers were encouraged to emigrate because they already had kin living in America. John Beheathland left for Virginia in 1636 "being about to go to his mother." He may have been the son of Robert Behethland, gent., a member of the first expedition of 1607.[104] Robert Cole's decision to emigrate to Maryland in 1652 was doubtless influenced by his Catholicism, but the choice of St. Mary's County may have been determined by the presence there of his "cousin," Benjamin Gill.[105] Henry Fleet's three brothers settled in Maryland during the 1630s and 1640s, and his nephews settled in Virginia around the same time.[106] Colonel Henry Norwood could have followed fellow royalists into exile in Europe or the West Indies in 1649 but instead chose Virginia. "The honour," he wrote, "I had of being nearly related to Sir William Barkeley the governor, was no small inclination to encourage me with a little stock to this adventure."[107] Peter Laslett characterizes the young gentleman emigrant as "no penniless seeker after a fresh start in a freer world. He went complete with capital to stock his plantation and introductions to the important people in the colony, many of whom were his relatives and had been his fathers neighbours.... The story of early Virginian planters' families illustrates the most important feature of English gentry of the time—the immense strength of the family bond and the extraordinary cohesion of the grouping of families by locality."[108]

Kinship was significant also in forging links between English provinces and major mercantile centers, particularly London. The career of Henry Corbin furnishes a good example. Born in 1629, he was the third son of Thomas Corbin, Esq., of Hall End, Warwickshire. He moved to London in his early twenties where he joined his brothers, Gawin and Thomas, who may have already been involved in the tobacco trade. Shortly after receiving a £400 legacy from his father, he sailed for Maryland in 1654 "to serve as the American arm of a transatlantic merchant partnership."[109] As we have seen, George Sandys of Norbonne, Kent, had city connections through his elder brother, Sir Edwin, leader of the liberal faction of the Virginia Company of London.[110] George Fitzgeffrey's brother, William, was of Staple Inn, London, at the time of their departure for America, while William Stone from Northamptonshire, who emigrated in 1633, was a nephew of Thomas Stone, haberdasher and merchant of the city.[111]

It is difficult to be precise about the degree of influence that London connections exerted on an individual's decision to emigrate, but sufficient evidence survives to suggest that many future settlers first arrived in the city to take up apprenticeships or work before moving on to the colonies. It made good sense for one member of the family to supervise business in America while other members remained in England. Many partnerships operated on this basis.[112] Younger sons of gentry, prominent yeomen, and provincial tradesmen flocked to the cities during the seventeenth century seeking opportunities in the burgeoning colonial trade.[113] As representatives of provincial families established themselves in London or Bristol, they facilitated the movement of brothers, nephews, and cousins from the shires. Cities and ports served as staging posts en route to the New World. They constituted a vital link in the chain of events that took people from their home parishes across the Atlantic to the shores of the Chesapeake Bay.

IV

Notwithstanding religious and political reasons, the major motivation for emigrating was economic. The overwhelming majority of free settlers set sail for the tobacco coast in the hope of making money and a comfortable living. During the tobacco boom of the 1620s, Virginia took on the feverish atmosphere of the Klondike gold rush. Those who survived the hazards of the environment and could secure enough labor to work in the fields stood to make handsome profits while the price of leaf remained high.[114] But after the collapse of the boom, settlers were obliged to build up their estates more gradually. Planters began the laborious process of clearing the land, building dwellings and barns, fencing in crops, planting orchards, and raising livestock. Tobacco remained the keystone of the economy, and planters were firmly wedded to transatlantic markets, but wealth was also generated, albeit slowly, by the central activity of the seventeenth century: farm building.[115]

Aside from careerists (such as government officials) and itinerant merchants, most settlers who emigrated after 1630 must have expected to stay in the Chesapeake for sufficient time to establish and develop a plantation. This does not imply that they chose to emigrate for good. As we shall see, there was a small but significant movement of people back to England throughout the century. Yet the economics of plantation agriculture did not allow for rapid returns on the initial investment, nor, in the main, was it feasible to leave a plantation in the hands of an overseer and return home. There was, consequently, no development of an absentee landlord class as in the case of the West Indies.[116] Running a successful tobacco plantation required the personal supervision of the owner to ensure that the many critical operations involved in cultivating, preparing, and marketing tobacco were carried out efficiently.[117]

Little direct evidence survives of what settlers thought of their new home in America. A few letters, however, reveal something of the reality of daily life in the Chesapeake and the concerns of the settlers themselves. One evident concern was to keep in touch with friends and relatives in England. Emigration undoubtedly represented a major upheaval in the social and emotional lives of colonists—it could hardly have been otherwise—yet moving to the New World did not necessarily mean that settlers completely severed all ties with their past. Recently, historians have begun to stress the social as well as political and economic links that influenced the transatlantic world in this period.[118] Communications were hampered by the distances involved and the haphazard organization of postal deliveries, but it is clear that regular correspondence between planters and factors, friends, and kin was commonplace.

Maintaining contact with family and events in England helped immigrants with the difficult process of settling down. Thomas Reynolds (or Rennalls), a mariner formerly of London, arrived in

Virginia in 1650 and took up a hundred-acre tract on Tanners Creek in Lower Norfolk County. In 1658, he wrote to his "very loving sister" in Bristol desiring to "heare from you & my child" (his daughter). He sent his regards to his aunt and "cousen James" and continued, "You shall receave a small token by ye gunner of Capt. Bond to drinke a pint of wine with my Aunte & my child. I shall make it better next year if I live."[119] Susana Perrin wrote to her son, John of York County, in 1648 informing him of the death of his father and enclosed "a smale peece of gould for your wife."[120] Sending "tokens" was an important aspect of keeping in touch. Michael Upchurch sent his father two rolls of tobacco and his mother an Indian basket and a pepper box, besides a variety of "exotica" (including two woodpeckers' crowns, a pair of flying hart's horns, two "mushcodds," and half a dozen Indian pipes) to his friends, John and Virginia Ferrar.[121] Correspondents writing from England often included news of important developments. When Francis Wheeler wrote to his father in Virginia in 1659 he included a description of the political turmoil in London: "Since the 9th of October here hath been another overturne in the Governmt. of this nation; ye soldyers turned out ye last long Parliament & for a while wee were without any setled Governmt. but ye Sword... & had not ye good hand of the Lord prevented what was feared, for aught I know this City might be turned into Ashes & the streets running with blood." He concluded, "Father I thinke it would be convenient for you to keepe a plantation; & something in Virg[ini]a the times being soe dangerouse here."[122]

Similarly, settlers frequently reported news of recent and significant events to their family and kin in England. "We have had many prognosticks of God's Judgment," wrote John Catlett to his cousin, Thomas, in 1664 "first a very Unseasonable yeare so yt[that] I can say nothing did prosper of the fruits of ye earth, 21y The coming downe of wilde beast amongst us more than ordinary such as bears and woolves... 31y The treachery of the heathen, the manner to long to relate... 41y At this very Junction of time there was a combination of severall servants, who had comploted first to arme themselves with their Masters armes & then 21y to make their owne termes which was their freedom & in case of denial to kill all that should oppose them."[123] His letter reveals a sense of loneliness and isolation that some colonists felt far away from home. Catlett lived in Rappahannock County, a frontier region that had only recently begun to fill up with settlers.[124] The parish in which he lived, "Sittingborne," was named after the parish in Kent from where he came, but apart from this, there was little to remind him of his birthplace. Sparsely populated and prone to Indian attack, it is hardly surprising that he felt vulnerable. His letter describes "ye remotenesse" of "ye Country" and the problems of communication: "I find that many of my letters never come to hand."[125]

While Catlett's vision of events tended toward the apocalyptic, the majority of letters illustrate more prosaic concerns: the price of tobacco, the impact of the Dutch wars, and personal circumstances. Lawrence Warde confided to his aunt in the summer of 1653 that though she might envy him "living in quietness," they had had "sad and distressing times for want of shipping to take away their tobacco because of the untimely war." The London fleet, he reported, came safely when they had almost given up hope of its arrival. Having neglected to provide for themselves from the Bristol ships, those depending on the London fleet were brought "to a great necessity."[126] Twenty years later, Nicholas Spencer wrote to his brother at the outbreak of the third Dutch war. "This violent warr will put A great obstruction in the freedom of trade especially in the supply to these remote parts."[127] Anxiety about the disruption of trade, cost of freight, and the price fetched by leaf in distant European markets was part of the warp and weft of a tobacco planter's life and serves as reminder of the dependence of colonists on English merchants and shipping.[128]

Bequests furnish further evidence of settlers' concern about friends and kin in England. Walter Irbye, of "Ackeemaake" in Northampton County, left his mother all his estate in Virginia and his house and land in "Hogstrapp" Lincolnshire. James Austen, gent., of Stafford County bequeathed his estate in Virginia and England to his "cousin" John Ashton, haberdasher of Covent Garden, London, and "cousin" John Foster of Wozbridge, Cambridgeshire. Some settlers followed the English custom of leaving a bequest to the poor of their native parish. Peter Hooker, who emigrated in 1636, bequeathed £1 to the poor of Chilcombe, Hampshire, besides £3 to his aunt, £1 each to his "Uncle Eger's children," and £3 to his "Cousin" Ann. The rest of his estate went to his brothers, John and Edward. Francis Dickison left Elizabeth Moore, his "wife before God," £40 as well as £2 to the poor of Northam and the same amount to the poor of Barnstaple, Devon.[129]

Wills confirm that many planters, middling and wealthy, owned property in England. Robert Wynne of Charles City County, gent., had a farm in Whitstaple, Kent, which he left to his eldest son and a house and oatmeal mill in Canterbury, called the "Lilly Pott," which he bequeathed to his youngest son.[130] John Perrin of York County inherited "a little house" in Bury worth £40 when his father died in 1648.[131] Thus, moving to the New World did not always entail selling up family land in England. Perhaps some emigrants believed they would one day return home, but probably the main reason for retaining property in England was that it made good economic sense in view of the vicissitudes of plantation agriculture. If the price of tobacco collapsed, at least there remained a nest egg in England. Family property could be leased or managed by kin and provided supplemental income until such time as it was passed on to children or relatives.

Links between the Old World and the New were maintained also by occasional visits back to England. Every year, scores of settlers sailed to London, Bristol, and other ports to see friends and kin, procure servants, and sell tobacco. Luke Petley arrived in London in 1656 intending "to see his friends." Baker Brooke, "planter in Virginia," returned to England in the same year "at the request of his Brother who sent for him."[132] Christopher Boyse and Richard Rutherford were in England in the mid-1630s to obtain servants.[133] Merchants frequently crossed the Atlantic, some virtually having *dual* residence.[134] On courthouse doors throughout the Chesapeake, notices of the intention of settlers to "go for England" were on public display every month of the year.[135] If the two- to three-month voyage was considered tiring and possibly dangerous, still there was a steady flow of people traveling between England and America.[136]

Once back in England, some colonists had no intention of returning to the Chesapeake. Family or business circumstances may have changed which made staying in England advantageous or they may have had enough of living in the colonies. Return migration was not large in scale, but the evidence suggests that not all settlers were committed to living in America permanently. As John Goode explained in 1676, "Here are many people in Virginia that receive considerable benefitts and advantages, by Parents, ... Friends and Correspondents in England, and many expect Patrimonys and Inheritances."[137] Even in the 1620s, sufficient people were leaving the colony to force the Assembly to address the issue. It was decided in 1626 that "there should be noe generall restraint of people from goeing for England, but that such as desire theire passes shall repaire to the Court held weekly at James Citty."[138] William Tucker and Maurice Thompson made their fortunes in Virginia before returning to London in the 1620s. William Ewen, a prominent early settler on the south side of the James River, returned to London in 1637 and eventually retired to Greenwich where he died. Major Robert Bristow and Otho Thorpe left Virginia after Bacon's Rebellion in the late 1670s.[139]

Little consideration has been given to the impact of return migration on the development of Anglo-American society in the seventeenth century. Returnees did not form an effective political lobby as West Indian sugar planters did. Most settlers who came back from the Chesapeake probably slipped back into English society imperceptibly, returning to the parish of their birth or taking up a trade in London, Bristol, or other colonial ports. But this is not to say that the influence of returnees was negligible. In the major cities there could be found men and women who had direct experience of living in the colonies; here was a fund of information about life along the tobacco coast. Cases concerning colonial affairs heard before the central courts in London, for example, drew on expert opinion of mariners, merchants, and settlers who were permanently or temporarily resident in the city. In London and Bristol, there must have been plenty of opportunity for prospective emigrants to talk over the realities of setting up a tobacco plantation with men who had firsthand experience. These contacts may have been vital in helping emigrants prepare for the venture—how much money to take, what goods and provisions were needed—as well as providing introductions once in the Chesapeake.[140]

Return migration, visits home, and the effort to keep in touch by letter or word of mouth all point to growth transatlantic community linked by ties of family, kinship, and trade. Free emigration to America should be viewed in this broad social and economic context. Such ties helped new arrivals to settle in and engendered a sense of continuity with the past. These characteristics set free settlers apart from the majority of emigrants—indentured servants. Their social world was considerably more circumscribed than their wealthier contemporaries, and their chances of ever returning to England were much more limited. They may have lost touch with their English backgrounds far more rapidly than free settlers.[141] The cultural consequences of different social origins and opportunities have yet to be explored.

V

Recent research on Chesapeake society has emphasized the unspectacular origins of free settlers.[142] Emigrants were neither typically scions of high-born families nor cavalier fugitives beloved of romantic fiction. The majority of free emigrants came from the middle ranks of England's mercantile community, lower tiers of provincial squirearchy, and various trades in towns and cities. However, the diversity of social contexts that contributed to emigration in the seventeenth century should not be obscured by bland generalizations. While a single motive, making a living from tobacco, attracted most settlers to Virginia and Maryland, their individual circumstances varied considerably. For some men who had traded to the Bay for years, settling in the Chesapeake represented no more than a logical next step in the production and marketing of leaf, a transatlantic partnership linking English ports to the Tidewater. To others, emigration must have been much more of an upheaval, perhaps a last desperate gamble to recoup losses at home or an attempt to escape from pressing creditors. The Chesapeake, like marginal areas in England, offered a refuge to those seeking sanctuary from political, religious, or financial difficulties. Finally, many English men and women saw in the colonies the opportunity for a new start. An abundance of land and the relatively small sums required to set up a tobacco plantation were the principal attractions of Maryland and Virginia.[143] Younger sons of minor gentry, tradesmen, and petty merchants had a chance to establish themselves in a manner that would have been impossible in England. Immigrants who survived the rigors of the environment and put down roots in their communities could expect to be called on to serve in various local offices or even at the provincial level. Thus, English merchants became Virginia or Maryland gentlemen.[144]

Whatever their origins, the influence of free emigrants on the social and economic development of the Chesapeake can hardly be exaggerated. If indentured servants provided the mass of laborers without which extensive plantation agriculture would have been impossible, free settlers provided the capital to establish the economic and political infrastructure of colonial society. They financed the transportation of servants, maintained and developed links with the great commercial centers, and constituted the backbone of government. Transatlantic connections founded on trade, family, and kinship were an enduring legacy and helped shape Anglo-American society long after the flow of settlers to the Chesapeake waned. As Maryland and Virginia entered the "golden age," the offspring of families established in the second half of the seventeenth century reaped the rewards of their forebears' enterprise.

Acknowledgments

I would like to thank Warren M. Billings and Paul G. E. Clemens for allowing me to incorporate unpublished research in this study. The Colonial Williamsburg Foundation generously permitted me to use their research library and the invaluable materials collected under the auspices of the Virginia Colonial Records Project (CW VCRP) and the York County Project. Most of the research was done while I was an ACLS-Fulbright Fellow at the Institute of Early American History and Culture in 1985–86. I am indebted to the American Council of Learned Societies, the Fulbright Commission, the American Historical Association, and the American Philosophical Society for funding and to Thad W. Tate and his staff for making my stay at the Institute particularly warm and friendly. Earlier versions of this paper were given at the University of York and the Boston Area Seminar in Early American History, and I am grateful for the helpful comments and encouragement I received from participants.

Notes

1. Henry Fleet, "Henry Fleet of Fleet's Bay, Virginia, 1600–1660," *Northern Neck Historical Magazine* 12 (1962): 1068–1076; Virginia M. Meyer and John Frederick Dorman, eds., *Adventurers of Purse and Person: Virginia, 1607–1624/5* (Richmond, 1987), 284–286; Nell Marion Nugent, comp., *Cavaliers and Pioneers: Abstracts of Virginia Land Patents and Grants, 1623–1666* (Richmond, Va., 1934), 1: 13, 14, 177, 259–260, 311, 316, 332. For the early fur trade, see J. Frederick Fausz, "Merging and Emerging Worlds: Anglo-Indian Interest Groups and the Development of the Seventeenth-Century Chesapeake," in Lois Green Carr, Philip D. Morgan, and Jean B. Russo, eds., *Colonial Chesapeake Society* (Chapel Hill, 1988), 47–98.

2. For Kentish genealogies, see William Berry, *County Genealogies: Pedigrees of the Families of the County of Kent* (London, 1830). Peter Laslett, "The Gentry of Kent in 1640," in T. H. Breen, ed., *Shaping Southern Society: The Colonial Experience* (New York, 1976), 32–47; Meyer and Dorman, eds., *Adventurers of Purse and Person*, 718–723; James D. Alsop, "Sir Samuel Argall's Family, 1560–1620," *Virginia Magazine of History and Biography* 90 (1982): 478–484.

3. Brian Dietz, "Overseas Trade and Metropolitan Growth," in A. L. Beier and R. A. P. Finlay, eds., *London 1500–1700: The Making of the Metropolis* (London, 1986), 115–140; W. E. Minchinton, ed., *The Growth of English Overseas Trade in the Seventeenth and Eighteenth Centuries* (London, 1969); Robert Paul Brenner, "Commercial Change and Political Contact: The Merchant Community in Civil War London" (Ph.D. dissertation, Princeton University, 1970), chaps. 1, 2, 4, 10; Fausz, "Merging and Emerging Worlds," 62.

4. John B. Boddie, *Seventeenth-Century Isle of Wight County, Virginia....* (Chicago, 1938), chaps. 2, 3, 15.

5. State Papers Domestic (SPD), Chas I, 16/414, nos. 71, 79, 80 (Colonial Williamsburg Foundation, Virginia Colonial Records Project, Survey Report 2877; hereafter CW VCRP).

6. SPD, Chas I, 16/475, no. 60 (CW VCRP, 3244).

7. CW VCRP, no. 879.

8. W. G. Stanard, comp., *Some Emigrants to Virginia....* (Richmond, 1915, 2d ed.), 50; British Library, Add Mss 34015, 2: 82.

9. A recent interpretation of free emigration to the Chesapeake that stresses the "cavalier" origins of influential settlers who arrived in the middle decades of the century can be found in David Hackett Fischer's *Albion's Seed: Four British Folkways in America* (Oxford, 1989), 207–418. See my critique of his views in "Cavalier Culture? The Social De-

velopment of Colonial Virginia," forthcoming in *WMQ*, 3d ser., 47 (1991).

10. James Horn, "Servant Emigration to the Chesapeake in the Seventeenth Century," in Thad W. Tate and David L. Ammerman, eds., *The Chesapeake in the Seventeenth Century: Essays on Anglo-American Society* (Chapel Hill, 1979), 51–95; David Souden, "'Rogues, Whores and Vagabonds'? Indentured Servant Emigrants to North America, and the Case of Mid-Seventeenth-Century Bristol," *Social History* 3 (1978), 23–41; Anthony Salerno, "The Social Background of Seventeenth-Century Emigration to America," *Journal of British Studies* 19 (1979): 31–52; David W. Galenson, *White Servitude in Colonial America: An Economic Analysis* (Cambridge, 1981); and Henry A. Gemery, "Markets for Migrants: English Indentured Servitude and Emigration in the Seventeenth and Eighteenth Centuries," in P. C. Emmer, ed., *Colonialism and Migration: Indentured Labour Before and After Slavery* (Dordrecht, 1986), 33–54; John Wareing, "Migration to London and Trans-Atlantic Emigration of Indentured Servants," *Journal of Historical Geography* 7 (1981): 356–378. For New England migration, see T. H. Breen and Stephen Foster, "Moving to the New World: The Character of Early Massachusetts Immigration," *WMQ*, 3d ser., 30 (1973): 189–222; Virginia DeJohn Anderson, "Migrants and Motives: Religion and the Settlement of New England, 1630–1640," *New England Quarterly*, 58 (1985): 339–383. Bernard Bailyn deals largely with servants in the late eighteenth century in *Voyagers to the West: A Passage in the Peopling of America on the Eve of the Revolution* (New York, 1986).

11. Genealogical material can be found in the *Virginia Magazine of History and Biography* and the *William and Mary Quarterly*, 1st and 2d series. Testamentary evidence is voluminous but not readily accessible, and the same can be said of court records. I have used CW VCRP extensively for references. Cases from HCA appear in Peter Wilson Coldham, ed., *English Adventurers and Emigrants, 1609–1660* (Baltimore, 1984). The county court records of Lancaster, Lower Norfolk, and York counties, Virginia, were examined in detail. For Maryland, I am grateful for the help of Lois Green Carr of the St. Mary's City Commission and Lorena S. Walsh of Colonial Williamsburg. Literary sources—letters, journals, diaries—are much less common, but see *William and Mary Quarterly* for examples of seventeenth-century correspondence. Propaganda literature providing advice to prospective settlers can be sampled in Robert Gray, *A Good Speed to Virginia* (London, 1609); William Bullock, *Virginia Impartially examined.* ... (London, 1649); anon., "A Relation of Maryland, 1635," and John Hammond, "Leah and Rachel, or, The Two Fruitful Sisters, Virginia and Maryland," in Clayton Colman

Hall, ed., *Narratives of Early Maryland, 1633–1684* (New York, 1910), 63–100, 277–300. Other examples can be found in Warren M. Billings, ed., *The Old Dominion in the Seventeenth Century: A Documentary History of Virginia, 1606–1689* (Chapel Hill, 1975), chap. 1.

12. Bailyn, *Voyagers to the West*, 24.

13. Henry A. Gemery, "Emigration from the British Isles to the New World, 1630–1700: Inferences from Colonial Populations," *Research in Economic History* 5 (1980): 179–231; John J. McCusker and Russell R. Menard, *The Economy of British America, 1607–1789* (Chapel Hill, 1985), 102–103, 214–217; Russell R. Menard, "British Migration to the Chesapeake Colonies in the Seventeenth Century," in Carr, Morgan, and Russo, eds., *Colonial Chesapeake Society*, 99–132; Gloria L. Main, *Tobacco Colony: Life in Early Maryland, 1650–1720* (Princeton, 1982), 10–16.

14. J. P. Greene and J. R. Pole, eds., *Colonial British America: Essays in the New History of the Early Modern Era* (Baltimore and London, 1984), chap. 1. For the development of Chesapeake society in the seventeenth century, see the essays in Lois Green Carr, Aubrey C. Land, and Edward C. Papenfuse, eds., *Law, Society, and Politics in Early Colonial Maryland* (Baltimore, 1977); Tate and Ammerman, eds., *Chesapeake in the Seventeenth Century*; and Carr, Morgan, and Russo, eds., *Colonial Chesapeake Society*. See also Edmund S. Morgan's highly influential *American Slavery, American Freedom: The Ordeal of Colonial Virginia* (New York, 1975); Main, *Tobacco Colony*; J. P. Horn, "Moving On in the New World: Migration and Out-Migration in the Seventeenth-Century Chesapeake," in Peter Clark and David Souden, eds., *Migration and Society in Early Modern England* (London, 1987), 172–212; Allan Kulikoff, *Tobacco and Slaves: The Development of Southern Culture in the Chesapeake, 1680–1800* (Chapel Hill, 1986); Darrett B. and Anita H. Rutman, *A Place in Time, Middlesex County, Virginia, 1650–1750*, 2 vols. (New York, 1984); and, most recently, James R. Perry, *The Formation of a Society on Virginia's Eastern Shore, 1615–1655* (Chapel Hill, 1990).

15. Horn, "Servant Emigration"; Menard, "British Emigration"; Abbott Emerson Smith, *Colonists in Bondage: White Servitude and Convict Labor in America, 1607–1776* (Gloucester, Mass., 1965; first pub. 1947), 238–241.

16. Russell R. Menard, "The Tobacco Industry in the Chesapeake Colonies, 1617–1730: An Interpretation," *Research in Economic History* 5 (1980): 109–177.

17. Thomas J. Wertenbaker, *The Planters of Colonial Virginia* (New York, 1958; first pub. 1922), 23–24.

18. "Part of a Letter from the Rev. Hugh Jones to the Rev. Dr. Benjamin Woodruff, F.R.S., concerning Several Observables in Maryland, 23 January 1698 [1699]," Royal Society Archives, London, LBC II (2): 247.

19. Menard, "Tobacco Industry"; Horn, "Servant Emigration," 87–94.

20. These estimates are based on the assumption that approximately 120,000 settlers emigrated to the Chesapeake in the seventeenth century, of whom between 70 and 85% were indentured servants. If, as is likely, the proportion of servants is nearer the upper band, then a figure of about 25,000 free emigrants is probable.

21. Clark and Souden, eds., *Migration and Society*, chaps. 1, 5; Horn, "Servant Emigration"; Salerno, "Social Background."

22. William A. Reavis, "The Maryland Gentry and Social Mobility, 1637–1676," *Maryland Historical Magazine* 14 (1957): 418–428.

23. Philip L. Barbour, ed., *The Complete Work of Captain John Smith (1580–1630)* (Chapel Hill, 1986), 3: 272.

24. Ibid., 2: 140–142, 160–162.

25. Bernard Bailyn, "Politics and Social Structure in Virginia," in James Morton Smith, ed., *Seventeenth-Century America: Essays in Colonial History* (Chapel Hill, 1959), 92.

26. Russell R. Menard, "Economy and Society in Early Colonial Maryland," (Ph.D. dissertation, University of Iowa, 1975), 32–36; Garry Wheeler Stone, "Manorial Maryland," *MHM*, 82 (1987): 5–6.

27. Russell R. Menard, P.M.G. Harris, and Lois Green Carr, "Opportunity and Inequality: The Distribution of Wealth on the Lower Western Shore of Maryland, 1638–1705," *MHM* 69 (1974): 81; Menard, "Economy and Society," 70–71, 111–141.

28. The phrase "gentleman-tradesman" is from Daniel Defoe, *Moll Flanders*, ed., by Edward Kelly (New York, 1975), 48; Martin H. Quitt, "Immigrant Origins of the Virginia Gentry: A Study of Cultural Transmission and Innovation," *WMQ*, 3d ser., 45 (1988): 629–655.

29. Brenner, "Commercial Change and Political Contact," 113–115, 126–127, 132; Stanard, *Some Emigrants*, 83–84.

30. Stone, "Manorial Maryland," 27.

31. Brenner, "Commercial Change and Political Contact," chap. 3; P. G. E. Clemens, "English Merchants Trading to Maryland, 1659–1683" (unpublished research). I am grateful to Dr. Clemens for allowing me to use this material.

32. Brenner, "Commercial Change and Political Contact," 76–77, 83–84.

33. Coldham, ed., *English Adventurers*, 23, 76, 78, 158.

34. N. T. Mann, "William Ball, Merchant," *Northern Neck Historical Magazine* 23 (1973), 2523-2529.
35. Brenner, "Commercial Change and Political Contact," 115.
36. Ibid., 126-127, 131.
37. Horn, "Servant Emigration," 57-59.
38. One hundred ninety-seven emigrants were from London and ninety-four from the surrounding counties of Kent, Surrey, Sussex, Essex, Middlesex, and Hertfordshire.
39. Bedfordshire, Berkshire, Buckinghamshire, Oxfordshire, Wiltshire, Gloucestershire, Hampshire, Dorset, and Somerset.
40. For Puritan migration, see Carl Bridenbaugh, *Vexed and Troubled Englishmen, 1590-1642* (New York, 1968) chap. 12; N. C. P. Tyack, "Migration from East Anglia to New England before 1660" (Ph.D. dissertation, University of London, 1951); Breen and Foster, "Moving to the New World," 189-222; Allen, *In English Ways*, chap. 6; Anderson, "Migrants and Motives," 339-383; and David Cressy, *Coming Over: Migration and Communication between England and New England in the Seventeenth Century* (Cambridge, 1987).
41. "Central England" includes Lincolnshire, Nottinghamshire, Derbyshire, Cheshire, Shropshire, Staffordshire, Herefordshire, Worcestershire, Warwickshire, Leicestershire, Northamptonshire, and Rutland. The "Northwest" includes Cumbria, Westmorland, and Lancashire and the "Northeast," Yorkshire, Durham, and Northumbria. Aside from Lancashire and Yorkshire, no county produced more than ten emigrants, although this is partly a function of the bias of the sources.
42. The same pattern applies to indentured servants; See Horn, "Servant Emigration," 66-74, and Souden, "'Rogues, Whores, and Vagabonds'?".
43. Peter Clark and Paul Slack, *English Towns in Transition, 1500-1700* (Oxford, 1976), 18.
44. Edward Bennett's career, described earlier, is a good example.
45. W. E. Minchinton, "Bristol—Metropolis of the West in the Eighteenth Century," *Transactions of the Royal Historical Society*, 5th ser., 4 (1954): 69-85; Minchinton, ed., *Growth of Overseas Trade*, 33-34.
46. Stanard, *Some Emigrants*, 20, 21, 82; Boddie, *Isle of Wight County*, chap. 28; WMQ 1st ser., 7 (1898-1899): 215 and 4 (1895-1896): 116-118.
47. Daniel Defoe, *A Tour Through the Whole Island of Great Britain*, ed. by Pat Rogers (London, 1971), 178-179. Bristol's population rose from about 12,000 in 1600 to nearly 20,000 by the end of the century; Clark and Slack, *English Towns*, 83. For London, see R. A. P. Finlay,

Population and Metropolis: The Demography of London, 1580–1650 (Cambridge, 1981), and Jeremy Boulton, *Neighbourhood and Society: A London Suburb in the Seventeenth Century* (Cambridge, 1987), 1–4, 13–59.

48. Beier and Finlay, eds., *London 1500–1700*, 2–4.
49. Ibid., 14.
50. Minchinton, ed., *Growth of Overseas Trade*, 36.
51. Dietz, "Overseas Trade and Metropolitan Growth," 130, 133.
52. Theodore K. Rabb, *Enterprise and Empire: Merchant and Gentry Investment in the Expansion of England, 1575–1630* (Cambridge, Mass., 1967), 25.
53. Ibid., 26.
54. A. L. Beier, "Engine of Manufacture: The Trades of London," in Beier and Finlay, eds., *London 1500–1700*, 147–156.
55. CW VCRP 880; Boddie, *Isle of Wight County*, chaps. 2–4; Brenner, "Commercial Change and Political Contact," 113–115, 126–127, 132.
56. Horn, "Servant Emigration," 58–60, 70–73, 83–84.
57. Menard, "Economy and Society," table II-2, 75.
58. Menard, "British Emigration," 117–121.
59. Horn, "Servant Emigration," table 3, 63.
60. Ibid., table 1, 57–59.
61. Wesley Frank Craven, *The Southern Colonies in the Seventeenth Century, 1607–1689* (Baton Rouge, 1970; first pub. 1949), chap. 3; Morgan, *American Slavery, American Freedom*, chap. 4.
62. Billings, ed., *The Old Dominion*, 27.
63. Substantial fortunes were made from tobacco and merchandising in the boom years of the 1620s. George Yeardley was said to have arrived in Virginia in 1610 with nothing more valuable than his sword, but when he visited England seven years later, after his first term as governor, he was able to spend "very near three thousand poundes." He was worth about £10,000 at his death; Morgan, *American Slavery, American Freedom*, 122–123.
64. WMQ, 1st ser., 6 (1897–98): 135; and 24 (1915–16): 205; Henry J. Berkeley, "The Berkeley-Berkley Family and Their Kindred in the Colonization of Virginia and Maryland," WMQ, 2d ser., 3 (1923): 186; PRO C24/525 pt. 2/17 [1626]; C24/572 pt. 1; C2 Chas I W99/38; Eric Gethyn-Jones, *George Thorpe and the Berkeley Company: A Gloucestershire Enterprise in Virginia* (Gloucester, 1982), 147.
65. SPD Chas I 16/475, no. 60 (CW VCRP 3244); Nugent, *Cavaliers and Pioneers*, 1: 104, 109, 123–124.
66. Complaints were made to county courts throughout the century

about debtors fleeing Virginia and Maryland; see Horn, "Moving On," and n. 135 below.

67. Perry Miller, *Errand into the Wilderness* (Cambridge, Mass., 1956), 101.

68. William H. Seiler, "The Anglican Parish in Virginia," in Smith, ed., *Seventeenth-Century America*, chap. 6; Morgan, *American Slavery, American Freedom*, chap. 3; Craven, *Southern Colonies*, 142–145, 177–182.

69. Martin Ingram, *Church Courts: Sex and Marriage in England, 1570–1640* (Cambridge, 1987), 85; Christopher Haigh, "From Monopoly to Minority: Catholicism in Early Modern England," *Trans. Royal Hist. Soc.*, 5th ser., 31 (1981): 129–147; John Bossy, *The English Catholic Community, 1570–1850* (London, 1975), 182–194, 278–282.

70. Ingram, *Church Courts*, 86.

71. Menard, "Economy and Society," 36; John Bossy, "Reluctant Colonists: The English Catholics Confront the Atlantic," in David B. Quinn, ed., *Early Maryland in a Wider World* (Detroit, 1982), chap. 6.

72. Menard, "Economy and Society," 33–34.

73. David W. Jordan, "Political Stability and the Emergence of a Native Elite in Maryland," in Tate and Ammerman, eds., *Chesapeake in the Seventeenth Century*, 249–250. See also, Lois Green Carr and David W. Jordan, *Maryland's Revolution in Government, 1689–1692* (Ithaca, 1974).

74. Bossy, "Reluctant Colonists"; Michael Graham, "Meetinghouse and Chapel: Religion and Community in Seventeenth-Century Maryland" in Carr, Morgan, and Russo, eds., *Colonial Chesapeake Society*, 242–274; Jordan, "Political Stability."

75. Trumbull Mss, no. 101, Berkshire Record Office (CW VCRP R10); Boddie, *Isle of Wight County*, 24–26.

76. Boddie, *Isle of Wight County*, chap. 2.

77. Lower Norfolk County, Virginia, Wills and Deeds B, 1646–1651, 92–93. There were 334 tithables in 1648 (tithables were taxable members of the community: slaves and males over sixteen; see Morgan, *American Slavery, American Freedom*, 400–401).

78. Craven, *Southern Colonies*, 229.

79. Stanard, *Some Emigrants*, 71, 78; J. C. Wise, *Ye Kingdome of Accawmacke, or the Eastern Shore of Virginia in the Seventeenth Century* (Baltimore, 1967; first pub. 1911), 105–109; Clayton Torrence, *Old Somerset on the Eastern Shore of Maryland: A Study in Foundations and Founders* (Richmond, 1935); Horn, "Moving On," 196–197; Babette M. Levy, "Early Puritanism in the Southern and Island Colonies," *Proceedings of the American Antiquarian Society* 70 (1960):

122–123, 130–133, 140; Hall, ed., *Narratives of Early Maryland*, 218–219, 235.

80. J. Reaney Kelly, *Quakers in the Founding of Anne Arundel County, Maryland* (Baltimore, 1963), 2.

81. B. Reay, "Quakerism and Society," in J. F. McGregor and B. Reay, eds., *Radical Religion in the English Revolution* (Oxford, 1986), 141, 145.

82. Kelly, *Quakers in the Founding of Anne Arundel County*, 29; Kenneth L. Carroll, "Thomas Thurston, Renegade Maryland Quaker," *MHM* 62 (1967): 170–192.

83. Kelly, *Quakers in the Founding of Anne Arundel County*, 1.

84. Aubrey C. Land, *Colonial Maryland: A History* (New York, 1981), 65; Graham, "Meetinghouse and Chapel," 242–272.

85. Russell Mortimer, ed., *Minute Book of the Men's Meeting of the Society of Friends in Bristol, 1667–1686*, Bristol Record Society 36 (1971): xii, xxvi, 11, 21, 26, 70, 92, 128, 194, 206.

86. Ibid., 49, 127–128, 194.

87. *WMQ*, 1st ser., 7 (1898–1899): 228.

88. Mortimer, ed., *Minute Book*, xxvii.

89. Reay, "Quakerism and Society," 143–144; CW VCRP 3747.

90. Ferrar Papers, Box II, no. 102 (CW VCRP C22).

91. Edward Hyde, Earl of Clarendon, *The History of the Rebellion and Civil Wars in England Begun in the Year 1641*, ed. by W. Dunn Macray, (Oxford, 1888), 5: 263.

92. Horn, "Moving On," 188; Richard L. Morton, *Colonial Virginia*, vol. 1, *The Tidewater Period, 1607–1710* (Chapel Hill, 1960), 167–168; "Note—Sir Thomas Lunsford," *Virginia Historical Magazine* 17 (1909), 26–33; Colonel [Henry] Norwood, "A Voyage to Virginia, [1649]," in Peter Force, comp., *Tracts and Other Papers Relating Principally to the Origin, Settlement, and Progress of the Colonies in North America from the Discovery of the Country to the Year 1776* (Gloucester, Mass., 1963), vol. 3, no. 10, 49.

93. Philip A. Bruce, *Social Life of Virginia in the Seventeenth Century* (New York, 1964; first pub. 1907), 61; Morton, *Colonial Virginia*, 1, 167–168.

94. See, e.g., Alan Everitt, *The Community of Kent and the Great Rebellion, 1640–1660* (Leicester, 1986), chaps. 6–8; David Underdown, *Royalist Conspiracy in England, 1649–1660* (New Haven, 1960); Craven, *Southern Colonies*, 247.

95. Morton, *Colonial Virginia*, 1: 166–168; Bruce, *Social Life*, 31, 76, 79.

96. For example, John Carter established a powerful family in Lan-

caster County in the 1650s; Richard Lee and Henry Chicheley settled across the Rappahannock around the same time. Edward Digges patented land in York County, George Mason in Northumberland, Joseph Bridger in Isle of Wight County. While it is indisputable that a small number of ex-royalist officers exercised considerable influence at both local and provincial levels in the second half of the seventeenth century, I do not believe "cavalier" immigrants dominated the social and cultural development of Virginia to the extent recently argued by David Hackett Fischer in *Albion's Seed*, 207–418.

97. Ida Altman, "Emigrants and Society: An Approach to the Background of Colonial Spanish America," *Comparative Studies in Society and History* 30 (1988): 182.

98. Ibid.; Quitt provides an alternative argument that stresses the lack of support given by family and kin to gentry emigrating to the Chesapeake, in "Immigrant Origins of the Virginia Gentry," 639–642.

99. Samuel Filmer married Mary Horsmanden, daughter of Warham Horsmanden who emigrated to Virginia in the 1650s. The Horsmandens were also related to the Codd family of Kent. Will of Samuel Fimer, 1670 (CW VCRP 3730); Stanard, *Some Emigrants*, 24; John B. Boddie, *Colonial Surrey* (Richmond, 1948), 67–72.

100. Anthony Fletcher, *Sussex, 1600–1660: A Community at Peace and War* (Chichester, 1980), chap. 1; Everitt, *Community of Kent*, chap. 1; Thomas G. Barnes, *Somerset, 1625–1640: A County's Government during the "Personal Rule"* (Cambridge, Mass., 1961), chap. 2; B. G. Blackwood, "The Marriages of the Lancashire Gentry on the Eve of the Civil War," *The Genealogists' Magazine* 16 (1970), 321–322. Gentry marriage ties may have been looser in the Midlands than in Sussex, Kent, and Lancashire; see Ann Hughes, *Politics, Society and Civil War in Warwickshire, 1620–1660* (Cambridge, 1987), 38–41.

101. Stanard, *Some Emigrants*, 34, 86, 93–94.

102. *WMQ*, 2d ser., 16 (1936): 302–303, 307–308, 310–311; Joan Thirsk, "Projects for Gentlemen, Jobs for the Poor: Mutual Aid in the Vale of Tewkesbury, 1600–1630," in Patrick McGrath and John Cannon, eds., *Essays in Gloucestershire History*. . . . (Bristol, 1976), 153.

103. Stanard, *Some Emigrants*, 73; Boddie, *Colonial Surry*, 36–40.

104. Will of John Beheathland, PCC PROB 22, 22 Oct. 1639 (CW VCRP 3985); Billings, ed., *The Old Dominion*, 18.

105. Lois Green Carr, Russell R. Menard, and Lorena S. Walsh, *Robert Cole's World: Agriculture and Society in Early Maryland* (Chapel Hill, forthcoming), chap. 1.

106. Fleet, "Fleet of Fleet's Bay," 1068–1076; Stanard, *Some Emigrants*, 34; CW VCRP 3730.

107. Norwood, "A Voyage to Virginia," 4.
108. Laslett, "Gentry of Kent," 45–46.
109. Rutman and Rutman, *A Place in Time*, 50–51.
110. Stanard, *Some Emigrants*, 73; Boddie, *Colonial Surry*, 36–40.
111. Stanard, *Some Emigrants*, 34, 78.
112. Brenner, "Commercial Change and Political Contact," 83–84; J. M. Sosin, *English America and the Restoration Monarchy of Charles II: Transatlantic Politics, Commerce, and Kinship* (Lincoln, 1980), chap. 1; Bailyn, "Politics and Social Structure," 98–99.
113. M. J. Kitch, "Capital and Kingdom: Migration to Later Stuart London," in Beier and Finlay, eds., *London 1500–1700*, 224–251; J. Wareing, "Changes in the Geographical Distribution of Apprentices to the London Companies, 1486–1750," *Journal of Historical Geography* 6 (1980); John Patten, *Rural-Urban Migration in Pre-industrial England*, University of Oxford School of Geography, Research Paper No. 6 (Oxford, 1973); A. J. Willis and A. L. Merson, eds., *A Calendar of Southampton Apprenticeship Registers, 1609–1740*, Southampton Record Series 12 (Southampton, 1968); Souden, "'Rogues, Whores, and Vagabonds'?"; Quitt, "Immigrant Origins of the Virginia Gentry," 635.
114. The best description of the 1620s remains Morgan, *American Slavery, American Freedom*, chap. 6.
115. Carr, Menard, and Walsh, *Robert Cole's World*, preface and chaps. 2–4.
116. Richard S. Dunn, *Sugar and Slaves: The Rise of the Planter Class in the English West Indies, 1624–1713* (London, 1973), 142–143, 161–163, 200–201.
117. Carr, Menard, and Walsh, *Robert Cole's World*, chaps. 2–4; Richard B. Davis, ed., *William Fitzhugh and His Chesapeake World. . . .* (Chapel Hill, 1963).
118. Greene and Pole, eds., *Colonial British America*, chaps. 1, 2, 6, 7, 13; Cressy, *Coming Over*; Sosin, *English America*.
119. WMQ, 1st ser., 7 (1898–1899), 112–113; Nugent, *Cavaliers and Pioneers*, 1: 187, 283, 285; Stanard, *Some Emigrants*, 71; Bristol Record Office, Deposition Book of Bristol, 1654–1657, f. 191r (BRO, 04439 2).
120. CW, York County Project: Deeds, Orders, and Wills (2), 434, 11 Nov. 1648.
121. "Ferrar Papers," Box X, no. 1031 (CW VCRP C. 85).
122. WMQ 1st ser., 5 (1896–1897): 122–123.
123. John Catlett, Sittingborne, Rappahannock to Tho. Catlett, Hollingborne Kent, 1 Apr. 1664 (CW Original Letters).

124. The county was formed in 1656 out of Lancaster; see Billings, ed., *The Old Dominion*, 82–83.

125. Most of the letter deals with Indian affairs. Catlett was killed by Indians six years later.

126. "Ferrar Papers," Box XI, no. 1036 (CW VCRP C. 85).

127. *WMQ*, 2d ser., 3 (1923): 134.

128. See, e.g., Fitzhugh's correspondence in Davis, ed., *William Fitzhugh*; Menard, "Tobacco Industry"; Terry L. Anderson and Robert Paul Thomas, "Economic Growth in the Seventeenth-Century Chesapeake," *Explorations in Economic History* 15 (1978), 368–387.

129. CW VCRP 4103, 3928, 3986, 3962.

130. CW VCRP 3718.

131. CW York County Project, Deeds, Orders, and Wills (2), 434, 11 Nov. 1648.

132. British Library, Add Mss. 34015, vol. 2, 6, 33.

133. Coldham, ed., *English Adventurers*, 58–59.

134. Ibid., 22–23, 25, 43, 76, 89–90, 153, 156.

135. John Biggs, for example, "sett up his name at the Court doore" in February 1649 "to give notice of his Intended voyage for England this present shipping," Lower Norfolk County, Virginia, Wills B, 107. Notices were also displayed on church doors: Mr Henry Branch, "bound out off [sic] ye Countrey this shipping and hath sett up his name three lords dayes at ye Churches of Trinity p[ar]ish in Lancaster County," Lancaster County, Virginia, Orders, etc., no. 1, 1661–1680, 194. The intention was to reduce the incidence of debtors fleeing the county undetected.

136. See the letter of Nicholas George to John Nicklis, October 1652. George's wife was reluctant to make the voyage to Virginia because of "ye dangers shee Conceaves are by watter," *WMQ* 1st ser., 11 (1902–03), 171; Horn, "Moving On," 193–96; Cressy, *Coming Over*.

137. Cited in Stephen Saunders Webb, *1676: The End of American Independence* (New York, 1984), 82.

138. McIlwaine, ed., *Minutes of the Council*, 116.

139. Horn, "Moving On," 194; Boddie, *Colonial Surrey*, 41–44.

140. Coldham, ed., *English Adventurers*, for HCA cases; CW VCRP, for examples of Chancery.

141. Horn, "Servant Emigration," The majority of poor former servants appear to have moved to other colonies, notably Pennsylvania and the Carolinas, rather than returning home; see Horn, "Moving On," 197–200.

142. Wesley Frank Craven, *White, Red, and Black: The Seventeenth-Century Virginian* (Charlottesville, 1971), 2–4; Menard, "British

Emigration"; and Bailyn, "Politics and Social Structure," 92–100. An exception is Fischer, *Albion's Seed*, 207–232.

143. Carr, Menard, and Walsh, *Robert Cole's World*, chaps. 2–4.

144. Reavis, "The Maryland Gentry," 418–428; Lorena S. Walsh, "Charles County, Maryland, 1658–1705: A Study of Chesapeake Social and Political Structure" (Ph.D. dissertation, Michigan State University, 1977), chap. 6. For a different view, see Quitt, "Immigrant Origins," 629–655.

Five

Recruitment of French Emigrants to Canada, 1600–1760

Leslie Choquette

The colonization of the Americas by Europeans in the sixteenth, seventeenth, and eighteenth centuries could not have occurred without effective recruitment. For promoters of French emigration to Canada, the problem of recruitment was particularly acute. Most nations involved in colonization needed to encourage emigration and settlement in the initial stages, when demographic ties between the colonies and the metropolis were still tenuous. In the case of Canada, however, such encouragement continued for the duration of the French regime, since the movement never became truly self-sustaining. "A tradition of emigration—like that which we see toward the Antilles—was not established toward New France, which did not pass for a country of rapid fortunes."[1]

Historians use the terms "myth," "dream," and "mirage" to explain the snowballing attraction of urban, Spanish, and West Indian destinations for French migrants in the seventeenth and eighteenth centuries. Canada did not succeed in capturing the French imagination to the same degree, and early enthusiasm appears less as a prelude to greater things than as a false start. On the eve of departure for New France in 1665, Jean Talon, the colony's first *intendant*, wrote excitedly that the ships were full to capacity and that prospective emigrants continued to arrive:

"Many people are presenting themselves for New France who mark their inclination by their eagerness and who, received in this manner, save the king the expense of the levy and of the advance that the [West India] Company made to those whom it is transporting."[2] Little more than a year later, Talon's tone was already one of disillusionment. "I will no longer have the honor," he wrote peevishly to Louis XIV, "to speak to you of the great establishment that I formerly indicated could be created in Canada . . . , since you know that there are not enough supernumeraries and useless subjects in old France to people the new one."[3]

Military emigration disappointed official expectations nearly as bitterly. In 1665, Talon wrote of the companies of the Regiment of Carignan, the first regular troops to be stationed in Canada, "I have been assured that more than half of them have supernumeraries. They all testify that they are going with joy to Canada, which makes me very hopeful about the usefulness of their service."[4] The adjustment of these troops to Canadian life was indeed extraordinary, with over three-fifths of them opting to remain,[5] but it was also unique. Recruiters of the *troupes de la Marine*, which served in the colony from the 1680s until the end of the French regime, found their job to be much more difficult. In 1687, the official in charge of recruitment in Le Havre informed the *ministre de la Marine* that "[w]e are currently working on the levy of the 100 soldiers whom you ordered me to raise. . . . I am going to raise them as we do for the navy, without indicating that they are to be sent to Canada, for we would have difficulty getting them on that footing."[6]

The situation improved somewhat, at least in terms of military emigration, in the final decade of the French regime. Perhaps this change would have been lasting, for whether internal or external, French migrations were intensifying at about the same time.[7] Be that as it may, the British conquest intervened and closed the book on emigration to Canada before it could truly surmount the objection "[t]hat it is a waste of time to work on New France, an intemperate country on account of the glacial sea that surrounds it, where the French can subsist only on what is brought from France."[8] From beginning to end, Canada suffered from a dubious reputation that inhibited emigration and made recruitment an urgent concern of all who desired the survival of the colony.

Contemporary views on recruitment crystallized in a system of Canadian colonization that underwent important modifications in the course of the French regime. Here I will consider both the structure and the functioning of this system from the earliest years of the colony up until the British conquest. The changing apportionment of responsibilities for recruitment, the disparate identities of the recruiters, and the geographic and social preferences implied by the recruiters' choices must all be examined in order to assess the failure, if failure there indeed was, of French attempts to colonize Canada.

Responsibilities for Recruitment

In France as in England, the early stucture of colonization emerged from a series of failed attempts as would-be colonizers discovered by trial and error which features to discard and which to retain. By the beginning of the seventeenth century, a viable organization had developed that prevailed until Louis XIV chose to increase the level of state intervention in this as in so many other spheres of French life. Before 1663, emigration took place within a framework of proprietorship and private entrepreneurship, although proprietors ultimately bore some responsibility to the crown. After 1663, the crown intervened directly in both administration and recruitment. Proprietors did not disappear until 1674, and chartered companies persisted until the conquest; the crown, however, succeeded in reducing them to mere partners in an essentially royal enterprise.

The first systematic attempts to colonize, rather than explore, America occurred in the mid-sixteenth century under the successive auspices of François I, Henri II, and Catherine de Médici. The resulting settlements differed in both location and intent. In Canada, the courtier, Roberval, agreed to work for "the augmentation and increase of our holy Christian faith and holy mother Catholic church,"[9] while in Brazil and Florida, lieutenants of the Protestant Coligny tried to establish New World refuges for their coreligionists. The state adopted a similar attitude toward each of these efforts regardless of religion. Although it provided subsidies to the initial expeditions, it expected the established colonies to support themselves. The founders and their associates, as *seigneurs* and traders, took full responsibility for future defense, administration, and recruitment.

Roberval's settlement succumbed to the Canadian climate and the two Protestant outposts to Portuguese and Spanish incursions. French colonization as a whole then fell victim to the Wars of Religion, remaining at a virtual standstill until the end of the century. When it resumed during the reign of Henri IV, the age of royal subsidies and of Protestant refuges was over. Henri distributed property rights and commercial monopolies in lieu of direct funding, and he reverted to François I's formulaic espousal of Catholic evangelism. A new framework for French colonization was now in place. Proprietors would finance colonization from the proceeds of commercial monopolies; they, not the crown, would bear responsibility for recruitment. Although Protestants would not be excluded, and indeed would figure among the proprietors, the official religion of the colonies and the metropolis would henceforth be the same.

The first decade of the seventeenth century witnessed the foundation of two French colonies in Canada: Port-Royal in 1604 and Québec in 1608. The initiative for both came from Pierre Du Gua de Monts, a Protestant officer who in 1603 became the exclusive proprietor of New France. The charter he received from Henri IV granted him seigneurial rights and a commercial monopoly over eastern North America from Philadelphia to Newfoundland; in return for these privileges, he agreed to transport sixty settlers across the Atlantic.

Port-Royal (today Annapolis-Royal in Nova Scotia) survived only until 1607; French Acadia, however, did not disappear owing to the first subinfeudation practiced within a proprietary colony. Acadian settlement resumed after a three-year hiatus under the direction of Jean Biencourt de Poutrincourt, a Catholic nobleman who had accompanied the first expedition to Port-Royal. A former participant in the Wars of Religion, Poutrincourt "had resolved to create an independent position in America and to have his family transported there, hoping to find more tranquillity than in Europe."[10] He had requested and received the concession of the Bay of Port-Royal (Fundy) on the condition of pursuing the work of colonization.

With Poutrincourt, colonial recruitment entered a new phase.

From the responsibility of a single overlord in possession of a commercial monopoly, it became a shared responsibility of the overlord and his seigneurs. The return on the latter's investments would come not from trade but from seigneurial revenues; the success of the enterprise would depend entirely on agricultural settlement.[11] Recruitment developed along these lines for nearly two decades, but it did not proceed quickly. Poutrincourt died a pauper in 1615 and bequeathed his *seigneurie* to his equally impoverished son, Biencourt. When Charles Turgis de Saint-Etienne de la Tour, a French acquaintance of Biencourt, inherited the colony in 1623, Port-Royal remained a trading post with no more than twenty year-round residents, none of them women.[12]

Meanwhile, the Canadian monopoly passed from De Monts, who lost it as a result of merchant complaints, to the comte de Soissons, who died, to the prince de Condé, who fell out of favor with Louis XIII, to the duc de Montmorency. Except for Soissons, all of these proprietors worked in tandem with a company of merchants, and all agreed to transport emigrants to the colony of Québec as a condition of their exclusive privilege. The obligation to recruit was never onerous; Condé and his associates agreed to send six families within eleven years, and Montmorency had fifteen years to transport six families of at least three persons each.[13] Despite the leniency of these quotas, proprietors proved reluctant to fulfill them. In 1627, when Richelieu prematurely revoked the most recent charter, Québec had a total population of eighty-four or eighty-five within its boundaries; of these, only about two dozen were true *habitants*.

Richelieu decided to restructure New France in 1627 and set about creating the organizational framework for an important settlement colony. The resulting Compagnie des Cent-Associés differed from earlier companies in scope rather than in structure. While it remained a private venture that possessed New France *"en fief et seigneurie,"* it brought together moneyed interests from a broad geographic and social spectrum.[14] Participation in the company did not entail *dérogeance*; on the contrary, Richelieu promised to ennoble twelve of the nonnoble associates. The company received a perpetual monopoly on the fur trade and a monopoly of fifteen years on all other trade except for the fisheries. During that fifteen years, it agreed to transport 4,000 indentured servants of both sexes to New France. Prospective immigrants had to be both French and Catholic, but foreigners and Protestants were not prohibited from residing in the colony on a temporary basis.

The domain of the Cent-Associés extended northward from Florida to the Arctic circle and westward from Newfoundland to the Great Lakes. In practice, however, their jurisdiction confined itself to Canada, and they exploited the monopoly directly only in Québec. In Acadia, the company had recourse from the beginning to *sous-seigneurs*, who themselves formed companies to subcontract a portion of the monopoly. The indentured servants recruited by these seigneurs counted against the total of 4,000 required of the company. The new seigneurs of Acadia belonged with one exception to the Cent-Associés, and the parent company looked favorably on their enterprises. The colonization of Acadia proceeded slowly nonetheless; jurisdictional disputes paralyzed the original seigneurs and their successors, and in 1654, the British occupied all of the colony except for Miscou and the adjoining coast. The French population at the time of the occupation, though it now included women, did not exceed 300 souls.[15]

In Québec, the Cent-Associés subsidized recruitment directly, but their early efforts came to naught when the British seized the colony in 1629. Although the British occupation ended after negotiations in 1632, the company's capital had dwindled dangerously, and subcontracting remained the only option in the Saint Lawrence as in Acadia. The system of subcontracting adopted in Québec differed from that practiced in Acadia in one major respect: seigneurs did not receive a portion of the monopoly. Instead, a single subsidiary, composed primarily of merchants from Rouen, agreed to manage the monopoly and to assume the company's responsibilities for a period of six years. The *compagnie particuliére*, which arranged for the transport of 200 immigrants in 1633,[16] did not bear the full burden of recruitment but shared it with the colony's seigneurs, who invested in their properties in anticipation of seigneurial revenues. Laurentian seigneurs included individuals, with or without the backing of companies, and collectivities such as the Jesuits and the Société Notre-Dame de Montréal.

The compagnie des Cent-Associés never recovered its initial

vigor, although in 1642, the year of Richelieu's death, it resumed direct exploitation of the monopoly for lack of a willing subcontractor. In 1645, it had recourse to a new expedient: reconcession of the monopoly, not to a company but to the inhabitants themselves in the form of a Communauté des Habitants. The Communauté, defined as everyone permanently domiciled in the colony, took upon itself the annual recruitment of twenty persons complete with "victuals and amenities."[17] Unfortunately, the Communauté derived no more profit from the monopoly than had its predecessors, and it successively tested a number of survival strategies ranging from subcontracting exportation (1652) to leasing trading posts (1653) to reconceding the monopoly to yet another subcontractor (1660). Recruitment thus depended on individual seigneurs and on the Communauté or the latter's commercial associates from 1645 until the reorganization of the colony in 1663. The only innovation in recruitment policy during this period consisted of a 1647 decree of the Conseil de Québec mandating French shipowners to transport one immigrant per ten tons of cargo on all ships bound for Québec.[18]

The Compagnie des Cent-Associés did not long survive the personal reign of Louis XIV. Seconded by Colbert, the young king revoked the company's charter in 1663 and brought the colony directly under the royal administration. The company, he claimed, had failed to fulfill essential obligations, among them defending the colony, transporting immigrants, and converting the Indians. While "the company was able to prove before the Parlement of Paris, based on the Admiralty registers, that 5,000 people had been transported to New France under its authority,"[19] the failure of definitive settlement was palpable. The New France of 1663 had a total of barely 3,500 inhabitants, several hundred of whom were Acadians under British occupation. By comparison, the combined population of British and Dutch North America was 90,000 in the same year, and New Englanders alone numbered 40,000.[20]

In reorganizing New France, Louis did not immediately reject the formula of the proprietary colony, but he modified it significantly. In 1664, he reconceded New France, together with the Antilles, to the newly created Compagnie des Indes Occidentales "*en toute seigneurie, propriété et justice.*"[21] The company received a long-term commercial monopoly in return for which it contributed to colonial expenses, but it no longer controlled administration, defense, or immigration. Convinced that the proprietary framework had proved insufficiently dynamic, the king reserved initiative in each of these domains to himself. The company's sole responsibility for recruitment consisted of supplying the colony with a sufficient number of priests.[22] For the first time in exactly a century, the crown returned to a policy of subsidizing emigration directly. Within months of the dissolution of the Cent-Associés, two ships of the royal navy set out from La Rochelle with about 300 passengers for Québec, and in the following two years, company ships transported over 700 emigrants at the expense of the king.

The system inaugurated by Louis XIV prevailed, with modifications, until the end of the French regime. Direct state intervention became a permanent factor of recruitment policy, although the extent of support varied according to the place of Canada within the royal priorities. In the first ten years of royal control, the colony received about 4,000 new settlers at the king's expense: 2,000 indentured servants, 1,000 soldiers, and 1,000 *filles à marier*.[23] In the eighteenth century, the bulk of royal emigrants consisted of soldiers from the *troupes de la Marine* or the *troupes de terre*, to whom must be added perhaps a thousand prisoners. The state no longer subsidized the passage of filles à marier and rarely arranged for the transport of more than a handful of indentured servants;[24] however, it did fund the deportation to Québec and Acadia of vagabonds, wayward *fils de famille*, deserters, *faux-sauniers* (salt smugglers), and other petty criminals.

The participation of merchants in recruitment continued pursuant to the decree of the Conseil,[25] although they often complied with it grudgingly or not at all. The king found himself obliged to renew its terms twice: in 1714 and 1716, ordinances required merchant ships to transport indentured servants to Québec or troop reinforcements in their place.[26] In response to complaints from the merchants, the king permitted them in 1721 to pay sixty livres into the royal treasury for each *engagé* that they failed to embark or, alternatively, to transport prisoners;[27] a circular of 1722 extended these conditions from Québec to Ile Royale, which in earlier years had been exempt.[28] Passive resistance continued, and in 1724 an exasperated king imposed a fine of 200 livres on those merchants who failed to embark the requisite number of emigrants. Even this draconian measure failed to alter the behavior of *armateurs* for Ile Royale, whom a final ordinance recalled to their duties in 1729. The obligation to recruit as a condition of trading had moved from the center to the periphery of French recruitment efforts. In the final century of the French regime, it was simply an ancillary feature of a recruitment system that relied far more heavily on direct state intervention.

Like state agents and merchants, Canadian seigneurs also continued to bear responsibility for recruitment. Organized recruitment by the habitants, however, ended with the dissolution of the Communauté in 1666. Seigneurs remained especially active agents of colonization in Acadia, where the loss of the mainland rendered the development of Ile Saint-Jean (Prince Edward Island) and Ile Royale (Cape Breton Island) an urgent concern.[29] Responsibilities for recruitment thus came to be shared among a broader spectrum of institutions and individuals in the course of the French regime. In the earliest years of the colony, trader-proprietors and seigneurs consented to recruit in return for colonial revenues; under Richelieu, a proprietary company, commercial and seigneurial subcontractors, and simple seigneurs took their place. During the personal reign of Louis XIV, recruitment became an actual affair of state, albeit with continued seigneurial and mercantile participation. The Canadian commercial monopoly entailed few obligations to recruit after 1663, but beginning in 1647, merchants grudgingly guaranteed a small but steady stream of embarkations.

The Process of Recruitment

The ways in which the various partners in Canadian colonization—traders, seigneurs, and public officials—carried out their responsibilities vis-à-vis recruitment helped to shape a distinctive French Canadian population. In geographic and social terms, they drew on a broad but unrepresentative cross section of French men and women. Ironically, urban and Atlantic elements played a disproportionate role in the formation of a nation that came in the nineteenth century to embody vanishing French values of rural traditionalism.

The Role of Merchants

The mercantile contribution to recruitment remained consistent in kind, although not in volume, throughout the French regime. As traders moved from the forefront to the background of recruitment efforts, they continued to target roughly the same geographic areas and social groups. The vicissitudes of mercantile recruitment were reflected in the identity of the recruiters, the number of emigrants they indentured, and the more or less speculative nature of their enterprises. The evolving servant trade of La Rochelle in the seventeenth and eighteenth centuries will provide an illustration of the changing nature of mercantile recruitment.

Companies and individuals involved in the Canada trade concentrated their recruiting on a single geographic arena: the great Atlantic ports. Rouen, Le Havre, Saint-Malo, Nantes, La Rochelle, Bordeaux, and Bayonne witnessed the majority of their efforts, although not in the same proportions. In particular, Rouen, La Rochelle, and Bordeaux successively dominated mercantile recruitment as they did Canadian commerce generally.

The decision of merchants to seek their recruits in the great ports had important implications for the geographic profile of Canada's indentured servants. By restricting the emigrant pool to natives, residents, and visitors to these ports, it guaranteed the preponderance among the emigrants both of the cities themselves and of the migratory circuits connecting them to the outside. These circuits were essentially dual in nature, embracing, on the one hand, the villages of the hinterland and the towns of the surrounding region and, on the other, the great cities of Atlantic, continental, and Mediterranean France. The indentured servants of La Rochelle, to give but one example, came from the port and its environs, the center-west as a whole, and urban centers as far afield as Paris, Limoges, Rouen, Dijon, and Marseille.[30]

The social parameters of mercantile recruitment were as broad, in theory at least, as its geographic profile was narrow. Although the state established guidelines for the selection of indentured servants, it did so in such a way as to allow considerable freedom of choice. As we have seen, the statutes of the Cent-Associés called for the recruitment of 4,000 men and women, all of them French and Catholic. Subsequent rulings dropped the explicit reference to nationality and religion,[31] while adding new provisions on age and height. Throughout the royal regime, merchants needed to seek out emigrants between the ages of eighteen and forty and measuring at least four feet in height.[32] The obligation to recruit women disappeared after 1663, when the state began to assure their emigration directly.[33] Merchants were responsible for embarking "*hommes de travail*" in proportion to tonnage,[34] and the royal edicts of the eighteenth century referred to "engagés" with no further gender specification. With regard to social class and profession, merchants had the discretion to recruit whomever they wished. The only reference to profession in the edicts concerned the double counting of certain artisans against merchant quotas after 1714.

Taking the port of La Rochelle as representative, mercantile recruitment produced a youthful and heavily male emigrant population in which the poor outweighed the rich and artisans outnumbered peasants. It is difficult to attribute this outcome to social selectivity on the part of the recruiters, for we have little evidence that they practiced it. While they might have paid special attention to artisans after 1714, this group was no more prominent among eighteenth- than among seventeenth-century emigrants and did not figure disproportionately in mercantile propaganda. Merchants framed their arguments, as best we can reconstruct them, to appeal to a broad spectrum of potential indentured servants, urban and rural, male and female. A poster sponsored by the merchant houses of Le Havre to promote emigration to the West Indies, for example, promised "the rank of master to artisans who indenture themselves; lumber, tools and farm animals to cultivators; as much land as they can cultivate [to everyone]."[35] As for women, they were lured through offers of a trade (cotton spinner) and of marriage.[36] The high proportion of males and artisans among La Rochelle's indentured servants thus resulted less from merchant demand than from the pressures of supply. Women, who lacked traditions of long-distance migration comparable to men's, presented themselves less readily for a voyage into the unknown, and peasants appeared in smaller numbers because of the resolutely urban focus of mercantile recruitment.[37]

Mercantile recruitment did not merely exhibit continuities, however; in the course of the French regime, it underwent structural transformations affecting both the identity of the recruiters and the scope and nature of their efforts. These changes proceeded in part, but in part only, from the state-mandated lessening of the mercantile responsibility to provide colonists. The continuous reassessment by the merchants themselves of the opportunities presented by the servant trade played a determining role as well, with the result that the evolution of mercantile recruitment depended on the complex interaction of private interest and public policy.

As viewed from La Rochelle, the vicissitudes of mercantile recruitment began with the decline of collective recruiters and their gradual replacement with individual merchants. The latter entered the market with a bang, retrenched somewhat, withdrew altogether in favor of sea captains, then made a cautious comeback just before the conquest. The speculative accomplishments of traders thus rose, fell, and rose again, only to succumb in the end to military defeat. Similar trajectories undoubtedly characterized other ports with long-term connections to Canada, such as Rouen. The example of La Rochelle, however, must suffice in the absence of a well-documented series of indentures from the Norman capital.

Commercial recruiters for Canada arrived somewhat tardily in La Rochelle, as a result first of commercial rivalry and later of systematic exclusion. The earliest titularies of the monopoly preferred to deal with Normans and Bretons, and Richelieu, while broadening the geographic base of the Canada trade, failed to extend it to La Rochelle. The absence of Aunisian merchants from the Compagnie des Cent-Associés was far from accidental;[38] Louis XIII ratified its charter of incorporation while preparing to lay siege to the Protestant port.[39] Even after the capitulation, La Rochelle's perceived disloyalty prevented recruitment from moving southward in the early years of Richelieu's new regime.

Recruitment reached La Rochelle between 1642 and 1645, when the Compagnie des Cent-Associés for the second time handled the Canada trade directly. The losses sustained by the Normans during the years of subcontracting made them amenable at last to Rochelais participation, and the objections of Richelieu disappeared with his death in 1642. Three mercantile recruiters worked out of La Rochelle in these years: a director and two employees of the company.⁴⁰ The director, who had previously operated in Normandy, now enlisted some seventy-five indentured servants in La Rochelle,⁴¹ and his clerks signed up another dozen. Most of these servants became direct dependents of the company, but a few agreed to work for specific Canadian seigneurs.

In 1645, the Communauté des Habitants took over from the company, and its representatives replaced the latter's as recruiters. Until 1652, when the Communauté itself turned to expedients to maintain the Canada trade, its appointees made irregular levies of labor in La Rochelle. As recorded in the *tabellionage* (notarial archives), their activities were on a smaller scale than those of the Cent-Associés,⁴² but they resembled them in kind. Most emigrants indentured themselves to the habitants collectively, while a few signed on by procuration with individual habitants.

The ruling on indentured servants passed by the Conseil de Québec in 1647 did not affect recruitment in La Rochelle, at least in the several years after its passage. Although it held shippers responsible for the embarkment of a minimum number of engagés, the efforts of the Communauté apparently sufficed to meet the quota. The first instance of recruitment by a Rochelais merchant did occur in 1648, but at the time the merchant in question had a financial interest only in shipping to the West Indies. His decision to send an indentured servant to Canada thus appears as an isolated attempt to test the Canadian labor market rather than as a response to governmental imperative.

In the final decades of the Cent-Associés, the struggling Communauté des Habitants ceased to recruit servants in La Rochelle and addressed itself instead to the city's merchants for the fulfillment of its multiple obligations. Of the ten merchants who responded to the call, six were Catholic and four were Protestant. The Protestants, in keeping with their greater economic weight in the merchant community, operated on a larger and more speculative scale than the Catholics.⁴³

François Péron, a Protestant, inaugurated the new phase of merchant recruitment in 1655 by embarking the annual quota of twenty servants required of the Communauté. The real innovation, however, occurred the following year, when Péron and his Protestant colleague, Jacques Pépin, recruited fifty-odd emigrants on their own initiative and for their own benefit. Péron, who entrusted the disposal of his servants to a *commis* (an employee), found the results sufficiently gratifying to renew the operation in subsequent years. By 1659, he had recruited some seventy emigrants for Canada, only three of them at the request of specific colonists.

Catholic merchants attempted to imitate their religious and commercial rivals, becoming involved in their turn in speculative recruitment. As early as 1657, a partnership composed of Antoine Grignon, Pierre Gaigneur, and Jacques Masse embarked thirty-three indentured servants on their own account. Apparently success eluded them, for the endeavor was not repeated. At midcentury, Catholics commanded risk capital with greater difficulty than Protestants, and most of them preferred the safer course of responding to specific demands for labor.

Between 1663 and 1713 collective recruiters reappeared in the form first of the Compagnie des Indes Occidentales and later of the Compagnie du Nord and the Compagnie d'Acadie. Individual merchants, however, continued to enlist the bulk of the servants, since Louis XIV had released the companies from most of their obligations to recruit. The royal regime thus failed to stem the atrophy of collective mercantile recruitment, which remained anemic in comparison to its high point under the Cent-Associés.[44]

The merchants, who now consisted primarily of Catholics,[45] destined fully three-fifths of their recruits for unknown bidders. This belated speculative success of the Catholics probably stemmed less from an elimination of their Protestant competitors than from the latters' withdrawal from a market judged insufficiently interesting.[46] In this period, few shippers began to delegate their recruiting responsibilities, minimal as they were, to the sea captains they employed; all was not well with the Rochelais servant trade.[47]

Between 1714 and 1730, the role of ship's captains increased to the detriment of the merchants. About half of the servants signed on with ship's captains, suggesting that the burden of complying with the servant legislation of these years fell increasingly on them. Fifteen captains served as recruiters, as opposed to only six merchants, and all embarked the servants on their own account. Profits as well as losses accrued to them, while the shippers concerned themselves more with inanimate cargoes. Trade remained on a modest scale, with fewer than half a dozen servants embarking per voyage. Several captains, however, recruited quite consistently, obviously viewing recruitment as a profitable sideline.

From 1731 until the end of the War of the Austrian Succession, the captains carried on the servant trade virtually alone. Only four merchants went before the notary with indentures, and although sixteen of the city's shippers were trading with Canada during the war years,[48] just one felt compelled to involve himself in recruitment. Neither the merchants nor the twenty-seven captains enlisted servants with specific Canadians in mind.

This situation changed only in the final decade of the French regime, when the Canada trade again appealed to a larger spectrum of La Rochelle's merchants. Not all of these merchants took a direct interest in recruiting servants, but their involvement increased to the point where they dominated the Acadian market and shared that of Québec more or less equally with ship's captains. Overall, about twice as many servants embarked in this as in the previous decade.

Mercantile recruitment thus moved from the realm of collective enterprise to that of individual enterprise in the course of the French regime, a development ratified rather than initiated by governmental policy. Individual merchants recruited more or less heavily, and more or less speculatively, in accordance with their own economic preferences. When they perceived the servant trade as lucrative, they recruited large numbers of emigrants on their own account, but when they did not, they restricted their efforts to fulfilling colonial commissions or delegated observance of the servant legislation to their ship's captains. In spite of these not inconsiderable transformations, mercantile recruitment remained consistent in its approach to prospective colonists. Recruiters, whether agents of companies, independent shippers, or sea captains, sought their servants in France's major Atlantic ports, primarily among a population of young males in modest economic circumstances.

The Role of Seigneurs

Seigneurial recruitment, with its emphasis on agricultural settlement, played a more important role in the pioneering stages of colonization than afterward. Its geographic focus therefore shifted from Québec and peninsular Acadia in the seventeenth century to Ile Saint-Jean and Ile Royale in the years after the Treaty of Utrecht. Canadian seigneurs consisted, as we have seen, of either collectivities or individuals, and within the category of individuals, of simple *rentiers* or *seigneurs-commerçants*. The seigneurial traders were confined to Acadia and individual or collective rentiers to Québec.

The servants recruited by seigneurs of all three types exhibited a broader range of geographic and social origins than those recruited through mercantile interest or obligation. While not disdaining the great ports, the seigneurs or their agents cast their nets more widely when seeking emigrants; their native localities, in particular, furnished a considerable number of recruits. Socially, they made an effort to indenture families and peasants as well as single, young townsmen, so their efforts resulted in the transplantation to Canada of a more representative cross section of the French population.

The Atlantic ports, or La Rochelle at any rate, held a significant but not preponderant place in seigneurial recruitment. In the seventeenth century, seigneurs like Claude de Razilly of Acadia and seigneurial representatives like Jérôme Le Royer de La Dauversière of the Société Notre-Dame de Montréal appeared personally in La Rochelle to seek out colonists for their respective establishments. Razilly indentured two servants there in 1636,[49] and La Dauversière, "residing ordinarily in La Flesche," recruited twenty-one while lodging with Rochelais merchant Jacques Mousnier in 1644.[50] These same recruiters also looked to La Rochelle at times when their own presence proved impractical. Razilly's cousin, Menou d'Aulnay, had already secured him a servant in the city in 1634,[51] and in 1652, Jacques Mousnier enlisted emigrants for La Dauversière by proxy.[52] After the Treaty of Utrecht, the seigneur of the Ile Saint-Jean, the comte de Saint-Pierre, formed a society with the merchants of La Rochelle for the peopling and exploitation of his seigneurie. At least 150 servants embarked there for Ile Saint-Jean in the early 1720s, perhaps the largest group of colonists to leave the Aunisian port in the employ of a single seigneur.

Seigneurial recruitment did not, however, begin and end with La Rochelle, or even with La Rochelle, Le Havre, and Bayonne.[53]

Unlike merchants, seigneurs sought some of their colonists in areas remote from the Atlantic and its commerce but familiar to them personally. Perhaps their behavior represents a conscious if sporadic attempt to bypass the anonymity of portuary recruitment, for seigneurs knew indentured servants not as negotiable commodities but as their own future *censitaires*.

The best-known case of local, seigneurial recruitment concerns Robert Giffard, the Percheron seigneur of Beauport. The scion of a quasi-seigneurial family from the environs of Mortagne (Orne), Giffard visited Canada as a ship's surgeon in the 1620s, then returned to Mortagne to ply his trade as a master apothecary. Perhaps he found the living too humble or the competition from the town's four other pharmacists too stiff. In any case, he chose to abandon the business in favor of settling in Québec, and he petitioned the Cent-Associés for a seigneurie in 1634.[54]

Giffard's main associates were brothers Jean and Noël Juchereau, sons of a local merchant and protoindustrialist who had made a fortune in wine, wood, iron, land, and anything else that he could sell. Their involvement with Canada brought them not only monetary benefits but enhanced social prestige; Jean's son, Nicolas, acceded to the nobility in 1692, well before his cousins in the French branch of the family.

The three recruiters succeeded in generating a wave of permanent departures that was quite unprecedented in the region. It continued, in fits and starts, for over thirty years, its end coinciding roughly with the deaths of Giffard and Jean Juchereau in 1668 and 1672, respectively. Although Giffard du Moncel, Juchereau du Maure, and Juchereau des Châtelets all held title to estates in the Perche, they did not, for the most part, look to these estates for their colonists. Emigrants came instead from bourgs and towns along the post road to Paris such as Mortagne and Tourouvre. Recruitment was thus local and direct, but it in no way depended on a preexisting relationship between censitaire and seigneur.

The Percheron example, while the most famous, was not unique in the annals of seigneurial recruitment. Neither of the seigneurial recruiters whom we observed in Aunis, Claude de Razilly or Jérôme Le Royer de La Dauversière, confined his activities to La Rochelle; both, in fact, recruited far more vigorously in their areas of origin. In 1636, Razilly, who owned estates in Touraine, enlisted 40 servants in Bourgueil and Chinon (Indre-et-Loire), and in 1653, Le Royer recruited 121 around his home in La Flèche. Like the recruits of Giffard, these emigrants came primarily from country towns well served by the means of communication and not from parishes under the seigneurial jurisdiction of the recruiters. Verron, Crosmières, and Malicorne (Sarthe), where the Le Royer family was ensconced, sent far fewer servants than La Flèche, while Beaumont-en-Véron (Indre-et-Loire) produced not a single permanent colonist for Razilly.

Only one bona fide case of recruitment on seigneurial estates has been established to date. It concerns Razilly's cousin and successor, Charles de Menou d'Aulnay, whose lands in Poitou served to increase the population of the Acadian seigneurie. An examination of the parish registers revealed that

> more than half of the acts passed in the parish of La Chaussée between 1626 and 1650 concern about twenty family names, which we find in 1671 in the first census of Acadia; and three precise acts, passed in 1627, 1645 and 1646, pertain directly to families (Brault, Brun and Chebrat) recorded in the Acadian census.... It thus appears that the seigneurie of Aulnay, possessed by the mother of Charles de Menou, could have been the cradle of about twenty of the oldest families who settled in Acadia.[55]

Menou's efforts, while startlingly successful, appear exceptional in every way. Seigneurial recruiters often sought out emigrants in their region of origin, and they probably used their social influence to persuade their interlocutors. This influence was not the authority of the traditional seigneur, however, but rather the general notability of any prosperous and respectable member of the community.

Seigneurs did not expand merely the geographic horizons of recruitment but its social horizons as well. Because of their interest in agricultural settlement, they made a greater effort than merchants to include peasants among their recruits, and for the same reason, they sometimes looked beyond single young people to constituted families.

Seigneurial writings stressed the importance of peasant emigration to the creation of a successful Canadian colony. As early as 1636, the *Jesuit Relations* carried the following "Advice to those who desire to cross over into New France":

There are so many strong and robust peasants in France who have no bread to put in their mouths; is it possible that they are so afraid of losing sight of the village steeple, as they say, that they would rather languish in their misery and poverty, than to place themselves some day at their ease among the inhabitants of New France.[56]

The Jesuits also suggested the channeling toward Canada of artisans whose mobility would otherwise carry them outside of French territory,[57] but peasants rather than artisans formed the cornerstone of their conception of the colonial edifice.

The seigneurial appeal to peasants, unlike that of merchants, did not remain on the level of semantics. Razilly's recruits from 1636 consisted of two salt producers and forty "peasants from Anjou,"[58] and except for a gunsmith and a carpenter, those of his cousin Menou d'Aulnay were all farmers [*laboureurs*] from Poitou. Peasants also outnumbered artisans among the servants indentured by La Dauversière in 1653[59] and among those enlisted in Tourouvre-au-Perche by Jean and Noël Juchereau.[60]

The recruitment of families sometimes accompanied that of peasants, for seigneurs viewed family farms as the essential building blocks of a stable colonial society. As the Jesuit Lejeune wrote in 1635, "[*I*]t all lies in employing many men to cut down and clear the woods, in order to distribute the land to the families whom we are and will be transporting."[61] The "peasants from Anjou" recruited by Razilly in the following year included six families of three to five persons each, and on a larger scale, many of the Percherons arrived in Canada in family units. Families did not, however, predominate in seigneurial recruitment because of the preference implied by Lejeune for adult males in the initial stages of settlement.

Seigneurial recruitment thus produced a more diverse group of emigrants in terms of regional origin, social background, sex, and age than did mercantile recruitment. While this recruitment was on a lesser scale throughout most of the French regime, its importance far exceeds its admittedly limited numerical scope. Emigrants located through the personal prestige of a recruiter were on the whole better candidates for permanent settlement than those raked together "*à la volée*"; ultimately, the provinces where seigneurial recruitment prevailed, such as Perche, Anjou, and

Maine, made a disproportionate contribution to the agriculture and population of French Canada.

The Role of the State

The state's role in recruitment, as portrayed in the voluminous correspondence between France and the Canadian colonies, remained reasonably constant through both space and time. The royal efforts in Acadia replicated those in Québec, and the recruiting duties assigned to particular bureaucrats by Colbert still attached to their successors at the time of the conquest.

At the top of the pyramid of recruiters stood the ministre de la Marine; in consultation with the king, he determined how many emigrants the state could and should recruit.[62] Although he delegated the actual task of recruiting, he involved himself in the minutiae of policymaking, providing his subalterns with specifications about whom and where to recruit.

Beginning in 1666, the minister relayed his will preferentially to upper functionaries within the naval bureaucracy. The administrators of Rochefort assumed the role of coordinating recruitment, partly because the port now became by fiat the principal base of the Atlantic fleet and partly because Colbert could rely on its *intendant de la Marine*, his cousin, Colbert de Terron. The domination of the Rochefortais remained absolute until the 1680s, when colleagues from Bordeaux and Le Havre became involved in recruitment, and visible thereafter. Even the participation of administrators from Bayonne, Nantes, and Saint-Malo from the early eighteenth century on did not pose a serious challenge to Rochefort's supremacy.

The naval officials, consisting of the intendants and their various subalterns—*commissionnaires* and *commissaires généraux, commissaires ordonnateurs, commissaires ordinaires, inspecteurs*—took responsibility for both military recruitment and civilian recruitment in the form of male, skilled labor. Although the state, as we shall see, subsidized other categories of civilian emigrants such as indentured servants, filles à marier, and prisoners, it did so under the auspices of recruiters from outside the naval establishment. The naval bureaucrats approached their military and civilian responsibilities in different ways. Civilian recruitment was often direct, but military recruitment involved further delegation of the commissions received from the minister, in accordance with the established practices of the metropolitan army.

Thanks to André Corvisier, we can sketch a clear picture of domestic military recruitment in the seventeenth and eighteenth centuries. Colonels and captains received an official mandate to recruit and worked to maintain troop strength at the stipulated levels. Sometimes they did so directly by enlisting soldiers themselves, but more often, they referred the task to their subordinates: lieutenants, sergeants, corporals, and even simple soldiers.[63] These "natural auxiliaries"[64] usually sufficed, but since the market for recruits, like a labor market, responded to supply and demand, they sometimes had to look elsewhere to meet their quota. In times of scarce manpower, they had recourse to intermediaries of all stripes who brought in recruits in return for a per capita sum. Former soldiers, innkeepers, merchants, petty judicial officers, members of the mounted constabulary, and relatives of the official recruiters might occasionally supplement their incomes by finding takers for the *"pain du roi."*

Soldiers made their way into the Canadian troops in much the same way. The men the commissaires relied on included a colonel, two majors, seven captains, four lieutenants, and a sergeant.[65] Those below the rank of captain acted in the name of their superior officers, engaging soldiers for the entire company or regiment. There is little direct evidence of civilian meddling in recruitment, but accounts of periodic fiascoes point to the participation of disreputable *rabatteurs* in the recruitment process.[66] In 1750, for example, the governor of Québec complained to the minister of the military recruiters in the following terms:

I cannot dispense... with representing to you that those who took care of raising these recruits have served the king very badly and have abused your confidence; here is the proof. You will be surprised that they accepted people disabled from birth, men between sixty and seventy years old, sailors from the royal navy, married men who brought with them wives and children, people of all nations, including a great many Spaniards who neither speak nor understand French; lastly, among the rest there are a number of knaves and scoundrels, certain of them repeat offenders who deserved to be on the galleys rather than to serve the king.[67]

Geographically, military recruiters for Canada did not exactly replicate the movements of recruiters of the domestic troops. These last combined local recruitment during the morte saison (off-season), among people known to the captain and his family, with *racolage* per se, or anonymous collective recruitment by way of poster and public drum beating in major cities such as Paris.[68] Canada's military recruiters relied primarily on the second, or impersonal, approach. Direct, local recruitment occurred in specific instances only; officers of the Swiss troops, which served on Ile Royale from the 1720s[69] "seem to have recruited in the vicinity of their family,"[70] and during the Seven Years War those of the Royal Roussillon moved outward from a home base in Roussillon and Catalonia.[71] Most of the time, however, recruiters had recourse to public announcements in urban squares, as stipulated by their superiors.

As with domestic racolage, the officer in charge of colonial recruitment "received from the king a 'route' that indicated the itinerary to follow."[72] More often than not, he centered his operations on a major port city such as Le Havre, Nantes, Brest, Rochefort, La Rochelle, Bordeaux, or Bayonne, then radiated out if necessary into the towns of the hinterlands. The orders of one Pannetié, an officer working out of Le Havre in 1687, permitted him to send recruiters from the port "into all the cities of this province."[73]

Paris provided far fewer recruits than did Atlantic France, for reasons that appear more financial than geographic. In 1717, when the recruiter, La Galissonière, requested an itinerary for Paris, the council balked; it informed him flatly that "it has esteemed necessary to have them raised in the Department of Rochefort, where they will cost infinitely less than in Paris."[74] This higher price may have been justified, for when troops did arrive from Paris in 1734, the governor and intendant of Québec wrote of them: "Those who were enlisted in Paris... are the best who have come here to date, for age as well as for... the other dispositions necessary for the service; those who were raised in Rochefort are very different... by their infirmities and other defects."[75]

Recruiters of the domestic troops, wherever they found themselves, addressed indiscriminately a broad segment of the male population. By law, they could not accept recruits under the age of sixteen, and they could not enlist anyone against his will; beyond these broad guidelines, anything was acceptable. In practice, even these minimal constraints did not always obtain. Underage boys enrolled, with or without a dispensation,[76] and prisoners entered the service for life regardless of their personal preferences. Nor were wayward sons, vagabonds, smugglers, and deserters the only victims of forced recruitment. Unscrupulous racoleurs chose to meet their quotas through impressment, which became almost an institution in areas of heavy recruitment. Several taverns in Paris, for example, "acted as 'ovens,' that is to say, places where unfortunates who had been lured in or kidnapped were shut up until they signed an enlistment."[77]

The same criteria applied to Canadian recruits, and a cavalier attitude toward them appeared to be equally prevalent. With regard to age, the ministry routinely set standards, which the recruiters just as routinely violated. In 1725, for example, lieutenant Paschot learned that his recruits "had to be between eighteen and thirty years of age,"[78] but within a week, he had received "a young man named Villars who is only fourteen years old" but "who absolutely wanted to enlist."[79] When recruitment proved difficult, as it often did during wartime, any lingering concern with age evaporated. The Canadians sometimes complained, as in 1712, when the governor of Québec wrote of the year's recruits that "all of these soldiers are mere children and it will take at least three or four years before they will be able to be in a position to render service."[80] Even Canadians, however, could be complacent; in 1696, Frontenac had described the new soldiers as "strong, pretty and alert," adding that "they are in truth very young, but in our experience young people adjust better to the country than the others."[81]

The policy toward prisoners changed for the worse during the French regime. In the seventeenth century, recruiters could not enlist them, no matter how desperate they were for manpower; but by 1702, the authorities had reversed themselves completely, permitting the family of one Henri-Claude Bernard to deport him from Nantes to Newfoundland, "where he will serve as a soldier pending further orders."[82] During the regency, recruiters began to enlist vagabonds as well; in 1717, La Galissonière received permission to embark twenty-eight of them, provided that they were healthy and that "in the meantime you keep the thing secret."[83] Sundry prisoners arrived with the Canadian troops up until the conquest.

The correspondence does not abound in examples of impressment, which was, after all, a distasteful subject, but it indicates that even in peacetime some abuses occurred. Isolated victims could obtain justice in the form of a discharge, if not a return to France; in 1702, a "young man from the region of Maine who was put by force into the reinforcements lately arrived in Canada" received his freedom.[84] Perhaps the most curious case involved a kidnapped priest, who spent two years in the Canadian army while awaiting the outcome of his appeal. After an investigation, the minister informed the governor of Québec that "M. Pierre Chauveau, who was sent to Canada among the new recruits of 1733, told you the truth when he stated to you that he was a priest. The Bishop of Orléans has sent me a certificate of his ordination."[85]

Unfortunately, when impressment took place on a larger scale, there was little that anyone could do. The infamous recruits of 1750 were not only crippled, aged, Spanish, naked, and criminal:

Furthermore, most of these soldiers had no enlistment, and they have complained stoutly, some that they had been taken by force, others by surprise and practically all that they had not been paid what had been promised for their enlistment.[86]

Their morbidity and mortality rates were elevated, even for the time, and those of them who found the strength to rebel were put down by force.[87] Such callous and irresponsible recruitment constituted an aberration, as the very vehemence of the documents shows, yet it stands as a reminder that at its involuntary worst, emigration preyed on some of the most vulnerable members of society.

Attention to age and freedom of contract, no matter how imperfect, does not completely define the social selectivity of Canadian military recruitment. Especially in the eighteenth century, Canadian recruiters sometimes received a more specific mandate; the colony needed not only soldiers but soldier-workers.

In the maritimes, where an exposed position made fortifications a prerequisite of effective settlement, the recruitment of soldier-workers seemed the ideal solution. The average soldier served in France for seven or eight years and for even longer in the colonies.[88] His advantage over an indentured servant, or *trente-six mois*, was therefore palpable, without even considering the pressing issue of defense.

At the turn of the century, recruiters began to target workers to fortify French Newfoundland. In 1700, the minister arranged for the arrival there of "a levy entirely composed of masons, stonecutters, and carpenters."[89] The following year, while deploring that "it is difficult, especially in the present situation where soldiers are being raised everywhere,"[90] he nonetheless managed to include "a few masons, stonecutters, carpenters, and other workers" among the seventy-one new reinforcements.[91]

The projected settlement of Ile Royale in 1714 called forth another wave of artisanal recruiting. Indeed, the minister described the artisanal competence of the island's soldiers as a matter "of utmost consequence."[92] As in Newfoundland, the building trades topped the list of desirable skills, but the range was somewhat wider, as befitting the scope of the establishment. According to the minister, "The trades that are the most necessary are those of mason, stonecutter, carpenter, joiner, blacksmith, and locksmith. Those of cooper, cobbler, and tailor would also be necessary but in small quantity."[93]

In Québec, the matter seemed less urgent, due both to the larger population and the vaunted artisanal capacities of the habitants. Shortages of skilled labor did exist, however, for in the words of the last intendant, "the Canadian is naturally a jack-of-all-trades but only for his own use."[94] Levies of workers for the Québec troops occurred more sporadically and tended to be more specialized than those for Ile Royale. The recruits ranged from tilers and potters (1717) to cordwainers (1732) to bakers and surgeons (1741). If conditions were favorable, heavier and more general labor recruiting could take place. After the Treaty of Aix-La-Chapelle, for example, the chief recruiting officer announced to the minister his success in enlisting "several masons, roofers, carpenters, blacksmiths, sawyers, a pavior, a stonecutter, a cooper, and several bakers."[95]

Military recruiters for Canada thus exercised more discretion than their domestic confrères, at least on occasion. The direct supervision they experienced from the naval ministry did not prevent them from yielding to familiar temptations such as cheating on age, nor did it completely eradicate impressment. It did, however, require them to fulfill specific commissions regarding skilled labor, which provided Canada with an important if temporary reservoir of artisans.

In addition to coordinating military recruitment, naval functionaries also fulfilled specific requests for civilian emigrants. The minister turned to the navy for artisans as well as soldiers, and many *ouvriers du roi* arrived in the colonies by way of the great naval bases. The involvement of commissaires, Rochefort's in particular, in supplying skilled labor for the colonies grew out of their domestic role of guaranteeing a work force in the royal arsenals. The Rochefort Arsenal employed four or five thousand workers in wartime,[96] who preoccupied administrators "in terms of both their recruitment in sufficient numbers and their professional competency."[97]

In recruiting civilians for the colonies, naval functionaries delegated their authority less readily than in recruiting soldiers. The correspondence refers to them consistently as *engageurs* in their own right; only François de Beauharnais, who as intendant of La Rochelle and Rochefort enjoyed a singularly elevated position, routinely passed recruitment orders along to his subalterns.[98] The commissaires accomplished the bulk of the work themselves, aided by the "*secours et facilités*" of provincial governors and intendants.[99] The sergeants, corporals, and other humble racoleurs who helped to enlist the troupes de la Marine played little part in the naval recruitment of skilled civilians.

Administrators frequently sought out workers in the ports within their jurisdiction,[100] but they also made efforts to locate them in zones associated with specific kinds of occupational competence. The best ironworkers, they assumed, came from Burgundy and Franche-Comté, the best chimney sweeps from Savoy, and the best building workers from Limousin and Auvergne. They obtained royal orders accordingly, such as that for a levy of masons, stonecutters, and carpenters "in the provinces of Le Puy-en-Velay, of Auvergne, of Bourbonnais, Limousin and Poitou" in 1720.[101]

Recruiters of such professionals worked at a disadvantage in that regions like the Velay had no obvious connection to Atlantic commerce. In contrast, the provinces of the *Massif central*, like Savoy, had a long-standing tradition of labor migrations, and while these migrations usually followed established routes, they could be diverted. Recruiters needed only to make a somewhat better offer than the workers knew they could obtain in their customary destination, and some of the more adventurous at least would willingly sign on for a stint in Canada.

Although naval functionaries and their deputies recruited the bulk of Canada's state-subsidized emigrants, the minister also commissioned recruiters without ties to the naval bureaucracy. The Compagnie des Indes Occidentales, hospital administrators, churchmen, prison officials, and the Ferme Générale provided the balance of the king's civilian recruits in the form of indentured servants, *filles à marier*, and prisoners.

The Compagnie des Indes Occidentales recruited indentured servants at the behest (and expense) of the crown, which relied on merchants to effect the large-scale levies characteristic of the early years of Canada's royal regime.[102] In 1665, Jean Talon described the company's efforts in La Rochelle to the minister:

> The West India Company, being obliged ... to transport 400 workmen to Canada, has ordered the directors who are here to raise 150 on its behalf through the levy that I am having carried out today on the deck of the ship. There are more than that number.[103]

Two years later, the company contracted for another levy of 400 men and appointed merchant Pierre Gaigneur to supervise recruitment. This time the results proved unfelicitous, and Talon wrote to Colbert,

> It is with much displeasure that I feel obliged to tell you that instead of 400 good men with whom you wanted to fortify this country ... I have received only 127 very weak, young and of little service; I want to believe that the raising of men in France for the war has removed the means of better succeeding from those who were employed in the choice ... of these passengers.[104]

The levy apparently prompted complaints from Bishop Laval as well, for at the time of the next shipment in 1669, Colbert assured him that all abuses had been corrected:

I have taken all possible precautions this year to receive only those men suited for work to be transported to New France. To this end I have asked Mr. Colbert de Terron (my cousin) to take care of [raising] the 200 people who will be carried on the vessel of M. Le Gagneur [Gaigneur].[105]

The state thus responded to the company's failure to recruit emigrants of quality by imposing a recruiter of its own choice; that this recruiter happened to be Colbert de Terron reflects its growing preference for naval supervision. Individually and in companies, merchants continued to enlist emigrants under the auspices of the crown; however, after 1669, they played a minor role in comparison to the naval functionaries whose direct dependence on the minister afforded him better control of the proceedings.

The recruitment of marriageable women also concerned the state in the mid-seventeenth century, for sexual imbalance discouraged male settlement and impeded population expansion. Private recruiters, whether French or Canadian, had limited success in embarking single women. Since women usually lacked traditions of long-distance migration, they did not respond en masse to the arguments that persuaded men. In 1666, three years after the departure of the first *filles du roi*, women still comprised little more than one-third of the Canadian population.[106]

The filles du roi of the 1660s and 1670s came in large part from the Hôpital Général of Paris, whose chief administrator, Christophe du Plessis de Montbard, had a long-standing interest in things Canadian.[107] Talon, who paid a visit to the institution on his return to Paris in 1673, described the selection process for the filles du roi as follows: "I have seen two of the directors who must give me... a list of the girls who are disposed to go to Canada and who are appropriate for the king's design."[108] The directors thus made a preliminary recommendation based on the inclinations and aptitudes of their wards and submitted it to the colonial authorities for ratification.

When institutions proved insufficient, state recruitment of women expanded to include the parishes of churchmen with an interest in colonization. In 1670, for example, Colbert asked the archbishop of Rouen, whose jurisdiction extended to Québec prior to the erection of a North American diocese in 1674, to "use the credit and the authority that you have over the vicars of thirty or forty of the said parishes [in the environs of Rouen] to see if they could voluntarily find in each, one or two girls to go to the said country [Canada]."[109] The Sulpiciens, whose Canadian ministry dated from 1657, also cooperated in recruiting women, for in 1673, Talon mentioned that a Sulpicien abbot, M. De Bretonvilliers, and the curé of Saint-Sulpice "ordinarily find well qualified ones in their parish."[110]

A willingness to emigrate did not in itself qualify a woman to become a fille du roi, as Talon's reference to the "king's design" suggests. What was at stake was her suitability, in terms that were phrased most explicitly by the minister in the following decade: "The king transports no women of ill repute [*femmes de mauvaise vie*] to the American colonies but gladly young ladies raised in hospitals who are healthy and have not been debauched."[111]

Recruiters thus concerned themselves first and foremost with the morality of their prospective charges, yet social background did not prove an idle consideration. The baron de La Hontan, a young army officer stationed in Canada from 1688 to 1693, insisted on the importance of class in the Canadian distribution of the filles à marier:

> The circumstances of their arrival were recounted to me, and I like to entertain you too much not to share them with you. This chaste herd was led to the conjugal pasture by old and prudish shepherdesses.... As soon as they reached the habitation, the wrinkled commandants inspected their troops, and having separated them into three classes, each band entered a different room. As they pressed each other quite closely on account of the smallness of the place, it made for a pleasant enough decoration. These were not three shops where love made up the showcases and displays; these were three fully stocked warehouses.[112]

For all its sarcasm, La Hontan's account accords with the more sententious comments preserved in the administrative correspondence. Recruiters began to seek out upper-class women in 1667 to bind seigneurs and officers to the colony. As Colbert informed Talon,

> And in case there were gentlemen or officers of the troops residing in the country who were not married or who found no one to marry owing to the disproportion between their quality and that of the people, I would try to have some well nourished and well brought up damsels sent from here to unite them.[113]

Apparently he kept his word, for six months later, Talon acknowledged the arrival of fifteen or twenty women "of some birth," "several of them true damsels and fairly well brought up."[114]

In the eighteenth century, the state ceased its large-scale shipments of indentured servants and filles à marier but compensated with the deportation of prisoners. Prison administrators dispatched poachers, wife beaters, and other common criminals to Canada throughout the 1720s, together with young people of good family locked up for correction in the hospitals.[115] The Ferme Générale, under the authority of Contrôleur Général Orry, took over from the prison wardens in the following decade and destined hundreds of smugglers for Canada between 1730 and 1746.

Strictly speaking, wardens and *fermiers* practiced selection rather than recruitment, since their recruits had no choice but to indenture themselves. The criteria for selection, as expressed to the Canadians, consisted of physical condition, occupation, age, and marital status; the preference went to healthy, young bachelors trained in useful trades.[116] Orry's correspondence, however, suggests a different reality, namely, that Canada also served as a dumping ground for the Ferme's undesirables. In the mid-1730s, deportation orders were issued to such incorrigible *chefs de bande* as Phillipe Guerry *dit le Dragon* and Simon Monny *dit la Mort*, and in 1734, the smugglers were so unsavory that the ship's captain in La Rochelle refused to embark four of them, including one who was stricken with "inveterate mange."[117] Needless to say, the Canadians soon caught on, but Orry exerted enough influence to maintain the convoys at a reduced level in spite of their complaints for another decade.[118] Regionally, the smugglers made up the most diverse group of all, coming from prisons as far afield as Amiens, Angers, Argentan, Auxerre, Bayonne, Boulogne-sur-Mer, Caen, Cambrai, Carentan, Château-Gontier, Chaumont-en-Bassigny, Coutances, Dijon, Saumur, and Valence.[119]

The participation of the state in recruitment thus ensured the emigration of a large and varied group of people in the final century of the French regime. Like the contribution of the merchants, it emphasized single young people at the expense of families and artisans at the expense of peasants, but like the seigneurial contribution, it exhibited a more even sex ratio and a geographic distribution extending well beyond the Atlantic ports. In terms of permanent settlement, recruitment by the state probably fell midway between mercantile and seigneurial recruitment for its efficacy. Certain of the state-subsidized emigrants, such as the filles du roi and some of the soldiers, proved to be excellent colonists, and others, specifically the prisoners, were required to remain whether they liked it or not. At the same time, however, many state-recruited soldiers and workers undoubtedly viewed their stint in Canada as temporary. For them, colonial emigration functioned analogously to a stay in the city or a foray into petty smuggling. It was simply one economic strategy among others, albeit a more unusual and adventurous one.

Conclusion

The combined recruiting efforts of merchants, seigneurs, and the French state resulted in the emigration of at least 30,000 men and women to Québec and of a further but indeterminate number to Acadia. In 1763, when the French formally ceded Canada to Great Britain, the population of Québec was 75,000, and that of the two Acadian islands was 5,000. The French residents of peninsular Acadia, under British jurisdiction since 1713, had already been deported in anticipation of the Seven Years War. Another 5,000 Francophones lived in what is now the United States and, depending on their location, passed to either the British or the Spanish. From Louisiana to the Gulf of Saint-Lawrence, New France in its entirety could boast about the same number of inhabitants as Nantes or Bordeaux and fewer than Marseille or Lyon. As for the capital, there were seven or eight Parisians for each French person in North America.

The slenderness of this achievement becomes even more apparent when considered in relation to British North America. In an identical time span, the British colonies absorbed some 700,000 immigrants of various European and African nationalities,[120] and their population at the Treaty of Paris stood at almost two million. Viewed in the context of demography, the British conquest of New France appears less as the strategic victory of Wolfe over Montcalm than as the unstoppable progress of a human steamroller.

Anglo-American historians have traditionally attributed the numerical inferiority of French North America to a lack of initiative on the part of ordinary Frenchmen, a situation made worse by the attempts of the state to compensate for it. Only the laissez-faire policies of the British, so the argument runs, could create optimum conditions for colonization.[121]

The French were not, however, reluctant to emigrate to America in general but merely to Canada in particular. The climate, with its harsh winter, mosquito-laden summer, and radically shortened growing season, and the continual wars with the Iroquois did little to boost the reputation of the colony. Even Voltaire, who once claimed "that if I were young, if I had my health, if I had not built Ferney, I would go settle in Louisiana," begged Chauvelin "on bended knee" to get rid of Canada.[122] In *Candide*, he penned a passage, ever infamous among Canadians, about the follies of the Seven Years War:

You know that these two nations [England and France] are at war about a few acres of snow in the neighborhood of Canada, and that they have expended much greater sums in the contest than all Canada is worth.[123]

The state was not altogether blameless, of course. Its mercantilist policies did inhibit Canadian economic development to a degree, and its paranoia about Protestant disloyalty closed Canada to the massive flow of Huguenot refugees who left for northern Europe and colonies such as New England and South Africa.[124] The refusal to welcome French Protestants was perhaps a fateful mistake, but it was really the only one. The French system of recruitment worked, providing the colony with both a core of permanent colonists and a floating population willing to contribute its labor on a temporary basis. A recent student of the New French population, Mario Boleda, has written, "Given all of the negative factors, we...should not be surprised at the feeble French immigration to Canada, but rather that a colony ever existed in the Laurentian Valley between the beginning of the seventeenth century and the middle of the eighteenth."[125] Yet exist it did, and while it ultimately proved unable to withstand British military might, its active or passive resistance to assimilation has guaranteed its integrity ever since.

Notes

1. Marc Gaucher, Marc Delafosse, and Gabriel Debien, "Les Engagés pour le Canada au XVIIIe siècle," *Revue d'histoire de l'Amérique française* 13–14 (1959–1961): 14: 594. All translations mine unless otherwise indicated.
2. Letter of Talon to Colbert, 24 May 1665. *Archives des Colonies* (AC), C11–A 2: 140.
3. Letter of Talon to Louis XIV, 11 November 1663. AC, C11–A 2: 216.
4. Letter of Talon to Colbert, 22 April 1665. AC, C11–A 2: 124.
5. Gustave Lanctôt, *Histoire du Canada du régime royal au traité d'Utrecht, 1663–1713* (Montréal: Beauchemin, 1963), 66.
6. Letter to the Minister, 23 January 1687. *Archives de la Marine* (AM), B-3 53: 48. The troupes de la Marine were troops that fell under naval jurisdiction, unlike the regular troupes de terre.
7. See, e.g., Olwen Hufton, *The Poor of Eighteenth-Century France, 1750–89* (Oxford: Clarendon Press, 1974): 70–71.
8. "Les Véritables motifs de messieurs et dames de la société Notre-Dame de Montréal pour la conversion des sauvages de Nouvelle-France," *Mémoires de la société historique de Montréal* 9 (1880): 66.
9. Cited in Marcel Trudel, *Histoire de la Nouvelle-France*, 3 vols. (Montréal: Fides, 1963–83), 1: 131.
10. Dr. Lomier, "Les Picards au Canada," *Bulletin de la société de géographie de Québec* 19 (1925): 11.
11. Actually, in the six years between Poutrincourt's concession and his first establishment, De Monts's monopoly was revoked. It was not, however, reconceded to Poutrincourt who, from 1609 on, simply participated in trade on the same footing as everyone else.
12. Trudel, *Histoire*, 2: 423, 440.
13. Ibid., 276; Georges Goyau, *Les Origines religieuses du Canada: Une épopée mystique* (Montréal: Fides, 1951), 84.
14. For a list of the original 100 associates and their successors, see Trudel, *Histoire*, 3, t. 1: 415–37.
15. Marcel Trudel, *Initiation à la Nouvelle-France: Histoire et institutions* (Montréal: Holt, Rinehart and Winston, 1968), 54.
16. Trudel, *Histoire*, 3, t. 1: 122.
17. Trudel, *Histoire*, 3, t. 1: 171.
18. Hubert Charbonneau and Yves Landry, "La Politique démographique en Nouvelle-France," *Annales de démographie historique* (1979): 33. Founded in 1647, the Conseil de Québec brought together the governors of Québec and Montréal, the superior of the Jesuits, and,

on a consultative basis only, elected representatives of Québec, Montréal, and Three-Rivers.

19. Lucien Campeau, *Les Cent-Associés et le peuplement de la Nouvelle-France (1633–1663)*, Cahiers d'histoire des Jésuites 2 (Montréal: Bellarmin, 1974), 152.

20. Trudel, *Histoire*, 3, t. 1: 399.

21. Lanctôt, *Histoire du Canada*, 44.

22. Ibid.

23. Lanctôt, *Histoire du Canada*, 264. These efforts profited Québec almost exclusively. The British returned Acadia to France at the Treaty of Breda in 1667, but the French reoccupation did not begin until 1670. The king paid to send fifty-five indentured servants and five filles à marier (girls intended for marriage) to Acadia in 1672, the same year he announced the end of major subsidies for emigration. See Lanctôt, *Histoire du Canada*, 255, 260.

24. There were exceptions to this rule. Colbert's son, Seignelay, for example, provided passage for about 200 indentured servants in 1684 and 1685. See Letter of De Meulles to the Minister, 1684, AC, C11–A 6: 399; Letter of the Minister to Arnoul, 8 March 1685, AC, B 11: 82.

25. In 1665, the Conseil Souverain, which replaced the Conseil de Québec, renewed the provisions of the 1647 edict on indentured servants. The captain of a merchant ship not already carrying royal emigrants could acquire a permit for Québec only by embarking one workman per ten tons of cargo. See *Jugements et délibérations du conseil souverain de la Nouvelle-France*, 6 vols. (Québec: Côté, 1885–91), 1: 269.

26. These ordinances did, however, sanction the double counting of masons, stonecutters, blacksmiths, locksmiths, joiners, coopers, carpenters, caulkers, and practitioners of "other useful trades." Royal ordinance of 20 March 1714, AC, C11–G 8: 55, and AC, B 36: 336; see also Letter of the Minister to the comte de Toulouse, 20 March 1714, AC, B 36: 121; Memorandum of the Minister to Vaudreuil and Bégon, 19 March 1714, AC, B 36: 338; Letter of the Council to Bégon, 16 June 1716, AC, B 38: 204.5; Royal ordinance of 15 February 1724, AM, B-3 368: 41.

27. Royal ordinance of 14 January 1721, AC, B 44: 56.5; Royal ordinance of 20 May 1721, AC, B 44: 161.5; Letter of the Council to Gaudion, 13 June 1721, AC, B 44: 56.5.

28. Circular to the intendants and commissaires of the ports, 9 April 1722, AC, B 45: 279.5; Letter of the Council to Marin, 29 April 1722, AC, B 45: 297.5.

29. Peninsular Acadia returned temporarily to English control between 1690 and 1697 and definitively after 1710.

30. See Leslie Choquette, "French Emigration in the Seventeenth and Eighteenth Centuries" (Ph.D. dissertation, Harvard University, 1988). The dissertation provides a demographic profile of French emigrants to Canada based on a sample of almost 16,000 emigrants, 14,000 men and 2,000 women.

31. Protestants perhaps emigrated to Canada more easily after the dissolution of the Cent-Associés; however, they were never free to practice their religion there before the conquest.

32. Trudel, *Initiation*, 71; AC, B 36: 336; AC, B 38: 204.5; AM, B-3 368: 41.

33. Although state-subsidized emigration of filles à marier ended after a decade, the more equal sex ratio that prevailed after 1673 probably rendered further arrivals of women less critical.

34. *Jugements et délibérations*, 1: 269.

35. Jean Le Goy, *Le Peuple du Havre et son histoire: Des origines à 1800* (Le Havre, 1980), 151.

36. Ibid.

37. Similarly, the relative youth of the indentured servants may have resulted as much from the propensity of the young to migrate as from legislative imperative. Assuming that they were observed, however, the edicts must have excluded some willing men in their early forties, as well as numerous adolescents below the age of eighteen.

38. The original hundred associates included Jean Tuffet, a Catholic who removed his operations from La Rochelle to Bordeaux for the duration and aftermath of the siege. Besides Tuffet and his son, one other Rochelais, Hersant, appeared briefly as an associate in 1643.

39. Trudel, *Histoire*, 3, t. 1: 7.

40. I relied, for nominative identification of the recruiters, on three sources: the series of contracts published in Gabriel Debien, "Les Engagés pour le Canada au XVIIe siècle," *Revue d'histoire de l'Amérique française* 6 (1952–53), and in Gaucher, Delafosse, and Debien, "Les Engagés"; on Marc Delafosse, "La Rochelle et le Canada au XVIIe siècle," *Revue d'histoire de l'Amérique française* 4 (1950–51); and on the manuscript list of Rochelais recruiters compiled by Archange Godbout, *Archives Nationales du Québec, Fonds Godbout*, art. 3.

41. The numbers cited throughout this discussion are only approximate. Lacunae in both the preservation and examination of the documents make it impossible to state exactly how many emigrants were recruited in a given time period.

42. Debien and Godbout uncovered under twenty indentures for this period.

43. In the third quarter of the seventeenth century, Huguenots dominated La Rochelle's overseas commerce; "on the list of the twenty-five principal shippers, twenty-one are Protestant, and they include those who financed the largest enterprises, the Pagès, the Allaires, the Godefroys, the Massiots." See Louis Pérouas, *Le Diocèse de La Rochelle de 1648 à 1724: Sociologie et pastorale* (Paris: SEVPEN, 1964), 137.

44. The companies recruited only 55 servants as compared with 128 for merchants in the same time period.

45. The Catholics included Pierre Gaigneur, Arnaud Péré, Alexandre Petit, Jean Péré, Jean Gitton, and Jean Grignon. Neither of the two Protestants, Daniel Biaille and Louis Allaire, recruited on a large scale, although Allaire figured among the city's most important merchants.

46. Religious persecution may have been a factor in the disappearance of Protestants as well.

47. In 1668, Heurtin became the first captain to dabble in the servant trade, and Duret followed suit in 1684. The captains, some of whom were Canadian, never embarked more than a handful of emigrants, but their trade was entirely speculative despite its small size; unlike merchants, captains did not recruit by proxy.

48. John G. Clark, *La Rochelle and the Atlantic Economy during the 18th Century* (Baltimore: Johns Hopkins University Press, 1981), 117–118.

49. Debien, "Les Engagés," 221.

50. Ibid., 376.

51. Ibid.

52. *Fonds Godbout*, 3.

53. Emigrants left Le Havre and Bayonne for Ile Saint-Jean in the early 1730s, after the expiration of Saint-Pierre's contract with the Rochelais. See Letter of the Minister to Beauharnais and Hocquart, 26 February 1732, AC, B 57: 602; Letter of the Minister to Saint-Ovide and Le Normant, 28 February 1732, AC, B 57: 640.

54. Joseph Besnard, "Les Diverses professions de Robert Giffard," *Nova Francia* 4 (1929): 325.

55. Geneviève Massignon, "La Seigneurie de Charles de Menou d'Aulnay gouverneur de l'Acadie, 1635–1650," *Revue d'histoire de l'Amérique française* 16 (1962–63): 471.

56. *The Jesuit Relations and Allied Documents*, ed. by Reuben Gold Thwaites, 73 vols. (Cleveland: Burrows, 1896–1901), 9: 187. Thwaites's translation.

57. *Jesuit Relations*, 7: 242.

58. Archange Godbout, "Le Rôle du Saint-Jehan et les origines acadiennes," *Mémoires de la société généalogique canadienne-française* 1 (1944): 22–23. Bourgueil and Chinon were actually on the Angevin border with Touraine.

59. Soeur Mondoux, "Les Hommes de Montréal," *Revue d'histoire de l'Amérique française* 2 (1948–49).

60. "Tableau des contrats d'engagement pour le Canada passés en l'étude notairiale de Tourouvre, 1646–1651," *Cahiers Percherons* 26 (1967): 45.

61. *Jesuit Relations*, 7: 242.

62. During the brief period of *polysynodie* (1715–1723), a Conseil de la Marine replaced the Ministère.

63. André Corvisier, *L'Armée française de la fin du XVIIe siècle au ministère de Choiseul: Le soldat*, 2 vols. (Paris: PUF, 1964), 1: 147–148.

64. Ibid., 168.

65. Namely, Karrer, colonel of a Swiss Regiment; Jacques de Pensens d'Espiet, major at Ile Royale; Daniel D'Auger de Subercase, captain and later major in the troupes de la marine; the marquis de Vaudreuil, captain and later governor; Chacornacle, captain; François Amariton, captain; Jean-Charles de Sabrevois, captain; the comte D'Agrain, captain; Gourville, captain; the marquis D'Aloigny de la Groye, lieutenant; Paschot, lieutenant; De Gannes, lieutenant; Vallier, lieutenant; and Loppinot, sergeant.

66. The only explicit reference to the recruitment of soldiers by civilians occurred in 1694, when the minister announced an augmentation of forty soldiers for the garrison of Plaisance. The letter reads: "Some merchants from Bayonne have contracted, in return for two vessels which the king has provided, to raise and transport the forty additional soldiers." Letter of the Minister to Du Brouillan, 10 March 1694, AC, B 17: 10.

67. Letter of La Jonquière to the Minister, 1 November 1750, AC, C11–A 93: 335.

68. Corvisier, *L'Armée française*, 1: 163–179.

69. Some Swiss may have been stationed in Québec as well. In 1730, Beauharnais and Hocquart warned the minister, "It seems important to us to destroy insensibly this type of independence that has slipped into and shown itself in several speeches made in Montréal by the inhabitants at tax time. . . . It is . . . in view of asserting the king's authority that we ask you for 150 Swiss from Karrer's regiment." Letter of Beauharnais and Hocquart to the Minister, 15 October 1730, AC, C11–A 52: 64.

70. Corvisier, *L'Armée française*, 1: 274.

71. Ibid., 410–411. The regional character of this regiment did, however, weaken in the course of the eighteenth century, and the change reflected itself in the composition of the Canadian troops. Of the sixty-five "Roussillonnais" who married in Canada in the 1750s and 1760s, forty-three came from the south or southwest, but there were also twelve easterners, four northerners, and three each from the Loire and the center. See Yves Landry, "Quelques aspects du comportement démographique des troupes de terre envoyées au Canada pendant la Guerre de Sept Ans" (M.A. thesis, Université de Montréal, 1977), 115.

72. Corvisier, *L'Armée française*, 1: 159.

73. Letter of the Minister, 4 February 1687, AM, B-3 53: 59.

74. Letter of the Council to La Galissonière, 29 June 1717, AC, B 39: 7.

75. Letter of Saint-Ovide and Le Normant to the Minister, 24 October 1734, AC, C11–B 15: 72.

76. Corvisier, *L'Armée française*, 1: 275.

77. Ibid., 186.

78. Letter of the Minister to Bégon, 8 May 1725, AC, B 48: 380.

79. Letter of the Minister to Bégon, 15 May 1725, AC, B 48: 387.

80. Letter of Vaudreuil to the Minister, 6 November 1712, AC, C11–A 33: 50.

81. Letter to the Minister, 1696, AC, C11–A 14: 119.

82. Royal order, May 1702, AC, B 23: 90.

83. Letter of the Council to La Galissonière, 21 July 1717, AC, B 39: 77.

84. Letter of the Minister to de Ramesay, 6 May 1702, AC, B 23: 73.

85. Letter of the Minister to Beauharnais, 19 April 1735, AC, B 63: 480.5.

86. Letter of La Jonquière to the Minister, 1 November 1750, AC, C11–A 95: 35.

87. After mentioning the high incidence of disease and death, La Jonquière wrote that "M. des Herbiers, Commander in Louisbourg, is in the same situation as myself. . . . He must have had the honor of informing you of the rebellion of the soldiers detailed in Port Toulouse." Letter of La Jonquière to the Minister, 1 November 1750, AC, C11–A 95: 335.

88. Corvisier, *L'Armée française*, 2: 605.

89. Letter of the Minister to Durand, 1 April 1700, AC, B 22: 72.

90. Letter of the Minister to Monic, 1701, AC, B 22: 187.

91. Letter of the Minister to Lhermite, 13 April 1701, AC, B 22: 199.

92. Letter of the Minister to Beauharnais. 9 April 1714, AC, B 36: 56.

93. Letter of the Council to La Galissonière, 22 April 1716, AC, B 38: 106.5.

94. Letter of Bigot to the Minister, 16 October 1748, AC, C11–A 92: 106.
95. Letter of Rousseau de Villejouin to the Minister, 1 October 1750, AC, C11–A 92: 347.
96. R. Mémain, *Le Matériel de la marine de guerre sous Louis XIV: Rochefort, arsenal modèle de Colbert (1666–1690)* (Paris: Hachette, 1936), 32.
97. Mémain, *Le Matériel de la marine*, 555.
98. Even Beauharnais sometimes took charge of recruiting himself, as when he engaged some twenty building workers for Ile Royale in 1714. See Letter of the Minister to Beauharnais, 23 March 1714, AC, B 36: 143; Letter of the Minister to Lhermite, 26 January 1714, AC, B 36: 419. More often, he relied on his subordinates in the naval and civilian administrations: the commissaires and the *sub-délégués*.
99. Royal order to D'Agrain, 28 January 1720, AC, B 42: 466. Orders to recruit bore a formulaic appeal to governors and intendants on behalf of the recruiter. This one reads, in its entirety: "His Majesty informs all governors, intendants and commissars...in the said generalities to give [him]...the assistance and facilities that he might need to carry out the said levy."
100. In 1750, for example, the minister commissioned the recruitment of fifty to sixty ship's carpenters in the ports of the kingdom. See Letter of the Minister to La Jonquière and Bigot, 15 April 1750, AC, B 91: 25; Letter of the Minister to Le Tourneur, 30 March 1750, AC, B 92: 77.5; Letter of the Minister to du Ronsay, 30 March 1750, AC, B 92: 79.
101. Letter of the Council to Beauharnais, 24 April 1720, AC, B 42: 175; Royal order to D'Agrain, 28 January 1720, AC, B 42: 466.
102. As we have seen, the company also recruited small numbers of servants on its own account in La Rochelle.
103. Letter of Talon to Colbert, 22 April 1665, AC, C11–A 2: 124.
104. Letter of Talon to Colbert, 27 October 1667, AC, C11–A 2: 306.
105. Letter of Colbert to Laval, 15 May 1669, AC, B 1: 144. Colbert's instructions to Colbert de Terron appear in AM, B-2 9: 68.
106. Hubert Charbonneau, *Vie et mort de nos ancêtres: Étude démographique* (Montréal: Presses de l'Université de Montréal, 1975). 41. The filles à marier who were recruited and dowered by the state in the mid-seventeenth century were known as the King's girls, or filles du roi.
107. A member of the Compagnie du Saint-Sacrement, Montbard became an associate of the Société Notre-Dame de Montréal in 1642. See Marie-Claire Daveluy, *La Société Notre-Dame de Montréal. 1639–1663, son histoire, ses membres, son manifeste* (Montréal: Fides, 1965), 197–199.

108. Memorandum of Talon, 9 March 1673, AC, C11–A 4: 28.

109. Letter of the Minister to the Archbishop of Rouen, 27 February 1670, AC, B 2: 15.

110. Memorandum of Talon, 9 March 1673, AC, C11–A 4: 28.

111. Letter of the Minister to Daguesseau, 24 May 1684, AM, B-2 53: 112.

112. François de Nion, ed., *Un Outre-mer au XVIIe siècle: Voyages au Canada du baron de La Hontan* (Paris: Plon, 1900), 17–18.

113. Letter of Colbert to Talon, 5 April 1667, AC, C11–A 2: 290.

114. Letter of Talon to Colbert, 27 October 1667, AC, C11–A 2: 306.

115. Letter of the Minister to Beauharnais and Dupuy, 4 May 1726, AC, B 49: 645; Letter of the Minister to the Bishop of Québec, 4 May 1726, AC, B 49: 674.

116. Letter of the Minister to Beauharnais and Hocquart, 25 April 1730, AC, B 54: 472; Letter of the Minister to Beauharnais and Hocquart, 8 May 1743, AC, B 76: 70.

117. Letters of the Minister to Orry, 17 January 1735, AM, B-3 373: 62; 31 January 1735, AM, B-3 373: 65; 15 February 1734, AM, B-3 373: 69.

118. His successor petitioned the minister unsuccessfully to renew them in 1750. See Letter of the Minister to the Comptroller General, 18 September 1750, AC, B 92: 217.5.

119. Origins of the convoy for Québec in 1739. See AC, B 68: 2.

120. Bernard Bailyn, *Voyagers to the West: A Passage in the Peopling of America on the Eve of the Revolution* (New York: Knopf, 1986), 25.

121. Recent Anglo-Canadian historiography has strayed surprisingly little from Francis Parkman's original formulations on this point; however, some authors do question Parkman's value judgments. Finlay and Sprague, for example, wrote in 1979, "In attempting to weigh English libertarianism and French absolutism, those who prefer size-growth of an economy will be forever troubled by the comparatively unimpressive economic development of New France.... Those who place human development above property rights, on the other hand, will forever defend the statism of New France and denounce the New Englanders." J. L. Finlay and D. N. Sprague, *The Structure of Canadian History*, 2d ed. (Scarborough: Prentice-Hall, 1984), 45–46.

122. Cited in Emile Salone, *Colonisation de la Nouvelle France: Étude sur les origines de la nation canadienne-française* (1905; Three-Rivers: Baréal Express, 1970), 429.

123. Voltaire, *Candide and Other Tales*, trans. T. Smollett, rev. by James Thornton (London: J. M. Dent, 1937), 180.

124. Half a million Protestants left France between 1660 and 1710. See Henri Bunle, *Mouvements migratoires entre la France et l'étranger*, Études démographiques 4 (Paris: Service national des statistiques, 1943), 12.

125. Mario Boleda, "Les Migrations au Canada sous le régime français" (Ph.D. dissertation, Université de Montréal, 1983), 128.

Six

Indentured Servants Bound for the French Antilles in the Seventeenth and Eighteenth Centuries

Christian Huetz de Lemps

Although the colonization of the French West Indies has given rise to numerous studies, most have focused on the evolution of black slavery rather than the immigration of white settlers in the seventeenth and eighteenth centuries.[1] Yet white immigration is fundamental to an understanding of social development in the islands, first because white settlers were responsible for fashioning plantation society and hence shaped the lives of hundreds of thousands of slaves shipped to the West Indies,[2] and second because the nature of emigration from France provides an excellent illustration of the relationship between French society and government and the colonies throughout the period.[3]

White immigrants were generally an extremely heterogeneous group.[4] Two main categories can be identified. The first of these consisted of freemen—adventurers, planters, and merchants but also tradesmen, government officials, and soldiers from whose ranks came the island colonies' managers and who established more or less close ties with France's four major colonial ports. Over the years, there emerged a white Creole society in opposition to "newcomers" just over from France; its vigor was enhanced by the fact that the colonists' interests very rapidly ceased to coincide with those of the French ports. While the major French merchants interested in trading with the Americas were determined to defend the principle of exclusive colonial and seafaring rights, the islanders were inclined to practice, or at least defend, the right of utmost commercial freedom to engage in commerce with whomever they wished.[5]

The second main category consisted of poor emigrants who were drawn by the American mirage or, more especially, were driven away by poverty and the struggle to survive in France. They lacked the means to pay their own passage and voluntarily indentured themselves to planters, merchants, or the captains of vessels for three years in the service of those who advanced the passage money or the person to whom they were later sold. These engagés played a vital part at the beginning of French colonization of the islands, since they provided the bulk of the labor force at a time when the mass importation of black slaves had not yet commenced. What was singular about the French islands, however, was that for a very long time after the local society had stopped being able or willing to take in this category of "lower-class whites," more still arrived, this time by order of the king who thereby attempted to strengthen the white population both to offset—only slightly, as it happens—the black masses and to provide the islands with the human resources necessary to defend them. Here I will deal mainly with the continued immigration of white servants, which many people in the islands and French ports considered an anachronism.

I

In defiance of the partition of the New World between the Hispanic powers, English, French, and Dutch colonization of tropical America took place in small islands untouched by Spanish colonists. The latter had too few men even to keep a firm hold over all the larger islands, and many of the small islands seemed to lack natural resources or were inhabited by hostile populations.[6] In 1623, the English under Captain Warner set foot on St. Christopher. That same year, it was wrested away by the French pirate, Captain d'Esnambuc, a gentleman fallen on hard times who had gone privateering just as in earlier centuries impoverished knights went "off to the Crusades." Richelieu's official recognition of his merits occurred at the very moment when d'Esnambuc set up the so-called St. Christopher Company in 1626 which was intended to be the counterpart of the Dutch Company, then so remarkably successful. It was in the name of the company that he embarked the first 530 settlers bound for the West Indies on February 24th, 1627. Of these, 350 perished from famine and disease in the first months after their arrival. Settlement initially involved the two extremities of the island; the richer central part was left to the English after an agreement between d'Esnambuc and Warner in May 1627. The establishment of a French presence on St. Christopher was followed by the settlement of Guyana (1628–1633), Martinique and Guadeloupe (1635), Tortuga and the north and west of Santo Domingo, Grenada, St. Lucia, St. Martin, and St. Bartholomew.[7]

There is little point in retracing the complex history of the appropriation of the Lesser Antilles, marked as it was by changes in sovereignty and numerous conflicts during the wars between the French, English, Dutch, and Spanish, not to mention the fighting against the Caribs. At the dawn of the eighteenth century, French-held territory consisted of four main areas: the west of Santo Domingo, which Spain finally acknowledged as belonging to France in 1697 (Treaty of Ryswick), Martinique, Guadeloupe and its dependencies, and Guyana. Colonization of the islands took place largely through a system of voluntary indentures. The principle was simple: all that was necessary was to provide poor immigrants with passage to the islands in return for their agreement to work for a master for a certain length of time. This was sanctioned by a genuine contract, signed before a notary, whereby the duration of the indenture was first established. A three-year duration was the general rule, hence the term "36 months" often applied to indentured servants.[8] They were given food and board and were clothed by their master; all these provisions very much recalled the apprenticeship contracts of the period. Likewise, when his term of service was over, the indentured servant was given a small sum of money to help him embark on his life as a freeman or, alternatively, return to France; also, in the early decades at least, he had hopes of obtaining a small concession of land. There was, however, one clause that made the indentured servant's situation very different from that of the apprentice: the master had the right to sell his indentured servant without the latter's consent. In this, the "engagement" (voluntary indenture) resembled a fixed-term slavery more than an apprenticeship.

Above all, what was traumatic for indentured servants was that they encountered a totally unfamiliar environment and were exposed to extremely harsh living conditions: hard labor, inadequate food, and parasites and diseases that were unknown and fearsome. The reality of the tropical world was far removed from the visions of ease and opulence bandied about by recruiters and missionaries,[9] who were impressed by, among other things, the absence of winter. At the beginning of the colonial period at least, the masters' lives were not always very different from those of their servants, and their relationships were frequently close as a result of common geographic origins and shared sufferings. In the early decades, recruitment was carried out by the company (which became the Compagnie des Iles d'Amérique in 1635), then by "former inhabitants"—independent colonists or former indentured servants who had succeeded and returned to their place of origin to find workers. Merchants increasingly assumed the task of recruiting for other colonists, but there was here a human element, in that the indentured servants knew who would be responsible for them on their arrival, even if their masters were to prove harsh and sometimes cruel.

From 1650 onward, the nature of indenture contracts changed; merchants and especially ship's captains were now the necessary go-betweens for these "engagements" and had the job of handing over the recruited engagés on their arrival. Thus, the groups they transported became, to some extent, anonymous, and the conditions of the indentured servants degenerated as they were increasingly regarded simply as units of labor. Pere du Tertre, who was generally optimistic about living conditions in the West Indies, was critical of the way servants were treated:

> The harsh manner of treatment meted out by the masters to their French servants indentured for three years is the only thing that seems to me to be worrying; for they are made to work to an excessive degree, are very badly fed and often obliged to work in the company of their slaves, which afflicts these poor people more than all the excessive hardships they suffer. There have been in the past such cruel masters that it became necessary to forbid them ever again to buy any such servants. I had knowledge

of one in Guadeloupe who had buried fifty on his land, having worked them till they died and not given them assistance when they were ailing. The reason for this harsh treatment is certainly that they will have them for only three years and take more care to spare their negroes than these poor men; the charity of the governors has much improved their conditions however through the decrees they have issued in their favour.[10]

The deterioration in the conditions of indentured servants in the latter half of the seventeenth century is reflected both in the cost of their labor and in their expectations as regards what the future would hold once their contracts were at an end. When this three-year contract expired, the indentured servant traditionally received a small endowment of 300 pounds of tobacco, this at a time (in the early colonial period) when it had an appreciable value, sufficient to start up a small plantation. In the late 1630s, however, the price of tobacco began to fall on the London and Amsterdam markets (and tobacco never again regained its former value).[11] Nevertheless, at the end of his contract, the engagé still continued to receive the devalued tobacco in the same quantity and could not therefore either return to France or start up for himself in favorable conditions. Certainly, if he joined forces with another freed servant there would be a slightly larger sum to set up a small undertaking; this was what was known as "*l'amatelotage.*" The partners themselves built a dwelling and in the first year sowed peas and potatoes and planted manioc (to make cassava) and banana trees while they cleared the land to find a place to grow tobacco. But this assumed that there was vacant land to give them.

In the French Antilles, the rate of settlement was relatively slow compared to many British islands. In Martinique and Guadeloupe, the scarcity of land only really became apparent in the 1670s and a long time after that in Santo Domingo, which had been colonized later. It was easy, therefore, to obtain a concession, as du Tertre remarked: "when the islands were first inhabited, each made a place for himself—those who came as freemen went to see the Governor who gave a wooded area 200 feet long and 1000 feet wide to clear; he gave as much to those who had finished their period of service."[12] Quite frequently, however, former servants who had acceded to land did not manage to keep their plots, since they were obliged to incur debts, either with the merchants who supplied their rations or labor or with other planters. They had to resign themselves to selling their land that was more or less cleared.

In reality the fate of engagés in the seventeenth century could vary considerably. A substantial number died more or less quickly through poverty and disease even before their contract had ended. This is probably the reason that very few of those who embarked in France in 1655 and the years that followed were listed in the census carried out in Martinique in 1660.[13] Among those who survived their term of servitude, some chose to return to France. Du Tertre himself observed that there was "a continuous ebb and flow of voyages from America to France and France to America." Others, who were incapable of making a living on their own, indentured themselves for a further period of three years or else joined the cohort of miserable wretches who were destined for an early death.

But there were those—not insignificant in number, especially among the earliest arrivals—who succeeded. Some owed their success to their dogged determination to make their land fruitful, their desire to increase their domain through land acquisition or sometimes through a timely marriage. These former servants then, in turn, became recruiters, entrusted a "commander" with the running of their plantation, paying him 2,000 pounds of tobacco annually, and stopped doing manual work—an unmistakable sign of their success. Others managed to create an enviable place for themselves as skilled craftsmen, who were often severely lacking in the islands. Du Tertre mentions the surgeon-barbers, pit sawyers, carpenters, tailors, coopers, and especially tobacco rollers.

The trade of tobacco roller is to be learned in the islands; there they are unofficial masters (as there was no corporation to impose a special task [chef d'oeuvre] to qualify as a Master) and it costs only the effort of learning; ordinarily it is poor ex-servants who take up this work. It is extremely lucrative and a lad who is good at it can have a lot left over by the end of the season, for they eat at the master's table; but as they work for only a part of the year most of them eat in a single season what they have amassed in the other.

It often happened, however, that when their three-year term of servitude was over—and sometimes even before—the engagés sought what for many epitomized the freeman's way of life: buccaneering in all forms.[14] Many of them only met with death during their privateering expeditions, but others acquired affluence and even fortunes much more quickly than would have been possible from toiling with their hands. One could mention Jean Roy, a former servant in Martinique who later became a planter there, thanks to "a few privateering expeditions." Or, better still, Pere Labat describes the career of Guillaume Pinel, nicknamed "the Provençal," a contrabandist, privateer, and merchant who operated from Martinique to Guadeloupe, St. Christopher, Tortuga, and mainland America, then invested in plantations. In 1660, he "employed no less than 35 servants and was considered one of the richest colonists."[15] The surgeon Oexmelin was himself a former servant and later chronicler of the "Distinguished Buccaneering Adventurers in the Indies."[16] It is noticeable that even among former servants who had gained wealth through buccaneering, success was maintained and continued through acquiring a plantation where they set others to work.

This instinct for land may be related to the origins of a good many engagés, which are known through the contracts of indenture signed before a notary. A special study of them has been made by G. Debien, whose work provides the basis for our knowledge of seventeenth-century emigration.[17] His main point is that indentured servants were largely recruited either in the ports of embarkation or in their rural hinterland, although some, and occasionally a substantial number of them, were found to come from other, sometimes quite distant, provinces of France. Initial departures were from Le Havre, the port for St. Christopher and Martinique, from Dieppe, especially for Guadeloupe, and also from La Rochelle, then Nantes and Honfleur from 1637 onward, as well as St-Malo and probably also from other ports in this period. For Dieppe, there were three towns that provided large contingents from 1653 to 1660: Dieppe, of course, but also Rouen and Paris. However, the Caux region and the rest of rural Normandy were the most important recruiting sources (56.8% of all engagés were from rural areas). In Nantes, from 1636 to 1660, the percentage of indentured servants from the town was higher than from rural areas, and they came from a wider area, even though

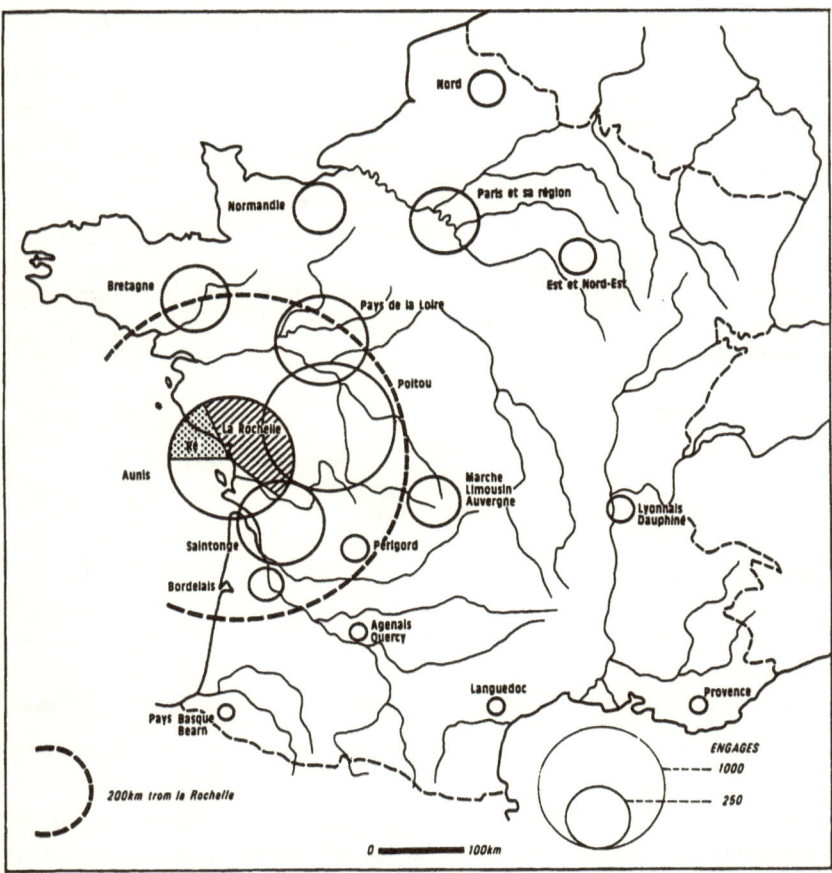

Fig. 6.1. Geographic Origins of Indentured Servants Embarking in La Rochelle, 1638–1715 (after G. Debien)

Brittany and the nearby Loire Valley region were still the main sources. This shows the extent of Nantes' influence along the Loire.[18]

In La Rochelle, where Debien has documented no less than 6,100 indentured servants from 1638 to 1715 and given the exact origins for some 4,000 of them, one finds the same preponderance from surrounding areas (Aunis, Poitou and Saintonge accounted for 2,263 known engagés, or 56.1% of the total) and the same

TABLE 6.1. *Geographical Origins of Indentured Servants Embarking in La Rochelle, from 1638–1715*

Surrounding regions 56.1%
Aunis	862	(La Rochelle 389, Ile de Re 159, Oleron 53)
Poitou	1,003	(Poitiers 99, Fontenay Le Comte 45, Niort 44, Les Sables 21 plus Olonne 13, Lucon 23, Marans 24, but only 2 from Noirmoutier and 4 from Yeu)
Saintonge	398	(Marennes La Tremblade 32, Tonnay Charente 15)

Pays de la Loire—Centre 14.8%
Anjou 129, Touraine 104, Orleanais, Gatinais, Blesois 87, Berry 46, Marche and Limousin 125, Maine 47, Auvergne 43, Bourbonnais 15

West 11.2%
Bretagne 274, Normandie 152, Perche 25

Paris region 6.8%
Paris 229, Paris region 44

North 1.8%
Picardie 55, Artois 6, Flandre française 11

East 1.8%
Champagne 43, Lorriane 29

Southeast 2.0%
Lyonnais 37, Dauphine 15, Provence 31

Southwest 5.5%
Languedoc 33, Guyenne 71 (Bordeaux 62), Bearn and Pays Basque 37, Périgord 55, Agenaid 17, Quercy 9

proportion of rural inhabitants (see fig. 6.1). Almost four-fifths of those who emigrated from the west of France came from rural areas, and half of those worked the land. But it is also striking that virtually all regions of France were represented and that the farther the distance from La Rochelle, the more urban areas were represented (table 6.1).[19]

La Rochelle seemed to make inroads into the natural catchment areas of Nantes and Bordeaux—proof that both these ports, Bordeaux in particular, only fitted out a limited number of ships for the colonies up until the late seventeenth century.[20] In addition, La Rochelle established itself as the main port for Canada, which was the destination of almost one thousand engagés, as opposed to just under five thousand for "the islands."[21]

The figures just quoted are, of course, provisional, since many notaries' archives have been lost; but they nevertheless enable us to draw two conclusions. First, the Antilles initially held a much greater attraction for settlers than did New France (Canada). Second, and more important, the numbers of French indentured servants in the seventeenth century were low in comparison to the considerable number of servants leaving for the English islands during the same period, despite the more favorable terms of service enjoyed by the engagés (Irish and English servants usually served from four to seven years compared to three commonly granted to French servants). St. Christopher and Barbados experienced a very rapid influx of English and Irish settlers in the 1630s and 1640s and soon became overpopulated.[22] Around 1660, there were no less than 26,200 whites in Barbados, 1,265 in the English part of St. Christopher, 2,347 in Nevis, 1,788 in Montserrat, and 1,539 in Antigua. In addition, there were about 33,000 black slaves in the British West Indies. At the same time, there were only 15,000 to 16,000 white settlers in the French islands and probably no more than 8,000 slaves.[23] In the British West Indies, white immigration reached its peak from about 1645 to 1647, much earlier than in the French islands, where the influx of white settlers was more leisurely. Although the transformation of the French islands' economies was under way, shifting from tobacco to sugar, Martinique and Guadeloupe were later and slower in turning to sugar crops for which masses of black slaves were used, in contrast to Barbados where slaves had largely replaced the white labor force from the 1650s onward.

The French islands' reorientation toward sugar went hand in hand with a political tightening up. The royal government attempted to impose the rule of colonial exclusivity on planters who had until then been accustomed to trading almost freely with the Dutch, who had largely contributed to the success of colonization and to the development of sugarcane.[24] This chiefly explains the revolts by planters in Martinique in 1665–1667 and in Santo Domingo in 1670–1671, as well as the later *gaoule* (colonists' uprisings) in Martinique in 1717.[25] At the same time, the wars against the Netherlands and England, marked by many military ups and downs,[26] took a severe toll of the white population, especially during privateering expeditions. They also led, however, to an increase in troops and renewed government determination to install a greater white population in the islands.

From the 1670s onward, there was the beginning of a rift between planters, merchants, and ship's captains, on the one hand, who considered indentured servants as increasingly unnecessary or at least as no longer justifying the effort and expense involved in transporting them, and the authority of the king, on the other hand, who, mainly for military reasons, wished to increase the numbers of white people.[27] This was why the king decreed in February 1670 that servitude would be reduced from three years to eighteen months because "various of his subjects" had ceased to consider moving to the islands because of their legitimate apprehension of placing themselves in the service of unfamiliar people whom they feared might not treat them well. This incentive was never implemented; subsequent contracts specified forfeiture of this advantage and the upholding of the three-year term of bondage until this latter disposition came back into effect in 1698. The gulf between official notions of the indentured servant's interests and local evaluation of the same continued to widen in the eighteenth century. The continuing immigration of "poor white people" at the behest of the king was nonetheless peculiar to the French islands and seemed anachronistic to the various economic actors who were resolutely convinced of the necessary preeminence of large slave plantations.[28]

II

As Debien noted, "the colonies go on taking in, assimilating or rejecting the never-ending flow of very different categories of men." This was still true of eighteenth-century Antillean society, in which the different categories of people—merchants, government servants, soldiers, freed servants, indentured servants, black slaves—continuously intermixed, even though the respective position of each of them had changed profoundly since the beginning of colonization in the seventeenth century. The number of independent newcomers from France—planters, merchants, government officials—increased in the eighteenth century, parallel to the economic boom and the increase of trade with France.[29] The numbers of slaves from Africa depended on the development of the plantation economy, the need to renew the labor force, and the vagaries of the slave trade. Finally, there were the lower-class white engagés who, as we have seen, played such an important part in French settlement during the seventeenth century. In the eighteenth century, no more mention is made of the engagés, except for periodic complaints about maintaining a system considered to be out of date. And yet their migratory flow continued, even if it no longer in any way resembled that of the previous century as far as its basic motivation was concerned. Colonization that was privately inspired and organized by tobacco planters, traders, and ship's captains was replaced by one willed by the state, contrary to the wishes of the planters and even more so to the wishes of the owners and masters of the vessels.[30] Private interests in the eighteenth century repeatedly maintained that indentured servants were no longer required in the colonies and would only swell the ranks of those on the fringes of West Indian Society—"vagabonds and pirates," as the Chamber of Commerce in Bordeaux pointed out in 1723.[31]

The purely economic or social arguments advanced by colonists and merchants were countered by the royal government's reasons of national interest. To continue to allow destitute white people to go to the colonies by dint of voluntary indentures was to increase the numbers likely to take up arms in the event of war against the invading Dutch or English; it was also a way of maintaining a balance of power between the black and white populations so as to avoid jeopardizing the very existence of the colony in case of revolt. Hence, the insertion in the decree dated 8 April 1699 of the clause obliging each "inhabitant"—that is, planter—to have one engagé to every twenty Negroes. Needless to say, this was just a pious hope, but it illustrates the royal government's desire to create a kind of white middle class from which a colonial militia could be recruited.

Royal expectations were embodied in legislation, issued on February 19, 1698, according to which ships bound for the Americas must henceforth carry with them a number of indentured servants proportional to their tonnage: three for ships under 60 tons, four for those between 60 and 100 tons, and six for ships over 100 tons. To encourage a certain quality of recruits, those who possessed a trade would count double, "in consideration of their likely usefulness to the colonies." The edict of April 8, 1699, supplemented the previous text in an attempt to put a stop to certain abuses in recruitment: indentured servants had to be at least eighteen years old and fit for work. The contract's duration was to be 36 months once again. Both these texts formed the basis for a policy that was ultimately to be continued and enlarged. From March 20, 1714, this obligation to embark indentured servants was extended to ships plying the route to Canada. The reasons for this were clearly outlined in the edict's provisions:

From what his Majesty has been informed that his measures obliging captains of merchant ships trading with the French islands in the Americas to embark a certain number of indentured servants, have met with the intended success, and being informed that the inhabitants of New France have need of them (as do those in the Islands) for their agriculture and other work, these establishments having much increased, it is feared that through a lack of new inhabitants it will be impossible not only to create more, but also to maintain those that exist, which would be damaging to the preservation and continued progress of the said country and to our merchants' trade there.[32]

Last, legislation on voluntary indentures, applicable to all the French colonies in America, was integrated into the regulation of November 16, 1716. This was to be the standard legislation until 1774, and its dispositions were repeated and clarified on several occasions during the century—an indication, above all, of the difficulties experienced in translating the royal wishes into reality in the face of opposition bent on circumventing the law in every possible way.[33] Hence, certificates of desertion had to be considered null and void in cases where there was legitimate suspicion of their being fraudulently acquired. Following that, certificates of disembarkation were demanded of indentured servants in the islands (edict of February 15, 1724), and those declared as possessing a trade, and thus accounting for two places, were required to furnish proof by means of a certificate from a master of the relevant trade designated by the authorities.

In considering indentured servitude in the eighteenth century, it must be borne in mind that fraud was a constant problem and that defrauders found many accomplices both in the ports and in the islands. Might not the very strict legislation of 1724 be due to the authorities' discovery in 1723 that scarcely one-third of engagés registered as leaving from metropolitan ports had in fact disembarked in the Indies? These reservations are all the more necessary because our basic sources, that is, notaries' contracts of indenture, ships' rolls, and so on, concern those who were supposed to leave and because only a few hundred of the certificates of disembarkation (which date anywhere from 1746 to 1765) have been preserved and authenticate the voyage to the Americas.[34]

If we oversimplify and say that from the seventeenth to the eighteenth century, there was a shift from a more or less spontaneous and popular colonization to a state-directed one, we can also see a change in the geographic basis of the system of indentures, connected with Bordeaux's rapid progress as a port with direct trade links with the islands.[35] In the seventeenth century, Bordeaux showed little interest in the colonies and scarcely fitted out any ships for this type of trade that was considered risky compared to the major fields of trade in which it was traditionally involved, such as the export of wine to northwestern Europe and Brittany. As late as 1699–1700, out of 53 ships leaving from Bordeaux for the islands, only 21 had been fitted out there, as opposed to 23 in La Rochelle.[36]

After the Spanish War of Succession, however, and for reasons that do not concern us here, Bordeaux established itself as an increasingly important center for fitting out ships for the colonies, soon becoming the major port in France, leaving Nantes the lion's share of trade between Nantes, Africa (slaves), the Americas, and back to France and leaving La Rochelle the trade with Canada. In the eighteenth century, then, Bordeaux was a place where one was certain of finding a ship bound for the islands and notaries who specialized in drawing up indenture contracts on request. People arrived from all other provinces of France to embark in Bordeaux. However, many ships fitted out for the islands in other ports—Le Havre, Rouen, Dieppe, St-Malo, Boulogne, Nantes, or even La Rochelle—came to Bordeaux to take on not only wine, brandies, and flour but also the necessary indentured servants. Some ships came occasionally from other places with one or several engagés recruited in their home port and completed their numbers in Bordeaux, where a common contract would be drawn up for all of them. Bordeaux thus appeared as a major center for voluntary indentures in the islands during the eighteenth century.

III

The first question to be answered is how many people were involved in all? An assessment can be made from the notaries' archives, which are quite abundant in Bordeaux, where the contracts can be located. The data can be cross-checked using the ships' rolls[37] where the names of indentured servants are listed and copies of their contracts are inserted. This latter source is useful also because it shows what percentage of ships actually carried the engagés. Unfortunately, the series of rolls is not continuous, and, with rare exceptions, the bundles give no complete years. From 1698 until July 1718, the "registers of ships' rolls for the islands"[38] give the names of indentured servants on board each ship but no indication of where they originally came from; they nevertheless make it possible to assess departures.

Our count is unfortunately very far from complete. Up until the present, we have identified some 8,500 indentures from 1698 to 1774, but, given the research yet to be completed, we can estimate an approximate total of some 13,000 leaving Bordeaux for America in the eighteenth century.[39] That would mean between 100 and 500 departures per year in times of peace. These figures may be modest, but they are far from negligible, and the example of the French Canadians shows that a limited population influx can have considerable long-term consequences. The fact that this was not the case with Antillean indentured servants can be attributed to a multitude of reasons that I will not analyze here.[40]

The frequency of these departures was not, of course, the same throughout the first three quarters of the eighteenth century. It depended, first, on the international political situation—the rate of departures slowed down, then came to a complete standstill in times of war—and the economic situation, since the number of engagés was in direct relation to the number and size of the ships. The degree of flexibility shown by the administration often favored a reduction in the number of indentured servants through financial or other alternatives to embarkation. Finally, during part of the regency (during the infancy of Louis XV, 1715–1723), compulsory indentures slightly overshadowed voluntary ones.

It was during the Spanish War of Succession that Bordeaux really began to show interest in fitting out ships for the colonies, hence the developing need that ships from Bordeaux comply with the edict of 1698. At the same time, however, recruitment was becoming so difficult that the royal government had to suspend implementation of the edict. The one issued on November 17, 1706, thus permitted that whenever, in times of war, it proved impossible to find the required number of engagés "due to recruitment for the armies," the captain of a ship could be released from the obligation by paying to the treasurer for the navy 60 "livres-tournois" per indentured servant missing.

The aftermath of the Spanish War of Succession was characterized by a very heavy increase in indentures for several years.[41] The rush of young candidates for the colonies was such that certain captains agreed to embark more engagés than they were obliged to. This situation was exceptional in the eighteenth century, however, both as regards the number of engagés and their characteristics. It did not last, and very soon there were renewed complaints about the difficulties in recruiting candidates, especially in Bordeaux from 1717 onward[42] and in La Rochelle and Nantes,[43] where merchants suggested replacing voluntary emigrants by salt smugglers ("faux sauniers"),[44] vagabonds, and beggars. The government soon gave backing to the idea of "compulsory indentures," and the decree of May 12, 1719, obliged captains to embark vagabonds who were sentenced to the galleys in the place of voluntary servants. These prisoners who embarked "by Order of the King" had no contract and had to serve five years as engagés. This measure applied especially, as we know, to compulsory embarkation for Louisiana via the Antilles. On July 5, 1720, Louis Alexandre de Bourbon, Count of Toulouse and Grand Admiral of France, indicated to the officers of the admiralty in Bordeaux that "the king having destined for the French colonies the various individuals who have been imprisoned in your town and are to be transported to Louisiana, it is my pleasure to inform you of this and to advise you that it is his Majesty's wish that these prisoners be handed over to the owners of French vessels bound for the Americas to serve as indentured servants.... It is the king's will that prisoners' wives and children who freely follow their husbands and fathers will each count as one indentured servant."

At the end of 1720, we find 58 prisoners embarking in Bordeaux in two months. And in 1721, out of a total of 371 indentured servants, 155 of them were "by Order of the King" and without contracts. In the following years, for which ships' rolls are unfortunately quite incomplete, there were 64 prisoners out of 195 engagés in 1722, 73 out of 95 in 1723, 46 out of 162 in 1724, but no more than 7 out of 213 in 1726. This was because the sending of prisoners to Louisiana only lasted for a time, and colonists in the Antilles were not at all anxious to see the dregs of metropolitan society disembarking in the islands.

Little is known of these prisoners who were taken on board in Bordeaux, but what can be discerned differs somewhat from the pathetic scene of departure of Manon Lescaut, who was in fact located by the Abbé Prevost in Le Havre, which, together with Rochefort, was one of the main ports of embarkation for prisoners.[45] In Bordeaux, there were no convoys of prisoners and only three to six prisoners per ship, very few women and few children. On December 2, 1720, however, Jacques Morel, a 41-year-old cartwright from Angers embarked with his 37-year-old wife, Ane, and their two children, 8-year-old Jeanne and 6-year-old Martin. This was an exception, nevertheless. In general, it was men, and young men at that, who embarked. There were only a dozen or so women, and out of 331 prisoners whose ages we know, only 2 were under 10 years of age, 7 between 10 and 14 years of age, 88 between 15 and 19 years old, 133 between 20 and 29 years old, 60 between 30 and 39 years old, 26 between 40 and 49 years old, and 6 aged 50 or over. The oldest was a man of 60 from the Savoy region. The average age (25.5) is, however, noticeably higher than that of voluntary indentured servants of the period.[46]

The geographic origins of some 270 prisoners are primarily outside of the region. There are no fewer than 111 Parisians, and other regions that figure prominently are the Ile de France (14), Maine (14), the Anjou (13), Normandy (12), Burgundy, Champagne, Picardy, and Brittany (11 apiece), Orleans (10), Poitou (7), Lorraine (6), and Savoy (5). What is striking is that regions near Bordeaux scarcely provide any prisoners: only 2 from the Saintes

Region, 2 from Perigord, and 2 from Toulouse. It is very likely, then, that a majority of prisoners embarking in Bordeaux belonged to chains of prisoners from Paris. The dozen or so foreigners among "compulsory servants" (3 from Liege, 1 from Anvers, 1 from Bruges, 2 Irishmen, 1 German, 1 Englishman, 1 Swiss) must have been rounded up in the capital, as also many vagabonds originally from areas more or less nearby. The reasons for the deportations are not known. In his edict of January 14, 1721, the king refers to "his subjects who defraud him, vagabonds and others" who must be sent out as engagés. But we only know that for 10 prisoners in 1724, it was a case of salt smuggling.

Compulsory indentured servants could not have been very well regarded by the ships' captains, who were surely not too sorry if some fled the ship. It was to remedy this situation that the edict of January 14, 1721, made the captains responsible for escapees: "those from whose ships the said prisoners shall have escaped in their port of origin shall be obliged to take on twice as many as those who escaped, with a fine of 60 francs for each prisoner not reembarked." The penalty was the same in the case of escape at a port of call.

The difficulties in providing prisoners for the major trading ports and the increasingly forceful complaints against the system, together with the very severe shortage of voluntary servants available, led the administration to allow missing indentured servants to be replaced, as during times of war, by a tax of 60 livres-tournois each (May 20, 1721). Shipowners and merchants wanted much more—the suppression of the system of indentures—and, on April 15, 1723, the directors of the Chamber of Commerce, "pressed by Bordeaux merchants' habitual remonstrances about their very frequent inability to take on engagés, suggested replacing that obligation with another: taking on ships' boys." "In any case," they continued, "the engagés are no longer useful in any way whatsoever; the country is sufficiently populated and we can no longer find employment for them and so they become pirates and vagabonds in the islands." Being unwilling to pay the tax of 60 livres-tournois in lieu of each missing engagé, the shipowners chose to defraud by putting forward bogus indentured servants who had, in fact, no intention of leaving.

The royal administration became annoyed at this resistance,

and the edict of February 15, 1724, rigorously defined the shipowners' responsibility in carrying indentured servants. Henceforth, a disembarkation certificate verifying their arrival was to be brought back if the fine of 60 livres-tournois (LT)[47] was to be avoided. This legislation remained in effect until the end of the indenture system in Bordeaux. There is no way of proving that it prevented fraud, since Bordeaux shipowners were liable to find many willing accomplices even in the islands.

The royal administration maintained its right to use the obligation on shipowners to carry indentured servants to have persons with some public function transported. In particular, it would, when necessary, have the "new levy of soldiers" transported, each soldier being the equivalent of one engagé. Thus, in 1740, we find a dozen or so ships with soldiers in lieu of indentured servants and 10 or so in 1749. Sometimes, too, ships embarked skilled craftsmen for public works "by Order of the King." Hence from 1750 to 1752, woodcutters, stonecutters, and blacksmiths set sail for Santo Domingo: "The captain is strictly advised to hand over the above-mentioned skilled craftsmen in the first port of call in Santo Domingo where he shall go to the Commissioner or whomsoever was acting as such and have the disembarkation certified in the margin." These workers had no contract, and we know nothing of how they were recruited; judging by their origins, it seems to have been on a regional basis.

Last, the government also habitually used indentured servants' places to transport officers, administrators, or people on a mission to the islands. This practice became more and more common following the Seven Years War. Government officials replaced varying numbers of indentured servants, depending on their position in the hierarchy. To give but one example, when the Bordeaux ship, the *Judith*, 350 tons, embarked for Santo Domingo on January 17, 1767, the following two persons counted for eight engagés according to the letter of the Duke of Praslin, dated September 22, 1766:

Monsieur le Chevalier de Seguiran, Squire of Aix-en-Provence, son of Sire Jean Baptiste de Seguiran, Assistant Public Prosecutor at the "Chambre des comptes, cours des Aides et Finances de Provence... counting for 4 engagés;

Monsieur Jacques Hachin, lawyer at the Parliament in Orleans, 28 years of age... counting for 4 engagés.

This went hand in hand with a very flexible system of "transport credit" for shipowners. Thus, as the *Judith* had embarked the equivalent of eight engagés in place of the six required, there was an inscription on the roll saying the shipowner would be dispensed from carrying two such engagés in his next ship for the colonies.

This increasing flexibility concerning the implementation of measures related to indentures was a sign that the administration was less and less concerned with them and was considering changing the measure to a kind of tax or renewable levy on shipowners. During the Seven Years War, there were many ships that set sail without taking any indentured servants. After the war ended, there was a sudden increase in the number of indentures: no less than 459 in 1764, 407 in 1765, 197 in 1766, and 299 in 1767. This flurry of departures did not last, however, and Bordeaux shipowners very quickly acquired the habit of automatically paying the 60 LT in lieu of engagés. On each ship's roll, the following mention was found: "Dispensed from taking on board six engagés, the Captain having paid the Treasurer of the Navy and colonies in this port the sum of 360 LT. Receipt dated... presented by the said Captain and returned to his person."

In certain cases, in place of payment, the shipowners again embarked government officials, journeymen, or soldiers but never again indentured servants. The end of the indenture system was made official by a decree of the royal Council of State on September 10, 1774, which acknowledged in its preamble "that the increased population in the Colonies and the rise in the number of black slaves imported have long brought about the cessation of indentures as practiced heretofore and the places that shipowners were under obligation to provide have been granted to persons whose passage to America was not indispensable to the service to the Colonies.... Indentured servants' places shall henceforth be taken by soldiers and journeymen, failing which the Captain shall pay 60 francs per unfulfilled place, the proceeds being attributed to the fund for the Navy's disabled persons, to pay the cost of transport for journeymen and other persons in the employ of his Majesty in the Colonies, or being used to help the poor disabled."

This was no longer anything other than a tax incumbent on shipowners and was a far cry from the initial concept of indentures as a means of promoting European colonization of America.

IV

Contracts of indenture are the main source for our research, and they furnish a certain amount of detail about emigrants to America. The degree of detail depended on what the engagé himself (often illiterate) was capable of saying, the clerk's efforts to understand him, and the material limitations of the standard printed contracts of the 1720s, where very little space was reserved for a description of the indentured servant. Within these limits, we have details for almost all of them (less than 2 percent of serious omissions on the contracts) concerning their name, frequently their parentage, age, geographic origins, trade, and whether or not they could write their name.

These were, first, young, even very young, men (no women), the large majority between 18 and 35 years of age. Two separate phases should be differentiated. During the Spanish War of Succession and its aftermath, with the increase of departures that followed the return of peace, there was a very large majority of extremely young persons aged between 15 and 19 years: more than 69.7 percent for the period between January 1713 and December 1717. A great majority of them are declared as being 18 years of age, and there are only a few instances of 17-, 16-, and even 15-year-olds. But these affirmations were made verbally or otherwise, probably to conform to the edict issued on April 8, 1699, by which a minimum age of 18 years was imposed. What is surprising is that there were indentured servants listed as being under 18 years and thus contravening the legislation. It is likely that an appreciable number of those declaring themselves as being 18 years old were really below the minimum age. Be that as it may, if we take the declared ages, we can conclude that the average age of indentured servants for the period from 1713 to 1717 was 20.2 years.

From the early 1720s on, the age structure changed significantly (fig. 6.2). There was now no one declared as being under 18, and for our period of reference, 1751 to 1756, 18- and 19-year-olds

Indentured Servants Bound for the French Antilles

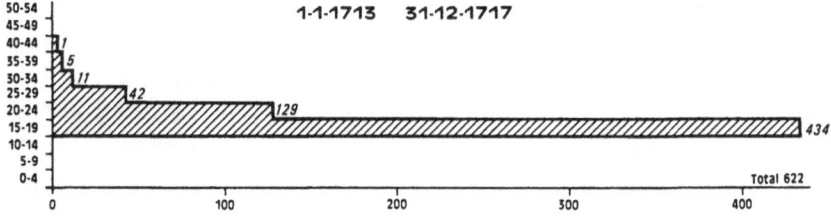

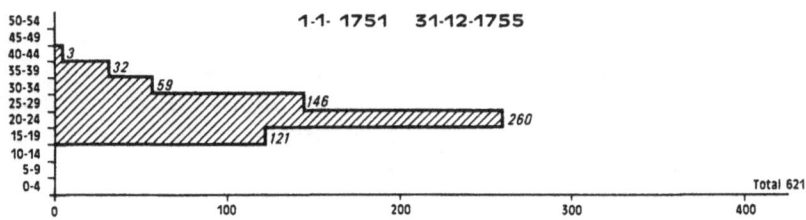

Fig. 6.2. Age Structure of the Servants Leaving Bordeaux

only accounted for 19.5 percent of all indentured servants. The large majority of those who left were young men: the 20 to 29 age group accounted for 65.4 percent of the total. Finally, the more mature 30- to 45-year-olds accounted for 15.1 percent compared to only 2.7 percent for 1713 to 1717. The average age is thus appreciably higher: 25.2 years in the period from 1751 to 1756.

The sharp contrasts in the ages of indentured servants just after the Spanish War of Succession and those for the half century that followed show up again just as clearly where their trades are concerned. For the period 1713 to 1717, the vast majority of very young men bound for America had no trade whatsoever; only 14.5 percent of them had one. Thereafter, from the early 1720s we find that all engagés, whatever their age, declared a trade. Underlying this, there was of course the edict of February 19, 1698, which stated that an indentured servant having a trade would count double. To supplement this, the regulation dating from November 16, 1716, specified that only those trades of use in the colonies would qualify: stonemasons, stonecutters, blacksmiths, locksmiths, carpenters, coopers, shipwrights, caulkers, surgeons, and so on. The chronic difficulties in finding engagés after 1720 must naturally have encouraged recruiters to valorize those they did find, to the fullest extent, by having them declare a trade. The royal government attempted to counter this type of fraud by requiring indentured servants claiming a trade to provide a certificate of their ability from a master of the relevant trade. (An edict of February 15, 1724, reiterated the regulation dating from November 15, 1728.) Was this just a vain hope, or was the ruling applied for only a very short period? In any case, we have found no trace of these certificates.

Whatever the case, a study of the trades first confirms how strong the spontaneous move to leave was in the years from 1713 to 1717. There was no necessity to cheat about trades, because there were more than sufficient "ordinary" engagés to fulfill the conditions laid down by the government. Does this mean that subsequent declarations concerning trades were by definition fraudulent? Not at all. One can, of course, wonder about the real professional training of such-and-such an 18-year-old surgeon (barber), writer, or goldsmith; they were, in fact, only apprentices. For the period from 1720 to 1770, indentured servants with a trade were older, on average, than in preceding years; it can be supposed that by the age of 25 or 30, possibly even 20, any man could have gained experience of one, or several trades. The list of trades would, of course, deserve a more detailed study; in addition to the well-known major regional specializations (e.g., woodcutters from the Limousin area), there were other trades that were frequently declared, perhaps because they were reputed to be useful in the islands (surgeons, refiners).

The geographic origin of the indentured servants is perhaps the most interesting element to emerge from the contracts of indenture. Our count (as yet only provisional) gave slightly more than 6,500 origins that are classified by major regions as shown in table 6.2, below.

These very rough figures call for some explanation, especially if they are compared to Debien's figures for La Rochelle in the previous century (table 6.1).[48] First, the variety of regions represented: indentured servants from all areas of France and from abroad embarked in Bordeaux (fig. 6.3). This pattern was not unique; La Rochelle, too, caught people from every part of

TABLE 6.2. *Geographical Origins of Indentured Servants Embarking in Bordeaux, 1698–1771*

Surrounding regions		
Bordeaux		741
Bordelais, Bazadais		918
Saintonge		322
Périgord		481
Quercy		135
Agenais		579
Regions south of Garonne, Gascogne, Western and Central Pyrenees, Landes		1,178
	Total	4,355 (66.9%)
Other parts of the "Grand Sud-Ouest"		
Aunis		53
Angoumois		96
Montauban		86
Toulouse		209
Albigeois-Rouergue		183
	Total	627 (9.6%)
"Centre Ouest"		
Pays de la Loire		205
Poitou		92
Centre du Massif Central		76
Limousin, V. de Turenne		189
	Total	562 (8.6%)
West (3.3%)		
Bretagne		166
Normandie		51
North		101
Northeast and East		170
Paris and Central Paris Basin		137
Languedoc		181
Provence		79
Colonies		44
Foreign Countries		36
	Grand Total	6,509

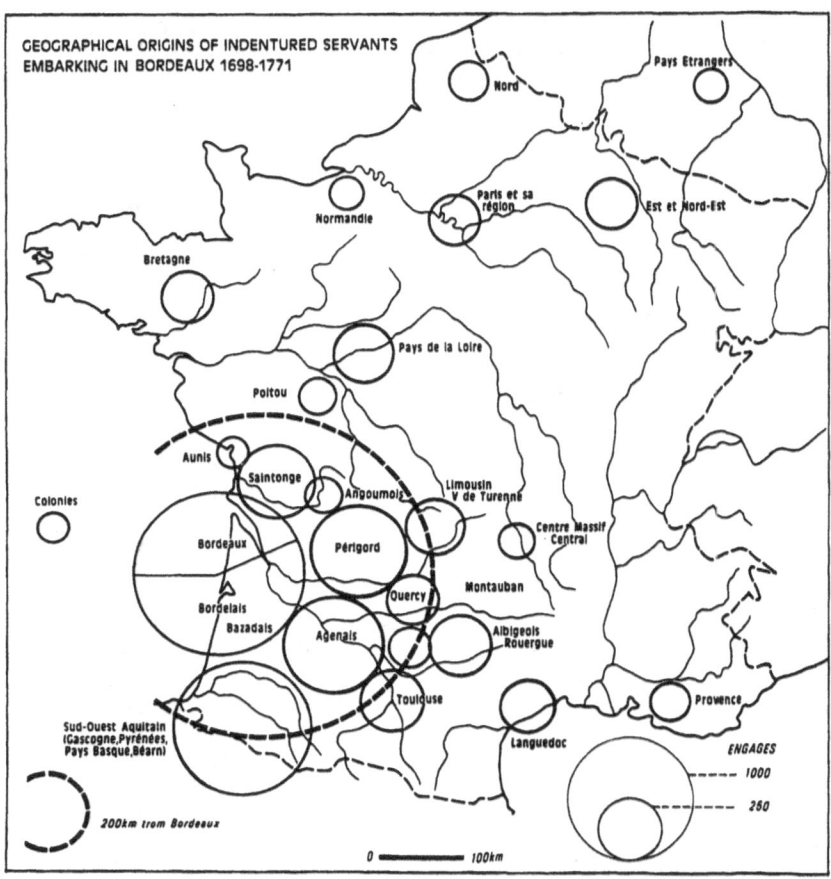

Fig. 6.3. Geographic Origins of Indentured Servants Embarking in Bordeaux, 1698–1772

France. Second, the regions that provided most engagés were Bordeaux's normal catchment areas: the Garonne Basin and the Adour Basin, since no ships at all were fitted out in Bayonne for the islands.

The "surrounding regions" are the most important, as in the case of La Rochelle. Northward, Bordeaux attracted people from the Saintonge, right up to the southern confines of the Aunis region and thus from the hinterland of La Rochelle. The situation is the reverse, therefore, of what it was a century before, when many engagés from the southwest of the Aquitaine region went to La Rochelle to embark. Last, it is striking to find that coastal areas were virtually uninvolved in the popular wave of emigration to America. The large battalions of engagés came from inland areas. It is even more remarkable in that nearly all French coastal areas (except for the Mediterranean coast and the Basque country) had almost constant contact with Bordeaux through their very active coastal navigation. For example, boats from the Ile d'Yeu sailed in the hundreds in the Gironde estuary each year, but servants from the area are noticeably absent in the lists. Could it be that maritime activities captured all its energies, leaving no room for a floating population, hence one that would migrate?

More detailed analysis of the indentured servants' geographic distribution within each major region, especially the Aquitaine Basin, reveals several important points that we shall only briefly touch on. One sees a fairly noticeable emphasis on the major riverbanks and valleys, which are often the most densely populated areas, of course, but which are also the ones that are most open to the outside world and where towns are preponderant. The farther away from Bordeaux, the more towns become an important source for indentured servants. Those from Brittany, Lorraine, the North, or the Paris Basin chiefly came from a small number of main towns, whereas servants from the Aquitaine area flocked to Bordeaux as much from rural parishes as from small and medium-sized towns. There are several possible explanations for this. First of all, when someone came from far away, it was normal to give the name of the nearest town, for example, as it is more likely to have been heard of. Or, it might indicate a process of uprooting that may be spread over more than one generation since departures from rural areas direct to America were rare; rather they were the culmination, in fact, of a more or less long-standing mobility and imply periods of living in one or more halfway towns. An illustration of this might be seen from the common occurrence of one and the same indentured servant listed on a ship's roll as coming from a certain town by dint of probably having stayed there for a variable period, and yet on the corresponding notaried contract, he is stated as belonging to a rural parish at a distance from that town.

Age, trade, and geographic origins are, of course, insufficient for a precise picture of these indentured servants' social, economic, and cultural circumstances. Other conclusions may be drawn, from the study of their signatures, for example. Here again there is a sharp contrast between the beginning of the century (before 1720), when very few of the young people who embarked could sign their names (less than 15 percent in the period from 1713 to 1717), and the period that followed, where there was a very rapid increase in the percentage of signatures, almost 60 percent from 1726 and approximately two-thirds thereafter.

Details of their physical appearance were rare, but occasionally mention was made of traces of smallpox or some other distinguishing characteristics. There are only a few examples of more detailed descriptions such as those of "Henry Loyer, shoemaker from Dax, 26 years of age, prominent chin, large nose, black hair...etc." and "Pierre Porteyron, shoemaker from Riberac in the Périgord region, covered with smallpox, long nose, prominent chin, large mouth, two warts on his left eye," both embarked on September 3, 1754, on the dogger boat, *Les Roys Mages*, from Saint-Valery sur Somme, bound for Louisburg. It may have been the appearance of Bernard Bernadou from Toulouse, a refiner aged 22, which caused the clerk to specify on April 25, 1755, "a wry neck bent over his shoulders." Few details of height are given either, even though the government had to issue a reminder on August 3, 1707, that indentured servants had to measure at least 4 feet (1.30 meters).

There are no details whatsoever about the motives for the young men's departures. Perhaps they were driven away by poverty and family tragedies (many had lost at least one parent, and often they are listed as orphans). Or perhaps they were attracted by the idea of far-flung adventure? At any rate, they frequently left their villages in twos (sometimes from the same family, brothers or cousins, or with the same trade, perhaps working together). These are only very bare glimpses, however, and only detailed research in their parishes of origin will help to clarify certain points.

It still remains to attempt to follow them on their long journeys. The vast majority of them left for the French islands. Of the 8,000 identified, 2,400 of them were bound for Martinique, 2,100 for

Santo Domingo, 500 for Guadeloupe, 2,300 for the "Islands" without further details, plus a certain number for "Martinique and Guadeloupe" and "Santo Domingo and Guadeloupe." There were also 6 bound for Grenada (1737–38), 3 for Marie-Galante (in point of fact, those bound for Guadeloupe sometimes continued on to Marie Galante), and 3 for St. Lucia. Other destinations did not figure prominently: 80 for Cayenne (half of those between 1764 and 1771) and for New France, 292 for Québec, and 42 to Ile Royale. The royal edict of March 20, 1714, little affected the Bordelais, who were not very interested in trading with Canada. Until 1752, therefore, we find only 71 engagés setting out for Québec and 19 for Ile Royale. Only during the period from 1752 to 1758 did many ships leaving from Bordeaux for Canada carry servants: 221 engagés for Québec and 21 for the Ile Royale. After the loss of Canada, there were 3 departures in 1764 for Miquelon. Louisiana, for which there were only 3 departures (in 1758), must be considered separately. As we have already seen, in fact, prisoners—and perhaps indentured servants, too—bound for Louisiana were listed as setting out for the Antilles, which was the first leg of their journey.[49]

The fate of most eighteenth-century indentured servants could not have been a very happy one.[50] Nevertheless, the phase of wholesale land clearance in a more or less wild and hostile environment was over, and the Antilles in the eighteenth century was a civilized place, possessing towns and facilities that might be the envy of many remote rural areas in France. But it was also a hierarchical society of slave "habitations" (plantations) and of small colonial towns, where there was no room at all for impoverished newcomers. Some of them managed to make a place for themselves on the plantations, especially in running the slaves' workshops, or else in "specialized" trades such as those of surgeon, refiner, and shipwright.[51] Others were able to integrate into urban societies and occasionally made a success of their lives there, as had some of their seventeenth-century predecessors in, say, skilled trades. But many of them would very quickly perish from disease or exhaustion or go off to swell the mobile ranks of vagabonds, pirates, or buccaneers in an era when the colonial world no longer had any place for them.

Notes

1. Much work has already been done by Gabriel Debien (see n. 17), but we still lack information about the eighteenth century and the fate of engagés in the islands.
2. In fact, some slaves arrived very early in the French West Indies, thanks to Dutch smugglers, but not in significant numbers.
3. See P. Pluchon, ed., *Histoire des Antilles et de la Guyane* (Paris, 1982).
4. See P. Butel in Pluchon, *Histoire des Antilles*, 163–192.
5. The growing gap between colonists' interests and the government's and traders' attempts to prevent smuggling led to riots in Martinique (1665–1667 and 1717, the well-known "gaoule") and Santo Domingo (1670–1671). See, e.g., Ch. Frostin, *Les révoltes blanches à Saint-Domingue aux XVIIe et XVIIIe siècles* (Paris, 1975).
6. For a geographic approach, see G. Lasserre, *La Guadeloupe* (Bordeaux, 1961), 2 vols.; idem., *Les Amériques du Centre* (Paris, 1974).
7. See G. Hanotaux and A. Martineau, *Histoire des colonies françaises* (Paris, 1929), t. 1, *L'Amérique*, 391–502.
8. This was much less than for servants in English islands, where the indenture was for four or five years at least and often lasted more than that. See Carl Bridenbaugh and Roberta Bridenbaugh, *No Peace beyond the Line: The English in the Caribbean* (New York, 1972); Richard S. Dunn, *Sugar and Slaves: The Rise of the Planter Class in the English West Indies, 1624–1713* (London, 1973); David W. Galenson, *White Servitude in Colonial America: An Economic Analysis* (Cambridge, 1981).
9. See, e.g., C. Rochfort, *Histoire naturelle et morale des isles des Antilles* (Amsterdam, 1658), and G. Debien and J. Le Ber, *Propagande et recrutement pour l'Amérique au XVIIe siècle* (Paris, 1954).
10. Jean-Baptiste du Tertre, *Histoire générale des Antilles habitées par les Français*, 4 vols., vol. 4 (Paris, 1667–1671).
11. See P. Butel, "Les temps des fondations," in Pluchon, *Histoire des Antilles*, 53–78.
12. Du Tertre, *Histoire générale*, t. 1.
13. J. Petitjean Roget, *La société d'habitation à la Martinique, un siècle de formation, 1635–1685* (Paris, 1980), 2 vols.
14. For buccaneers, see, among numerous titles, P. Butel, *Les Caraïbes au temps des filibustiers* (Paris, 1982), and, of course, Oexmelin (see n. 16).
15. R. P. Labat, *Nouveau voyage aux isles de l'Amérique* (numerous editions, e.g., Paris, 1742), 8 vols.
16. Alexandre-Olivier Oexmelin, *Histoire des aventuriers filibustiers*

qui se sont signalés dans les Indes (numerous editions, the best being Trevoux, 1774), 4 vols.

17. These contracts are a source of inestimable value, See, e.g., Gabriel Debien, *Le peuplement des Antilles Françaises au XVIIe siècle: les engagés partis de La Rochelle (1683–1717)* (Le Caire, 1942); *Les engagés pour les Antilles (1634–1715)* (Paris, 1952); *Les Poitevins aux fles* (Noirt, 1952); *Colons, marchants et engagés à Nantes au XVIIe siècle* (Le Havre, 1952); in collaboration with Abbé J. Le Ber, *Propagande et recrutement*.

18. See Jean Tanguy, "Les premiers engagés partis de Nantes vers les Antilles (1636–1660)," *Actes de 97e Congrès des Sociétés Savantes* (Nantes, 1972), Paris, 1977, t. 2, 53–81.

19. G. Debien, *Les engagés partis de La Rochelle*.

20. For Nantes, see P. Jeaulin, *L'évolution du port de Nantes: Organisation et traffic depuis les origines* (Paris, 1931), and for Bordeaux, T. Malvezin, *Histoire du commerce de Bordeaux depuis les origines jusqu'a nos jours* (Bordeaux, 1892), 4 vols., t. 2: XVIe et XVIIe siècles, t. 3: XVIIIe siècle.

21. H. Robert, *Les trafics coloniaux du port de La Rochelle au XVIIIe siècle (1713–1789)*, Bull. Soc. Ant. de l'Ouest, 1949, 135–172; E. Garnault, *Le commerce rochelais au XVIIIe siècle* (Paris, 1887–1900), 5 vols; Delafosse, *Histoire de la Rochelle* (Toulouse, 1985).

22. See Bridenbaugh and Bridenbaugh, *No Peace beyond the Line*.

23. H. A. Gemery, "Emigration from the British Isles to the New World, 1630–1700: Inference from Colonial Populations," *Research in Economic History* 5 (1980): 179–231; Jack P. Greene, *Pursuits of Happiness: The Social Development of Early British Colonies and the Formation of American Culture* (Chapel Hill and London, 1988), table 8.1, 178–179. John J. McCusker estimates that approximately 19 percent of the population of the French West Indies was black in 1650, 36 percent in 1660, 58 percent in 1680, 74 percent in 1700, 85 percent in 1730, and 90 percent in 1770; see "The RumTrade and the Balance of Payments of the Thirteen Continental Colonies, 1650–1775" (Ph.D. dissertation, University of Pittsburgh, 1970), p. 2, 712.

24. Pluchon, *Histoire des Antilles*.

25. J. Petitjean Roget, *La Gaoule: La révolte de la Martinique en 1717* (Société d'Histoire de la Martinique, Fort de France, 1966).

26. N. M. Crouse, *The French Struggle for the West Indies, 1665–1713* (London, 1966).

27. C. Huetz de Lemps, "Les engagés au depart de Bordeaux (fin XVIIe–XVIIIe siècle)," in *L'Atlantique et ses rivages* (Bordeaux, 1984), 133–154.

28. Roget, *La société d'habitation*.
29. Pluchon, *Histoire des Antilles*, chap. 5.
30. L. Vignols, *Les Antilles françaises sous l'ancien régime... L'institution des engagés (1626–1774)* (Paris, 1928).
31. Departmental Archives, Gironde, C 4269.
32. It is true that the king permitted those who wished to be dispensed from carrying engagés to take on board in their stead two soldiers recruited for his Majesty's companies garrisoned in the said territory of New France.
33. For the legislation, see Valin, *Nouveau Commentaire sur l'ordonnance de la marine du mois d'août 1681* (La Rochelle, 1776), 2 vols.
34. See the very rich notarial series in Departmental Archives, Gironde (3E).
35. P. Butel, *Les négociants bordelais, l'Europe et les îles au XVIIIe siècle* (Paris, 1974).
36. C. Huetz de Lemps, "Géographie du commerce de Bordeaux à la fin du regne de Louis XIV," *EPHE, Civilisations et Sociétés*, no. 49 (Mouton, Paris et La Yaue, 1975).
37. Departmental Archives, Gironde, 6 B 350 to 469.
38. Departmental Archives, Gironde, 6 B 78 to 80.
39. Not including prisoners embarking "by Order of the King," who will be discussed later. See C. Frostin, "Le peuplement pénal de l'Amérique aux XVIIe et XVIIIe siècles," *Annales de Bretagne et des Pays de l'Ouest* (1978).
40. See, e.g., Pluchon, *Histoire des Antilles*, chap. 7, 163–192, and the numerous publications on the demography of French Canda.
41. C. Huetz de Lemps, "Géographie du commerce de Bordeaux."
42. Departmental Archives, Gironde, C 4268, 14-1-1717.
43. B. N. Pap. Margry, 9828, fols. 14, 15.
44. Those involved in salt smuggling to avoid the *gabelle* (salt tax). See B. Briais, *Contrebandiers du sel* (Paris, 1984).
45. Abbe A. F. Prévost, *Histoire de Manon Lescaut et du Chevalier Desgrieux* (London, 1733).
46. Departmental Archives, Gironde, 6 B 365–380.
47. 1 livre-tournoi = 20 "sols," 3 livres-tournoi = 1 "écu." One gold écu weighed between 3.12 and 3.20 grams.
48. It would, of course, be of interest to compare indentured servant movements with those of passengers bound for the islands. This is being undertaken by J. P. Poussou and I, and on a larger scale migrations to Bordeaux have been exceptionally well analyzed by J. P. Poussou in his thesis, "Bordeaux et le Sud Ouest au XVIIIe siècle: croissance economique et attraction urbaine" (Paris EHESS, 1983).

49. For Louisiana, M. Giraud, *Histoire de la Louisiane française* (Paris, 1958), and E. Lauvriere, *Histoire de la Louisiane française (1673–1939)* (Paris, 1940).

50. Vignols, *Les Antilles françaises.*

51. See, e.g., L. Chanleau, *La société à la Martinique au XVIIe siècle* (Caen, 1966); P. de Vaissiere, *Saint-Domingue, la société et la vie créoles sous l'Ancien Régime* (Paris, 1909).

Seven

Harnessing the Lure of the "Best Poor Man's Country": The Dynamics of German-Speaking Immigration to British North America, 1683–1783

Marianne Wokeck

In the century from the founding of Germantown in 1683 to the end of the American war for independence in 1783, more than 100,000 German-speaking immigrants streamed into colonial British North America.[1] The vast majority of these newcomers landed at Philadelphia, and many settled in Pennsylvania. Compared with migrations from the British Isles, the influx of German settlers occurred late—after most colonies were founded. It came in response to a variety of official and private settlement schemes that depended on luring foreign Protestants to take up and develop land as far north as Nova Scotia and as far south as Georgia. Colonial governments and private colonizers alike found Germans an attractive source of settlers; in turn, German emigrants responded favorably to several different promises of free land, low taxes, and religious toleration.

In the beginning, only fairly wealthy people could afford the high cost of relocating from Germany to America, since few of the colonizers in America included free transportation among their incentives to settlement. This financial filter kept the numbers of immigrants small until British merchants in Rotterdam devised a system that allowed emigrants with limited means to cross the Atlantic on credit and redeem debts incurred for their passage by a period of servitude in the colonies. This financing feature of the German emigrant trade coupled with favorable reports about opportunity in the colonies and effective recruiting networks in southwestern Germany brought about a mass relocation that transplanted as many as 50,000 Germans in the years around the middle of the eighteenth century. This was over two decades before immigration from Ulster peaked on a similar scale in the 1770s[2] and generations before proportionately comparable waves of European mass migration reached the United States in the nineteenth century.[3]

An overall outline of German immigration to eighteenth-century America is the object here. In particular, where did the stream of settlers originate and what was its nature? How did the flow of immigrants change over time, and what are the implications of those shifts for the dispersal of Germans in the colonies and hence for their chances of adaptation and acculturation in the New World?

While the story of the German migration to the American colonies has been told before, some parts of it are much better known than others. Two fundamentally different approaches stand out among the conventional versions. German and Swiss scholars have most often examined aspects of emigration (or Auswanderung), concentrating largely on circumstances in Europe and reasons that pushed migrants to leave their homelands.[4] This focus makes sense in light of the familiarity these particular historians have with the sources that detail the character of regions with substantial out-migration. Conversely, American historians—members of an immigrant society—have focused on immigration (or Einwanderung), putting to use their training in the analysis of records that throw light on the characteristics of European migrants pulled to settle in America and the situation they encountered there.[5] The advantages of telling the story from the perspective one knows best are clear; and many important details come to light only after close scrutiny of local circumstances. Still, the story is not complete unless the views from both sides of the Atlantic are incorporated into an integrated understanding.[6] Weighing both push and pull factors and assessing their interplay has been on the agenda of migration history for some time; yet the realities of mastering more than one language and more than one set of sources are daunting and have slowed results.[7] Consequently, progress in the general study of immigration has been mostly in two areas, namely, the formulation of theories that dissect the processes of migration and the analysis of manageable test cases such as the Scandinavian migrations to nineteenth-century America, which are characterized by relatively small numbers and superb records.[8] Nevertheless, both kinds of studies—the theoretical and the particular—offer valuable insights on how to approach issues of immigration, even when the numbers of migrants are large and the sources as scattered and uneven as in the German case.

First establishing the general features of the transatlantic migration from eighteenth-century Germany is especially important because it makes it possible to relate contributing elements meaningfully to the overall pattern and to each other. Three basic elements determined the nature of German migration to the American colonies: the various conditions in southwestern Germany encouraging emigration; the opportunities that settlement in America offered; and the recruiting and transportation networks that facilitated and channeled the migration flows. Together, these strands interacted in a pattern whose numerical results became a strong surge of migration from the shallow beginning of 1683 until the middle of the eighteenth century, when this wave forcefully crested, and then a relatively rapid decline of German newcomers landing in America through the twelve years leading up to the American Revolution (see fig. 7.1). As the tide of German immigration swelled, peaked, and subsided, its composition altered from a predominance of families often headed by mature men to relatively fewer families of smaller size led by younger males. The makeup of the flow also changed from a majority of migrants who could pay their fare in advance to a large percentage who counted on indentured servitude to finance their relocation. The composition of the migration evolved over time, too, in terms of the areas from which Germans set out for the American colonies. The Palatinate, Württemberg, and Hesse provided a steady supply of set-

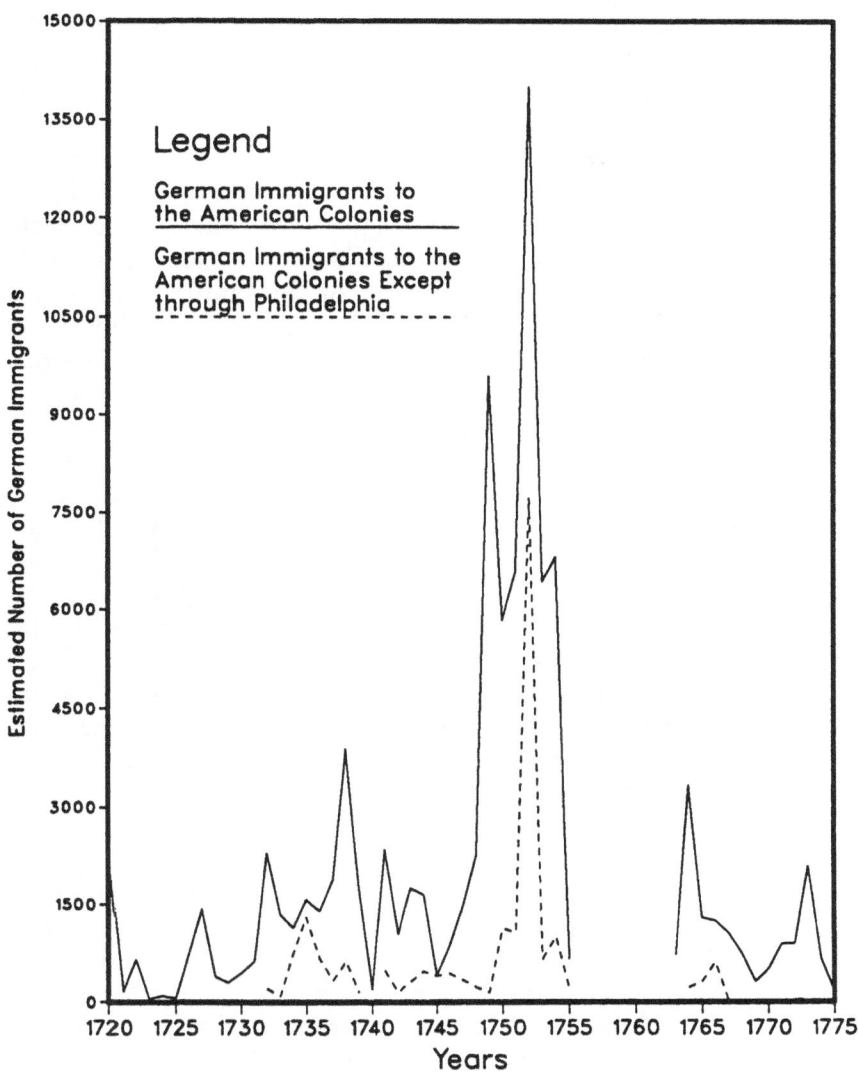

Fig. 7.1. German Immigrants to the American Colonies, 1720–1775

tlers throughout the period; but as the flow of migrants increased, most Protestant areas in southwestern Germany, including the Swiss cantons of Basel, Bern, and Zurich as well as Alsace and Lorraine, and also some territories in northwestern Germany contributed to the migration stream. Similarly, the destinations in the colonies varied as the influx of immigrants changed over time. Philadelphia, after the earliest years, was overwhelmingly the most prominent port of arrival, but German immigrants landed in all of the colonies, especially at the height of the immigration wave around 1750. In the end, examination in these terms of how different strands of people were interwoven in successive temporal phases by dynamics of push, pull, and transportation to form a characteristic pattern of historical relocation reveals that the German migration to the American colonies in the eighteenth century evolved to become the prototype of later, nineteenth-century, transatlantic mass migrations. The ways in which German relocation before the American Revolution brought together elements of recruitment, transport financing, and ethnically supported adjustment to the new land distinguished this migration from the servant[9] and slave trades[10] and unsystematic English and Irish migrations[11] prior to 1750. In its nature, it was thus more like the movements of many European groups yet to come and represents the transition from early modern to truly modern transatlantic migrations.

For a century after the siege of Vienna in 1683, an area centered along the Rhine and roughly bounded by the Moselle, Main, Neckar, Danube, and Weser rivers supplied almost 500,000 settlers to a number of regions outside of the territories that comprised the Holy Roman Empire, in particular, Hungary, Russia, British America, and to a lesser degree, France and Spain.[12] The reservoir from which these migration streams flowed represented no "core"[13] but rather more generally and more loosely a region of crisscrossing political and cultural currents where, especially along the Rhine and its tributaries, important and far-reaching informational and commercial networks operated and shaped response to change. Although the population history of southwestern Germany is complex, two characteristics stand out. Strategically located at major crossroads of European trade, the area was much depopulated by the ravages of the Thirty Years War and its social and economic infrastructure severely damaged.[14] Rebuilding in the second half of the seventeenth century was spectacularly successful. Much of this, however, depended on immigrants from neighboring territories, especially from Switzerland, which had suffered only indirectly from the war.[15] The inflow of new settlers seeking out opportunities in the Palatinate, Württemberg, and many of the smaller territories bordering the Rhine was highly segregated, however. Protestant migrants followed the invitations of Lutheran or Reformed lords; Catholics acquired residence under Catholic rulers. By the end of the seventeenth century, the region on the whole—a checkerboard of territories distinct in terms of religion, the composition of their populations, and their customs and laws—had largely, albeit unevenly, recovered and shifted from being an area of in-migration to one of out-migration.[16] Opportunity in southwestern Germany had now declined for a substantial proportion of its inhabitants and thus encouraged them to look elsewhere in their quest to improve their prospects and those of their children.

Against this background, long-range migration in eighteenth-century Germany evolved in a distinctive pattern. The major flows usually originated in particular areas, followed a set path, and adhered to some intrinsic timing. While in direction the streams often diverged, they sometimes converged.[17] Tracing these movements, one can distinguish five significant migrations. Throughout the eighteenth century, the most persistent and numerically the strongest flow drew migrants from Catholic territories to eastern colonies of the Habsburg empire. This relocation reached impressive peaks in the 1720s, 1760s, and 1780s. Russia offered her invitation to settlers late—after the Seven Years War—but could persuade emigrants from both Protestant and Catholic territories to heed the call. Prussia, in contrast, had relied on Huguenot refugees in the late 1680s and Protestants from the Archbishopric of Salzburg in the early 1730s for colonization; but in the 1760s, it, too, extended a settlement offer to Protestants in southwestern Germany. The largely Protestant migration to British North America contrasted with the streams flowing east not only because of its transatlantic direction but also because of its different magnitude: it captured only about 13 percent of the total long-range migration from Germany.[18] In addition, it followed a different phasing, with major peaks around 1710 and 1750. Although Spain was intent on securing her borders with Portugal through German settlements and France transported Germans to Cayenne in the early 1760s, only a relatively few—mostly Catholics—relocated under Spanish or French aegis.

In a composite overview of these different migration streams, two features stand out.[19] Until the end of the Seven Years War, Austria, Prussia, and America gained settlers who originated from the same general area of out-migration but whose particular territorial origins rarely overlapped, separating especially Catholics from Protestants into divergent emigrations. As Russia became a participant in the quest for settlers, the wave of eighteenth-century emigration crested in the 1760s, and the different recruitment efforts competing for potential emigrants overlapped in many territories. The next wave of flows to the East in the 1780s re-created this crisscrossing pattern, albeit displaying slightly less competitive intensity and shifting its geographic center from the Palatinate to Württemberg.

This rough outline of the major peaks and troughs of the long-range migration from southwestern Germany lays some groundwork for thinking about the reasons that prompted migration streams to swell and subside. To begin, when correlating numbers of emigrants with periods of war and peace, it is evident that times of war hindered any large-scale movement of people over long distances.[20] No simple, clear-cut pattern emerges, however, when testing whether and to what degree emigrants responded to political instability, agricultural crises, economic recessions, religious persecution, raised taxes, harsh conscription laws, or other likely reasons for widespread discontent.[21] Apparently, all such adverse circumstances were contributing factors in the decision to migrate to faraway places, but any one was rarely sufficient cause to leave home. Even the combination of two or more adversities often failed to set the process in motion.[22] Rather, the "push" factors inherent in political oppression and economic instability endemic to the whole region constituted the necessary background against which other dynamics came effectively into play.

Since war hindered long-range migration, and since adverse conditions at home alone did not cause migration streams to swell, the high correlation of the opening of new areas for colonization[23] with peaks in the migration flow suggests that potential emigrants from southwestern Germany were in large part "pulled" to relocate as they perceived a shortfall between their current position and future prospects at home compared with opportunities offered in distant lands. The lure of sufficient land, low taxes, and exemption from pressing obligations like conscription was strong, yet often not strong enough to sway people actually to leave their homes. As many promoters of private and governmental settlement schemes discovered, active recruiting was necessary for a good offer to catch on.[24]

The prerequisites for an effective recruiting effort were generally well known. In particular, the Austrian, Prussian, and Russian governments were most successful in their quest for settlers when they followed a certain strategy. First of all, cooperation by the authorities in the areas targeted for recruiting was essential.[25] The territorial authorities' permission to distribute promotional literature, their guarantees to protect the recruiting agents, and their willingness to process any applications for emigration speedily were critical components when establishing an effective local recruiting network. Such official support, or at least tolerance, not only gave agents free rein but also represented a stamp of approval for the whole operation. This often translated into a competitive edge.[26] Persuading locally respected people to support the recruiting effort or, better still, to sign them as emigrants was another useful device in the quest for settlers. Recruiters likewise often chose a centrally situated inn as their operational base to take advantage of the local communication network focused there.[27] They also concentrated their efforts on winning an area's minister or printer for their cause because men in these and similar positions could shape public opinion.[28] In any situation, the agent had to be convincing in his presentation to win commitments from potential emigrants. Among the many ploys devised to achieve that goal, positive communications from relatives, friends, or neighbors who had already emigrated were extremely valuable as such personal reports lent special weight to any official claim. To receive these endorsements—usually in the form of letters but sometimes by personal visits—it was crucial that the organization of the transport and the initial settlement went smoothly.[29] A newly settled area's good reputation then aided recruiters in building respect and credibility, thus contributing significantly to the effectiveness of their future efforts in winning still more settlers.

Most settlement schemes organized by governments on a large scale operated more or less in this fashion, their success depending on the skill and resourcefulness of their recruiters and agents to capitalize on the imbalance between the realities potential emigrants faced at home and their expectations for better circumstances in a distant land. Competition in this quest for settlers was sharp and at its height produced the all-time eighteenth-century peak of German emigration in the mid-1760s when Austria, Prussia, Russia, and France all courted potential emigrants.[30] Within this overall, international context, the migration to British North America stands out because it was not the result of a *concerted* government effort. Yet many of the recruiting mechanisms that fueled the German migration flow to America were the same as those that shaped the migration streams to the East.

Foreign Protestants first became a source for settlement projects in the American colonies when William Penn invited Quakers in the Rhineland to settle in Pennsylvania in 1682.[31] He published a promotional tract that extolled the virtues of his new colony for continental Europeans and used fellow Quakers—foremost among them Benjamin Furly, merchant in Rotterdam—as agents to attract suitable investors and help organize their move across the Atlantic.[32] Although the number of emigrants from Germany persuaded to settle in Germantown in 1683 was small compared to newcomers from England who made their homes in Pennsylvania, reports of their success in the New World inspired others to devise settlement schemes for foreign Protestants in the American colonies. In the early years of the eighteenth century, several entrepreneurial Europeans, like Francis Louis Michel, Johann Rudolph Ochs, and Christoph von Graffenried, explored possibilities for German settlement in America and negotiated with the British colonial administration and with some proprietory governors to find mutually satisfactory arrangements for relocating Germans to the frontiers of the New World.[33]

The advantages of such settlement schemes seemed compelling to everybody involved. The enterprising colonizer himself obtained often extensive tracts of land at comparatively very low prices, which he could use as an investment for profit, status, and influence in a foreign land or a safe haven for his flock.[34] The British government and most colonial administrations welcomed such suggestions for large-scale settlement, because giving up undeveloped land in America cost little and new settlers promised profits through improvements to the land, better security against hostile Indians and warring Europeans, and increases in revenue and trade. Both the central British administration and colonial governments discouraged undue speculation, however, by stipulating settlement requirements. These usually granted the developer final title only after a specified number of settlers had taken up land within a given time period. The settlers gained from such arrangements between entrepreneurs and foreign governments because they could pursue opportunities in distant lands without having to bear the costs and risks of exploration and of organizing their own relocation. Authorities in the areas of out-migration welcomed and even actively supported such schemes as long as they perceived them as a means of relieving population pressure on the limited resources in their territories or of ridding their lands of troublesome and burdensome citizens.[35]

This was the theory. In practice, the returns on most of these arrangements were much less clear-cut. The risks often outweighed profits; and organizational failure and discontent among settlers brought many endeavors to a halt before yields met expectations. The German immigrant flow to the American colonies and the pattern of its dispersal reflect widely varying levels of success in both private and governmental settlement schemes. William Penn's invitation to continental Protestants to take up residence in Pennsylvania readily produced imitators, who published and distributed their own promotional tracts and thus drew more general attention to settlement opportunities in the American colonies. Distinctive in Pennsylvania's attraction, however, were Penn's connections with coreligionists in Rotterdam. These links with the Anglo-Dutch business community at the mouth of the Rhine proved critical in establishing a migratory mechanism for German emigrants to cross the Atlantic. Quaker merchants in Rotterdam were instrumental in devising a transportation system that allowed emigrants with limited means to move in large numbers to the American colonies.[36] This market mechanism in the immigrant supply system for Pennsylvania made that flow different from (more successful than) all its American competitors and a precursor of transatlantic mass migration in the modern era.

In many respects, 1709 was a pivotal year in the German migration to the American colonies. Vicissitudes of political instability caused by France's aggressive expansion into the Rhineland and acute agricultural crisis brought on by the extremely harsh winter of 1708 combined with widely distributed glowing reports about settlement opportunities in America and a very liberal naturalization policy under Queen Anne to prompt about 13,000 people from southwestern Germany to leave their homelands.[37] This represents the second largest transatlantic outflow in any single year of the eighteenth century. The British government, from whom the emigrants expected help in relocating in America, was totally unprepared to receive such a mass exodus from the Palatinate and neighboring principalities. The municipal authorities in Rotterdam, the port where the Germans awaited transshipment to England, similarly found their resources for charitable aid overstretched.[38] In the end, about one-third of these "Palatines," as Germans became indiscriminately known, settled in America—the majority (2,344) of them in New York where they were transported as government redemptioners to produce naval stores, some (650) in North Carolina where they filled the ranks of Ritter's and Graffenried's settlements, and some others arriving much later in Philadelphia after they had first been settled in Ireland.[39] Of the German emigrants remaining in England, many died, the Catholics were returned to the continent, and even many Protestants went back to Germany—disillusioned and poor.[40]

Although the promise of the "golden book"[41] had ended in disappointment for many, its effects redirected and redefined the terms under which German emigrants ventured across the Atlantic. While the English government was confronted with many foreign Protestants eager to settle in the American colonies but unable to afford the relocation without help, transports organized on a relatively small scale determined the way in which emigrants would arrange the voyage. In particular, a few merchants in Rotterdam with Quaker and Mennonite connections, such as Jacob Telner and Benjamin Furly, who had direct contact with Pennsylvania and personal interests in the colony, were instrumental in aiding German emigrants bound for the colonies to make suitable transportation contracts with shippers engaged in trade between Rotterdam, England, and America.[42] Transportation of passengers and their goods to the American colonies was governed by the English navigation laws. This meant that only British citizens could engage in this trade; that transport had to be in British-owned vessels, which were operated by predominantly British crews; that only household goods were duty-free; and that all vessels carrying German migrants destined for the colonies had to clear customs in a port in Britain. Violation of the laws could result in forfeiture of the ship and the goods it carried, a risk hardly worth taking.

For the British merchants in Rotterdam, the matching of emigrants seeking transatlantic transportation with suitable vessels became an increasingly profitable middleman's function. Until the 1730s, two kinds of contracts were most commonly arranged. In the first, individual emigrants or a group of them, usually families and neighbors traveling together, would agree with the shipper or captain of a ship about the terms of the voyage.[43] The initial contact was often through a factor in Frankfurt, a mercantile center on the Main River which was also the residence of an envoy of the English government. In a second type of arrangement, the organization of a transport rested in the hands of a recognized leader. He became responsible for the necessary arrangements for the voyage and payment for the passage.[44]

In the first three decades of the eighteenth century, the majority of German emigrants depended on governmental and charitable aid to finance their relocation.[45] Although Queen Anne and her ministers supported the idea of settlement of foreign Protestants in the colonies, they had anticipated few direct costs. This was based on an assumption that emigrants too poor to finance the move across the Atlantic would not follow the invitation to settle in America. The Palatine mass emigration of 1709 proved them wrong. In the end, it cost the government enormous sums.[46] The semiofficial sponsorship of the German settlement projects in North and South Carolina and Georgia was less costly for the British government because these projects attracted settlers with some capital of their own or the developers could draw on other sources to finance the relocation and first years of settlement.

Although at first numerically less impressive, those emigrants who decided to settle in Pennsylvania in fact paved the way for the steadily rising migration flow to the American colonies in the first half of the eighteenth century. Two factors in particular contributed to that development. Reports about settlement opportunities in the Delaware valley were generally positive,[47] and a moderate climate, religious toleration, and a "quiet" government were added attractions when compared to features known about other colonies.[48] This reputation especially impressed potential emigrants who lived in territories where religious intolerance and political oppression made life difficult. Anabaptists, Baptists, Schwenckfelders, and Moravians were among those who responded favorably to such reports about opportunities in Pennsylvania. They tended to fare well when they relocated because they could rely on networks among coreligionists that enabled them to evaluate opportunities abroad realistically and to plan their move properly and that often afforded them tangible help along the way or on settlement.[49] In turn, they sent favorable reports home and in effect, if not in words, invited others to join them.[50]

The relatively small numbers of Germans who arrived in Pennsylvania before 1727 reflect the difficulties and above all the costs of relocating overseas. Among those drawn to settle in the American colonies, only few could afford to pay the fare for the voyage, especially if all family members were to travel together.[51] Since the ability to move overseas was so closely tied to the wealth of the potential emigrant, it is not surprising that the early immigration flow at first increased only slightly as the information of settlement opportunities in America spread beyond the circles with direct Quaker and Mennonite connections. The large numbers who came in later years, however, suggest that the majority of potential emigrants then ranked among the middling and poorer sorts of southwestern Germany who made their living mostly as farmers and artisans. It took some method of financing to enable this bulk of likely migrants to move across the Atlantic. That was where the role of the Rotterdam merchants was crucial in shaping the history of eighteenth-century German immigration to America.

With the popularity of Pennsylvania on the rise, two developments came together to allow an extraordinary broadening of the base of potential immigrants to the American colonies. Early on, successful immigrants encouraged those who planned to follow in their steps to bring not only their families but also servants. They reported that land was cheap but labor dear and that such sponsorship of emigrants too poor to pay their own way represented a sound investment.[52] Most such arrangements were informal and agreed on in Germany before all members of such an extended household set out on their journey. The other crucial element of change was that some merchants in Rotterdam apparently decided to accept a number of passengers traveling "on credit." The collateral was the emigrant's willingness to serve a master in America for five years in exchange for the price of the voyage. This selling of contracts for indentured servitude in the colonies was common practice in the English and Irish colonial trade.[53] In the 1720s, it was adapted to the German context.

Further, the merchants involved in the German immigrant trade soon developed indentured servitude in a novel form. In the early 1720s, they found that a considerable number of Germans successfully settled in Pennsylvania were willing to redeem the fare costs of poor immigrants, especially when such newcomers were relatives, friends, or former neighbors.[54] At first, the proportion of German immigrants who relied on friends in the Delaware valley to redeem them in this way was relatively small.[55] As the immigration flow began to swell, however, the practice became more widespread,[56] and merchants devised standard procedures for dealing with passengers traveling on credit. On embarkation in Rotterdam, passengers unable to pay their fare signed a contract that stated how much time they had in Philadelphia to get in touch with those whom they expected to defray the cost for the voyage. If they were unable to locate their friends in the time allowed—usually two weeks—the redemption of their outstanding debts was opened to general bidding from anyone willing to invest in their labor.[57] Unlike the practice common since the early seventeenth century in the English and Irish trade, where the length of servitude was a fixed term but the price negotiable, contracts for German redemptioners took the variable amount of outstanding passage debt as their fixed base and adjusted the length and terms of service accordingly.[58] This feature was particularly useful for families whose total fare debts were high but whose teenage children could take on indentures that would defray more than the cost of one passage. Flexible terms of servitude to adjust to variable amounts of outstanding debt on landing and a large number of children who became indentured servants to finance the relocation of their families characterized the German redemptioner system for the rest of the century.

The success of this system depended primarily on two factors: the willingness of the Rotterdam merchants to extend credit to poor emigrants and conditions of the labor market in the American colonies which made investment in bound labor attractive. The merchants found a number of ways to ensure reasonable returns on transporting Germans to the American colonies. Their strategies for making the German passenger trade a profitable business included striving for a high ratio of passengers per ship and a pricing policy that favorably balanced their costs for recruiting passengers, chartering, outfitting, and provisioning ships with the fare payments they could realistically expect to receive.[59] The other side of the equation, the receptiveness of the colonial labor market to German immigrants, especially indentured servants, eluded control, and even gauging it correctly was difficult. As German immigration to the American colonies became regularized and more dependable, however, Pennsylvania gained predominance among all possible destinations and maintained this position throughout the eighteenth century. Its favorable reputation among immigrants accounted for some of this development. Beyond that, the readiness with which newcomers from Germany not only found a way of making a living themselves but succeeded in doing so at a level that allowed them, in turn, to hire other German immigrants distinguished Pennsylvania's immigration still further from that of New York, the Carolinas, Georgia, and other colonies with early German settlements. Although masters without German roots did acquire indentured servants from Germany, the vast majority of redemptioners were bound to former countrymen.[60]

Colonies that depended mostly on slaves or convicts for their labor or that had relatively few Germans among their white population had less use for such non-English-speaking indentured servants. Consequently, merchants who transported a significant proportion of redemptioners were more likely to land their passengers in Pennsylvania, where they could expect enough buyers. This situation thus reinforced Pennsylvania's popularity among shippers and passengers, so that the rest of the colonies attracted German immigrants in large numbers only if unusually strong incentives pulled them that way. The English government's settlement project in Nova Scotia in 1750–1752, Samuel Waldo's scheme for New England in the same period, and North Carolina's offers of land bounties for foreign Protestants before and after the Seven Years War each diverted some part of the westward migratory flow from Germany to America;[61] yet none of those ventures produced the kind of self-generating momentum that drew ever larger numbers of German immigrants to the Delaware valley up to the 1750s.

The success of this distinctive interplay of Pennsylvania's good reputation and the willingness of the merchants to extend credit to emigrants unable to pay for the voyage in advance depended, like all settlement ventures, on a recruiting mechanism to advertise these options. In the 1720s and 1730s, most recruiting networks were personal and very informal.[62] Letters and especially visits from earlier migrants to the "new land" (hence the term "newlander") provided powerful incentives for potential emigrants to leave home. Although the newlanders acquired a bad name, it is important to remember that this negative reputation was based on the abuses and exploitation in the trade that occurred at the very height of the westward migration. Then, even a small percentage of dishonest agents could generate many personal cases of deceit and fraud. These, in turn, found much publicity as homeland officials used such horror stories to discourage more potential emigrants from leaving for America.[63] On the whole, however, newlanders provided valuable services to emigrants as well as to colonizers (and to themselves), and many did so honestly.

In the early years, migrants returning to visit their homelands had to have compelling reasons to make the arduous and expensive trip. Many went back to settle inheritances.[64] Most seem to have returned only after they had succeeded in the New World—enough so to impress relatives, friends, and neighbors with their accomplishments.[65] Customarily, newlanders carried letters from other immigrants and sometimes also powers of attorney that enabled them to collect inheritances for those settled in America.[66] Acting as go-between in these ways, the newlanders easily expanded the network of their own personal contacts. On their journey back, they were often accompanied by migrants eager to follow their example, taking advantage of making the move in the company of an experienced traveler. In turn, newlanders seem to have thrived on this leadership role. The money they collected for themselves and for others allowed them to invest in goods with high resale value[67] and also to finance, on commission, the passage of poor emigrants whose relatives or friends had offered redemption on arrival in the colonies.

As more newlanders returned and cast an ever wider net of contacts that inspired still further emigration from southwestern Germany, and as groups of migrants traveling down the Rhine and its tributaries became a regular feature of river traffic in late spring and early summer, local authorities in the areas of out-migration showed concern about rising numbers of departures,[68] and the merchants in Rotterdam increasingly realized the recruiting potential of newlanders for their own transport operations. Until 1739, when the United Provinces of the Netherlands required the merchants to post bond for all German migrants bound for the colonies in order to prevent transients from becoming charges of Dutch taxpayers,[69] many emigrants seem to have traveled to Rotterdam before they contracted with a particular shipper for their transatlantic passage. Thereafter many migrants signed contracts for the voyage before they reached the Dutch border, with the boatmen who transported the travelers down the Rhine often acting as recruiters for the Rotterdam merchants.

Competition among the handful of companies seriously involved in the German passenger trade heated up when groups of emigrants collected close to the Netherlands border awaiting permission by the Dutch authorities to proceed.[70] To gain a competitive edge, merchants offered newlanders free passage and other incentives[71] for advising their contingent of emigrants to contract with a particular shipper. Such arrangements between merchants and newlanders proved profitable enough so that, as the migration wave crested around midcentury, each firm involved in the trade had a regular recruiting network in place which relied heavily on newlanders.[72] The effectiveness of newlanders in stimulating emigration, and generally organizing and guiding the transport of emigrants down the Rhine and preparing for the voyage, was curtailed only when local authorities banned newlanders from operating in their territories.

Over the years, the informal recruiting networks of newlanders, who first operated alone and later often worked in close cooperation with the merchants of Rotterdam, developed into a system that rivaled those organized by the Austrian, Prussian, and Russian governments. The fundamental difference was the essentially private, market-driven nature of the ventures that drew German migrants to America, even those that were initiated, sanctioned, or supported by colonial governments.[73] Increasingly, the North American colonies became a familiar place in the imagination of potential emigrants as colonizers of different kinds publicized their schemes and as pioneering groups—often with direct connections to the settlement's entrepreneur or following a chosen leader—had relocated in the New World and communicated their success to those left at home. When such explicit or implicit invitations to settle in America were combined with an immediate stimulus, such as the visit of a newlander, they translated a general readiness to migrate into many particular resolves to relocate to America, especially as the costs and logistics of the move seemed less daunting if one had the assistance and company of an experienced migrant.

Whatever reasons newlanders had for their return to their places of origin, pride of their achievements in the new land and a keen sense for profits that they could realize through the importation of goods as well as labor became driving forces behind their ventures in the old country. Inheritances released to a newlander provided the bulk of both starting and operating capital for these endeavors. Savings of those who decided to emigrate and who entrusted the arrangement of their affairs to a newlander contributed to this investment fund, and commissions newlanders received from merchants for delivering passengers onto their ships were still another source of liquid capital.[74] Since the merchants recouped their recruiting costs through creative pricing of the passage fares they charged, the emigrants themselves in the end bore the costs of recruitment.[75] In exchange, German immigrants to America could take advantage of an increasingly established transportation system that enabled even those with limited cash assets to relocate overseas.

In simplified terms, three characteristics generated the dynamics that distinguished the eighteenth-century migration flow to the American colonies from those destined for Eastern Europe. First, while starting from similar backgrounds of widespread discontent with conditions and prospects at home and promising opportunities in distant lands, the westward migration stream became more *self-generating* as successful immigrants first reported favorably and then invited and helped relatives, friends, and former neighbors to settle in America. Crucially, they became willing to extend their support to strangers of their own language and general cultural background whose passage debts they redeemed in exchange for labor. Further, this feature of assisting (and exploiting) unknown fellow countrymen, which had started in an informal and personal way, was soon developed into a formalized system for funding relocation. The Rotterdam merchants engaging in the German passenger trade initiated this development as they adapted the existing custom of binding English and Irish servants to masters in the colonies to the special family-focused and ethnically distinct characteristics of the swelling German migration by offering passage on flexible credit, redeemable in several possible ways on arrival in America. They profited from this more open fare policy because their returns increased proportionately with the number of passengers each of their ships carried. Third, in their quest for ever greater numbers of emigrants, the merchants systematically exploited the cooperation of those former immigrants who returned to Europe on business and were willing to use their contacts and personal ethnic identity to recruit still more passengers for the merchants and guide them to the right ships at the port of embarkation. The roles, risks, and profits changed for these three groups of active participants in the German passenger trade—the migrants, the merchants, and the newlanders—as the intensity and the composition of the migration flow varied. Conversely, the pattern of the migration over the eighteenth century also reflects the way interaction evolved and changed over time among these participants who shaped and channeled the stream of Germans across the Atlantic.

In this distinctive development over time in the dynamics of the eighteenth-century German immigration flow to the American colonies, determining its size and composition offers some important insight into the distribution and relative importance of the various German settlements in North America. In theory, measuring the German migration is easy. In reality, the data at hand are less satisfactory than they might be; hence their analysis is more open to interpretation. All southwestern German territories required their residents to seek permission before moving out of the land, regardless of the reason for leaving or the distance involved. In many cases that included a petition for manumission from feudal bondage by which most rural inhabitants were traditionally tied to the lord of the land.[76] Although the precise bureaucratic procedures required for obtaining permission to leave the country differed from territory to territory, the principles were very similar: local and regional authorities alike insisted on their right to determine who was allowed to leave so that they could prevent those whose productivity they valued highly from taking up residence elsewhere, while encouraging those who were likely to be a burden to the community to seek their fortunes in someone else's region of responsibility.[77]

In light of this overriding fiscal interest in controlling out-migration, many records have survived. Some of the local and regional German archives have been systematically searched for this kind of evidence and already have yielded much information.[78] Unfortunately, many of the important details are missing or incomplete. Foremost among these shortcomings of the records are a lack of consistent information about the intended destination of all the migrants, their motives for leaving, their socioeconomic status, and their ages and family situation. Some of these details can be gleaned indirectly from within the documents of bureaucratic control or from other sources, but the necessary coordination of records is often difficult and always time-consuming. Quite a few vital pieces of information elude detection in the official records altogether because migrants with little stake in the community and no intention of returning often simply left without the necessary permission.[79] In short, while many emigration lists exist, they are geographically and chronologically scattered and their quality varies considerably, with bureaucratic bias especially marring their value for analysis.

The situation is even worse with regard to immigration lists. Records detailing the arrival of foreigners in the American colonies are probably more scattered and less complete than those recording their departure.[80] Among the varied arrival sources, the ship lists of German passengers landing in Philadelphia are an exception.[81] Although far from ideal, these allow much insight into the nature of the migration through Philadelphia. Further, in conjunction and in comparison with knowledge about German immigrant ships known to have landed elsewhere, they suggest the overall pattern of German immigration to eighteenth-century British North America.

Three distinctive periods characterized the flow to the Delaware valley.[82] From the founding of Germantown in 1683 until the middle of the eighteenth century, German immigration to Philadelphia rose at first slowly, then after 1727 fairly rapidly. This flow was not even across time. It shows distinctive peaks roughly coinciding with the periods of unrestricted transatlantic traffic. During this early phase, the average annual number of ships with German immigrants increased (from an average of three in the late 1720s to an average of seven in the late 1740s). So did the number of passengers per ship (from an average of about 170 in the late 1720s to a little over 200 in the late 1740s). In the late 1720s, on average a little over 600 Germans landed in Philadelphia each autumn; in the late 1740s, that number had tripled to almost 1,800. In 1749, with the end of the War of Austrian Succession, German immigration through Pennsylvania peaked, with more than 9,500 newcomers landing in Philadelphia that fall. For the next five years, until the beginning of the Seven Years War which seriously curtailed regular traffic across the Atlantic, the annual figures continued to be very high, averaging over 5,600 immigrants per year, many of them crowded in very large numbers onto an average of twenty ships per year. When immigration resumed in 1763, the trend was one of rapid decline, to which the onset of the American Revolution brought a complete stop until 1783. At the same time, further incidences of very crowded ships disappeared, and several vessels carried no more than one or two dozen German migrants.

This pattern of rise, peak, and decline in the number of arrivals found parallels in the composition of the migration flow to Philadelpia. Until the mid-1750s, the proportion of families among the German immigrants was high. The evidence for this is threefold. First, the rising numbers of women and children in the ship lists parallel that of men.⁸³ Moreover, the frequency with which the same last names appeared sequentially in ship lists did not change significantly during this period, although there are indications that pairings of fathers and sons gave way to combinations of brothers and cousins.⁸⁴ This internal documentary evidence about the large number of families is further corroborated by the research of those who have traced passengers on the ship lists to their places of origin.⁸⁵ These investigations have demonstrated very high incidences of extended family migration; in addition, they have found that neighbors tended to travel—and settle—together and that families relied on the exploration of one or more of their members before all or most of them, in smaller groups or individually, followed later. When German migration resumed after 1763, the pattern changed. Although throughout the eighteenth-century migration, there were always ships that carried relatively large numbers of single, young men, the proportion of this kind of passenger rose during the twelve years preceding the Revolution. The decline of the number of families arriving in Philadelphia in this late period is evident from relatively much sharper decreases in the numbers of women and children compared to those of men and also from the falling incidences of the same last name appearing in sequential order on the ship lists.

Yet how much does the flow and composition of the German immigration through Philadelphia reflect the movement of Germans to all the North American mainland colonies? In sheer numbers, the stream to the Delaware valley represents three-quarters of the total flow, or about 76,500 immigrants through Philadelphia compared with a total of 101,900 German newcomers estimated before 1783.⁸⁶ The distribution over time and place of the estimated 25,400 immigrants who landed in colonies other than Pennsylvania, furthermore, also follows a distinctive pattern (see fig. 7.1). It repeatedly reflects a strong local lure of initial settlement that failed for some reason to generate direct immigration over the long term. The first such peak occurred in 1710 and involved the settlement of "Palatines" from the 1709 mass exodus in New York and North Carolina. The second total colonial peak around 1720, which includes the migration of about 2,000 Germans to French Louisiana, falls, strictly speaking, outside of the parameters of the German immigration to the British colonies of North America but conforms to the model of unsustained flows outside of the Delaware valley.[87] In the 1730s, Germans landed in a variety of ports to settle in Georgia,[88] the Carolinas,[89] and New York. As these widely scattered experiments explored settlement opportunities outside of Pennsylvania, their combined numbers almost equaled those of immigrants headed for Philadelphia in some years. In the boom around 1740, sporadic direct migration to Georgia and the Carolinas was renewed and New England also tried to lure foreign Protestants, but overall, the numbers were small. When German migration to America peaked between 1749 and 1755, the "spillover" effect in the ports of entry other than Philadelphia was most pronounced. During that period, almost 2,400 Germans landed in Nova Scotia; 1,500 in New England; 1,700 in New York; 600 in Maryland and Virginia; 4,300 in the Carolinas; and 500 in Georgia.[90] When migration resumed in 1763 after the Seven Years War, South Carolina attracted most immigrants outside of Philadelphia, but in the mid-1760s, these arrivals numbered in the hundreds rather than the thousands during the peak in 1752. After 1720, Pennsylvania's increasingly numerous and prosperous population of ethnic Germans and the success of Philadelphia merchants in establishing a profitable trade in German passengers to the Delaware valley which effectively barred competition from outsiders[91] created a persistent dominance of Philadelphia over other ports of entry.

In comparing the whole transatlantic German migration flow to America with the portion that came through Philadelphia, the overall pull of the Delaware valley proves to have been overwhelming and to have dominated the pattern of immigration in terms of both numbers and composition, even though there were scattered years when other colonies competed successfully with Pennsylvania for emigrants from Germany (1710, 1720, 1735, 1752, 1766). Since this one port's role was so dominant, two questions about the representativeness of the Philadelphia ship lists take on critical importance. How complete is this compilation of German immigrants' names arranged by ship and its date of arrival in Philadelphia, and how accurate is it? The answer about the completeness of the ship lists is fairly simple. Gleanings from a variety of sources, ranging from shipping contracts registered in Rotterdam to Philadelphia newspapers,[92] reveal that relatively few ships carrying German passengers escaped the registry procedure set for Pennsylvania. For the period covered by the ship lists (1727–1775), only thirty-one ships (8.33%) were omitted from the list,[93] mostly because they arrived with many sick passengers on board or with too few immigrants altogether to submit to the normal registration procedure of which the ship lists are the administrative results.[94] Other ships escaped inclusion because they were misrouted, wrecked, or encountered other serious problems during the voyage.[95]

The answer about the inclusiveness of the record of passengers who appear in the ship lists as compared with the migrants leaving southwestern Germany is more complicated. Two different kinds of evidence about emigration nonetheless suggest that fairly high percentages of emigrants in fact appear on the ship lists. The most fruitful approach to matching emigration records with the immigration lists is the painstaking exploitation of local records, mostly church records. This has been done for two areas in Germany.[96] The results from these efforts show that 90 percent of the emigrants headed to America who appear as such in the records of the northern Kraichgau and the western Palatinate can be traced to the Philadelphia ship lists.[97] Although the superiority of local records over regional compilations is undisputed in the search for German emigrants, documents for the larger geographic units, too, provide an important, even if flawed, collective perspective. When cross-referencing the migrants who are listed as destined for the colonies in the regional records of Baden and Breisgau with the Philadelphia ship lists, almost two-thirds have been identified as newcomers to the Delaware valley;[98] and that percentage is probably substantially too low since the names of women and children are much underrepresented on the ship lists. Based on the regional records of the Rheinpfalz and Saarland,[99] only one-third of the emigrants who indicated they were going to America are known to have taken the route through Philadelphia.[100] The reasons for these regional differences are as yet unclear. They may simply reflect differences in record keeping.[101] They also indicate that Philadelphia was not a uniformly popular destination among those bound for the American colonies. Other evidence, such as the emigration from the canton of Zurich,[102] suggests that certain areas in southwestern Germany—following the lead of successful local pioneers—established distinct preferences for a particular

American colony or settlement. Whatever the reasons for such distinct patterns of distribution, however, the percentage of those who migrated through Philadelphia and appear in the ship lists was very high. Consequently, this compilation represents a very important source for the study of the eighteenth-century German flow to the American colonies.

Despite the homeland variations by region that may have shaped the distribution of German immigrants among the different gateways for settlement in the American colonies, Philadelphia received about three-quarters of the migration. Furthermore, the flow and composition of migrants into this port is relatively well documented and hence offers some important insights into how the migration dispersed and adjusted after newcomers landed in Philadelphia. In the early years, before the registration of German immigrants became regular in 1727, most Germans arrived with their families in groups including coreligionists or neighbors and settled in Pennsylvania, some as close to Philadelphia as Germantown and others out at the frontier. As more Germans followed the example of the pioneering groups after 1727, settlement was pushed first westward and then south into Maryland, Virginia, and the Carolinas.[103] Germans newly arrived in Philadelphia had to travel increasingly farther to reach areas where land was still cheap. This was in a phase of the migration when proportionately fewer immigrants brought with them the resources to farm independently right away. Since an increasing number of German immigrants financed their relocation with the help of relatives or former neighbors, who redeemed their passage debts on arrival in Philadelphia, fewer were free to follow their own inclination when choosing where to set up farm or shop. Their place and initial mode of adaptation to New World life were governed temporarily by the local market for German help, especially within the social and ethnic network established from Pennsylvania southward by previous German immigrants, not just a general Pennsylvania labor market.[104]

In midcentury, at the height of the immigration, thousands of Germans arrived each fall, and a large proportion of them depended on fellow countrymen to pay for their move across the Atlantic and to employ and subsidize them during the first years in the New World. Many immigrants found that when they indentured their children, much of the family's debt on arrival could be paid off and some of the cost of starting out anew was lowered because the children were taken care of in someone else's household. Although this financing strategy for relocation to America was common among German immigrants, three-fourths of whom traveled in family groups,[105] it is uncertain how much they viewed indentured servitude for themselves or their children as an employment opportunity, as an educational opportunity, or as a last resort. It is clear, however, that the willingness of other Germans already established in the colonies to invest in the future labor of newly arrived immigrants was a crucial element in fueling the migration. Without this incentive, the pool of potential immigrants to a given place in America remained relatively small, and merchants found it unprofitable to offer fares on credit unless they could count on others to assume the risk.[106] Once this mechanism was tried and proven, it remained in place even when the influx of Germans slowed rapidly in the twelve years preceding the American Revolution. Since it was the transaction of shippers to Pennsylvania and the now large existing German community of the Delaware valley which established the effective way to bring in German settlers and place them not only satisfactorily but profitably into New World life, the role of Philadelphia remained central even as the bulk of new settlement moved largely southward out of Pennsylvania.

The significance of Philadelphia as the most popular port of entry for German immigrants to the American colonies is twofold. After a slow start, its dominance in the German passenger trade remained unsurpassed for five decades, from the 1720s to the 1770s. Although the successful promotion of Pennsylvania in the 1680s had stimulated similar approaches for a number of German settlement projects in several other colonies, only Pennsylvania succeeded eventually in drawing a steady and growing number of German immigrants. A solid reputation for opportunity, the willingness of those already settled in the province to assist newcomers in relocating and starting a new life, and the readiness of some Rotterdam merchants to adapt the English system of transporting indentured servants to America to the characteristics of the German migration for the sake of profiting from the transatlantic transportation of German passengers as part of their complex trade, all came together to create a system that allowed large numbers of emigrants of limited means to move to the New World under conditions both more intricate and more flexible than the trade of African slaves or the seventeenth-century model of servitude for English and Irish single, young adults.

The mechanisms of favorable information, family, local, and ethnic networks, and cheap dependable transportation worked to coordinate and capitalize on the forces of push and pull in getting German migrants across the Atlantic. They also regulated the ways in which German settlement was channeled first into Philadelphia and its hinterland and then beyond the Delaware valley to western Pennsylvania and southwest to the Great Valley. Families of coreligionists and neighbors tended to settle and move together. As they made their homes farther away from Philadelphia, they drew more family members, friends, and former neighbors to join them. As the distances to new settlements grew longer from Philadelphia, however, more German immigrants depended on outside help to finance their relocation and more newcomers or recently freed servants found it increasingly harder to obtain land cheaply. Since this decline of opportunities in the American colonies coincided with vigorous recruiting efforts to settle lands in Eastern Europe, the transatlantic flow of Germans ebbed, and those who continued to be drawn to the West seem either to have followed in the footsteps of relatives and former neighbors or to have taken advantage of a well-established migration path. Other colonies desirous of German settlers—the Carolinas, Maine, Nova Scotia, and even New York—did not succeed, before the Revolution, in establishing the kind of interacting system of merchant profitability and ethnic reinforcement that made Philadelphia the colonial center of German entry to America.

This distinctive pattern of the German migration through Philadelphia, finally, foreshadowed in three important ways later movements from Europe to America. The systematic role of the merchants, who devised a profitable system of cheap transportion that allowed potential emigrants to take advantage of opportunities overseas, became a standard feature of such migrations. The willingness of the pioneering groups and their descendants to assist financially poor relatives and countrymen with their relocation constituted another dynamic crucial in generating and maintaining the migration flow. This was achieved among colonial Germans by redeeming passage debts, while the mechanism for nineteenth-century immigrant groups was to send prepaid tickets. The third change introduced in the German migration through Philadelphia in its early and peak phases was the large proportion of families among the newcomers.[107] This differed from most British and Irish migrations in the seventeenth century (except for prosperous religious minorities like the Puritans and Quakers) but was repeated in the late eighteenth-century migration of Ulster Scots and then in many other subsequent flows, starting with family relocation before shifting toward more single young men and women. In its characteristic patterns of constituting a major business, counting heavily on ethnic identity and support, and building on family migration rather than merely a job market for young single adults, then, the German immigration to the British colonies of North America presages the nature of many later mass migrations from Europe to the Americas.

Notes

1. It is important to remember throughout that the German-speaking immigrants represented a diverse group of settlers who spoke many different dialects of German. In English eyes, however, this diversity was largely lost, as all German-speaking settlers were simply "Dutch" or "Palatine" foreigners.

2. For an assessment of recent estimates of Irish immigration to America, see Marianne S. Wokeck, "Irish Immigration to the Delaware Valley before the American Revolution," in David B. Quinn, ed., *Ireland and America, 1500–1700* (forthcoming).

3. A still useful classic statement about nineteenth-century European mass migration to the United States is Marcus Lee Hansen, *The Atlantic Migration, 1607–1860: A History of the Continuing Settlement of the United States* (Cambridge, Mass., 1940).

4. Two notable examples are Andreas Blocher, *Die Eigenart der Zürcher Auswanderer nach Amerika, 1734–1744* (Zurich, 1976), and Wolfgang von Hippel, *Auswanderung aus Südwestdeutschland* (Stuttgart, 1984).

5. E.g., Carl Wittke, *We Who Built America* (Cleveland, rev. ed. 1964 [orig. publ. 1939]); Albert B. Faust, *The German Element in the United States with Special Reference to Its Political, Moral, Social, and Educational Influence* (New York, rev. ed. 1927 [orig. publ. 1909]); William T. Parsons, *The Pennsylvania Dutch: A Persistent Minority* (Boston, 1976).

6. Recently, A. G. Roeber commented on the underdeveloped state of German scholarship about the migration to the American colonies in "In German Ways? Problems and Potentials of Eighteenth-Century Social and Emigration History," *William and Mary Quarterly*, 3d ser., 44 (1987): 750–774.

7. See Allan Kulikoff's lament about the methodologically unsystematic nature of migration studies as reflected in the recent literature, "Migration and Cultural Diffusion in Early America, 1600–1860," *Historical Methods Newsletter* 19 (1986): 153–169.

8. For an example of the latter, see Harald Runblom and Hans Norman, eds., *From Sweden to America: A History of the Migration. A Collective Work of the Uppsala Migration Research Project* (Minneapolis, 1976).

9. For recent discussions, see David W. Galenson, *White Servitude in Colonial America* (Cambridge, 1981), and James Horn, "Servant Emigration to the Chesapeake in the Seventeenth Century," in Thad W. Tate and David L. Ammerman, *The Chesapeake in the Seventeenth Century* (Chapel Hill, 1979), 51–95.

10. See, e.g., Herbert S. Klein, *The Middle Passage: Comparative Studies in the Atlantic Slave Trade* (Princeton, 1978).

11. See, e.g., Charlotte Erickson, *English Immigration to America*, Ellis Island Series (New York, forthcoming); Audrey Lockhart, *Some Aspects of Emigration from Ireland to the North American Colonies between 1660 and 1775* (New York, 1976); Robert J. Dickson, *Ulster Emigration to Colonial America, 1718–1775* (London, 1966).

12. This estimate is based on Hans Fenske, "International Migration: Germany in the Eighteenth Century," *Central European History* 13 (1980): 344–346. It should be noted that Fenske treats the German migration to Prussia as intranational and that he does not include migration from Switzerland in his estimates.

13. Although the concept of core and periphery has recently gained much popularity, it does not fit in this German context. Bernard Bailyn, *Voyagers to the West* (New York, 1986), 8–28.

14. See, e.g., Wilhelm Abel, *Geschichte der deutschen Landwirtschaft vom frühen Mittelalter bis zum 19. Jahrhundert*, 2d rev. ed., Deutsche Agrargeschichte, vol. 2 (Stuttgart, 1967); Karl Kollnig, *Wandlungen im Bevölkerungsraum des pfälzischen Oberrheingebiets* (Heidelberg, 1952).

15. See, e.g., Heinz Schuchmann, *Schweizer Einwanderer im frühen kurpfälzischen Streubesitz des Kraichgaus*, Schriften zur Wanderungsgeschichte der Pfälzer, no. 18 (Kriserslautern, 1963).

16. See, e.g., Werner Hacker, *Auswanderung aus dem südöstlichen Schwarzwald zwischen Hochrhein, Baar und Kinzig insbesondere nach*

Südosteuropa im 17. und 18. Jahrhundert (Munich, 1975); Ernst Kirsten, *Raum und Bevölkerung in der Weltgeschichte*, vol. 1. Bevölkerungs-Ploetz, 3d ed. (Würzburg, 1965), 101.

17. Lowell Colton Benion, "Flight from the Reich: A Geographic Exposition of Southwest German Emigration, 1683–1815" (Ph.D. dissertation, Syracuse University, 1971, esp. chaps. 3 and 5). Analysis of two regional emigration listings confirm this conclusion. Migration from Baden and Breisgau to the American colonies follows a distinct pattern of peaks and troughs over time which differs from that set by migrants to America from the Rheinpfalz and Saarland. Werner Hacker, *Auswanderungen aus Baden und Breisgau: Obere und mittlere Oberrheinlande im 18. Jahrhundert archivalisch dokumentiert* (Stuttgart, 1980); *Auswanderungen aus Rheinpfalz und Saarland im 18. Jahrhundert* (Stuttgart, 1987).

18. Fenske estimated that in the eighteenth century, about 800,000 Germans relocated permanently over long distances. Fenske, "International Migration," 13: 344–346.

19. Benion, "Flight from the Reich," figs. 5–2, 5–3, 5–4.

20. See, e.g., ibid., 305–307.

21. Hacker chronicles years of crises for Baden and Breisgau and the Rheinpfalz and Saarland. Those years correlate somewhat with peaks in emigration, but the fit is far from satisfying. Hacker, *Auswanderungen aus Baden und Breisgau*, 34–41; *Auswanderungen aus Rheinpflaz und Saarland*, 23–26, 28–29.

22. Analysis of the nineteenth-century migration of Swedes to America called attention to the cumulative importance of a general acceptance of long-range mobility as a response to adverse conditions—most certainly a situation given in eighteenth-century southwestern Germany. Similarly, in Ireland, where overseas migration was generally well established, migration to colonial America increased in response to specific unfavorable conditions, especially when bad harvests and economic recession occurred simultaneously. Runblom and Norman, *From Sweden to America*, 318; Louis Michael Cullen, "Economic Development, 1691–1800," in T. W. Moody and W. E. Vaughan, eds., *A New History of Ireland* (Oxford, 1986), 4: 144–151, 162.

23. These periods often coincided with the onset of peace; in the case of the eighteenth-century German migration to America, most notably the end of the War of Austrian Succession in 1748.

24. John Dick, who sought German Protestants for Nova Scotia, and Samuel Waldo, who competed with him to win settlers for Maine, both learned that merely publicizing an attractive settlement offer was insufficient bait to get potential emigrants to sign up for their respective proj-

ects. Winthrop Pichard Bell, *The "Foreign Protestants" and the Settlement of Nova Scotia: The History of a Piece of Arrested British Colonial Policy in the Eighteenth Century* (Toronto, 1961), 132–142; H. A. Rattermann, "Geschichte des deutschen Elements im Staate Maine," *Der deutsche Pionier: Erinnerungen aus dem Pionier-Leben der Deutschen in Amerika*, vols. 14–16.

25. Conversely, the withdrawal of such support seriously hindered recruiting efforts, and an outright ban on recruiting stopped most agents from operating.

26. For example, John Dick explained to the Board of Trade in 1751 that he needed a document that legitimized his status as their official representative because his competitors claimed such status for themselves and had thus unfairly won the support of the local authorities. Bell, "Foreign Protestants," 168, 170–171.

27. Taverns and public houses in general were places where recruiting efforts naturally concentrated and where handbills describing a settlement project or announcing the dates of departure could be posted, subscription lists could be kept, and emigrants traveling together to larger collection places could conveniently gather.

28. It is difficult to assess how much the support of a man of local prominence figured into the decisionmaking of potential emigrants; Bell, "Foreign Protestants," 167. For example, Heinrich Ehrenfried Luther—a well-connected printer and newspaperman who actively supported Samuel Waldo's settlement scheme in the middle of the eighteenth century—was only moderately successful in winning settlers for Maine; Ratterman, "Geschichte des deutschen Elements im Staate Maine." Conversely, potential emigrants also interpreted official warnings and recruiting bans as signs of defensive reaction to particularly attractive settlement offers.

29. The importance of favorable reports home was widely recognized. Consequently, recruiters were often quite ingenious in securing letters that could serve as invitations, while officials intent on curbing recruitment efforts strove to confiscate such communications and published instead those that talked of difficulties and disappointments. See, e.g., Bell, "Foreign Protestants," 156, 184.

30. See Benion, "Flight from the Reich," fig. 5–4, for the areas of out-migration at that time; and Fenske, "International Migration," 344–346, for the estimated number of migrants.

31. Richard S. Dunn and Mary Maples Dunn, eds., *The Papers of William Penn* (Philadelphia, 1982–1987), 2: 591–597, 5: 264–269, 276, 302–307, 320–323.

32. The workings of this network is the focus of William I. Hull,

William Penn and the Dutch Quaker Migration to Pennsylvania (Swarthmore, 1935).

33. Francis Louis Michel negotiated with William Penn, among others, for land for settlement and the exploitation of mines. He toured the colonies twice on exploratory trips in the early 1700s to find the most suitable location for his venture. Johann Rudolph Ochs, a Bernese seal cutter who settled in London in 1711, was convinced of the potential of German settlement in Pennsylvania and actively supported such projects. Georg Ritter, a member of the Bernese town council, won the approval of the Bernese authorities in 1705 to propose to the English government his plans to transport about 500 persons to settle in America. Christoph von Graffenried, son of a Bernese patrician and founder of New Bern, North Carolina, sought land in America to ameliorate his financial situation. Ritter's and Graffenried's ventures came to fruition at the time of the 1709 exodus from the Palatinate; they took advantage of this exceptional source of settlers and transported 650 Palatines to North Carolina. *The Papers of William Penn*, 4: 600, 602n, 606, 635, 639, 666, 674–675; William J. Hinke, ed., "Report on the Journey of Franz Louis Michel, from Berne, Switzerland, to Virginia, October 2, 1701–December 1, 1702," *Virginia Magazine of History and Biography*, 24 (1916): 1–43, 113–141, 275–288; Leo Schelbert, "Swiss Migration to America: The Swiss Mennonites" (Ph.D. dissertation, Columbia University, 1966), 155–161, 165–166.

34. As noted above, Michel, Ochs, Ritter, and Graffenried differed considerably in their motivations for becoming involved in settlement projects in the American colonies.

35. In 1708 and 1709, the Bernese authorities, for example, sought to deport unwanted Anabaptists by way of settling them in the American colonies. Schelbert, "Swiss Migration to America," 178–181.

36. Archibald Hope and his sons, Isaac and Zachary, were most prominent in the early years of German migration to the American colonies. Their firm remained active in the trade almost throughout the entire colonial period. For their Quaker connections, see Jacob M. Price, "The Great Quaker Business Families of Eighteenth-Century London: The Rise and Fall of a Sectarian Patriciate," in Richard S. Dunn and Mary Maples Dunn, eds., *The World of William Penn* (Philadelphia, Pa., 1986), 261, 263, 375.

37. The standard work on the 1709 mass exodus is still Walter Knittle, *Early Eighteenth-Century Palatine Emigration* (Baltimore, repr. ed. 1966); see also, Henry Z. Jones, Jr., *The Palatine Families of New York: A Study of the German Immigrants Who Arrived in Colonial New York in 1710*, 2 vols. (Universal City, Calif., 1985).

38. "Copies of Dutch documents at Rotterdam and The Hague relating to early German immigration, 1709," Dutch West Indies Company, box 3, folder 8, Historical Society of Pennsylvania, Philadelphia, Pa.

39. Pennsylvania in the end received only a few of the Palatines who emigrated in 1709. *The Papers of William Penn*, 4: 657.

40. Henry Z. Jones and John P. Dern, "Palatine Emigrants Returning in 1710," *Pfälzer—Palatines*, Beiträge zur Bevölkerungsgeschichte der Pfalz, vol. 2, ed. Karl Scherer (Kaiserslautern, 1981), 53–77.

41. Many of the published reports that had lured these migrants from southwestern Germany to the American colonies were conveniently bound together as a book that had a title page with golden lettering, hence the name. Knittle, *Palatine Emigration*, 14.

42. In the mass exodus of 1709, Palatine emigrants were shipped from Rotterdam to England in vessels used for the transport of military troops. Under normal circumstances, Germans bound for the American colonies found passage to England in ships on their return voyage after carrying a variety of commodities from English ports to Rotterdam. As long as Queen Anne's liberal naturalization law was in effect (1710–11), emigrants generally journeyed to London before sailing to America. After 1712, direct routes across to America—with a stopover in Cowes to satisfy the requirements of the navigation laws and to take on additional supplies—became the norm.

43. See, e.g., the July 2, 1722, charter party between Thomas Pillans, shipper, Richard Cupitt, captain, and George Peter Hillengass, Jacob Vollenweiler, and Daniel Hill for 53 or 54 persons with their chests, provisions, and baggage. O[ude] N[otariel] A[rchief] 2096/333, Gemeentelijke Archiefdienst Rotterdam.

44. Graffenried, for example, had such a leadership role, even though the English government agreed in the end to pay for the transportation of the Palatines to North Carolina. Schelbert, "Swiss Migration," 165.

45. These were primarily the Palatine emigrants of 1709 who were eventually settled in New York and North Carolina.

46. Knittle, *Palatine Emigration*, 169, 181–185.

47. Since William Penn and especially his continental agent, Benjamin Furly, recognized the value of promotional literature, they published extensive information about Pennsylvania. A number of their tracts found wide distribution and made Pennsylvania known beyond the circles of Quakers and those sympathetic to them. For some examples of this promotional literature about Pennsylvania, see *The Papers of William Penn*, 5: 264–269, 276, 302–307, 320–323.

48. New York gained a bad reputation among emigrants not only because of the poor treatment the Palatines received there as government

redemptioners but also because the land policy of the colony made it difficult for immigrants to obtain land in their own right. Although conditions for acquiring land were better in the Carolinas than in New York, generally circumstances were less favorable than in Pennsylvania. Nevertheless, largely Swiss settlers continued to migrate there until the middle of the century when a generous land bounty system attracted more migrants from Germany. By comparison, Georgia, which had become the new home of Protestants from Salzburg after their crisis in 1732, drew numerically relatively few additional German settlers. Altogether less than 3,000 Germans settled in Georgia up to the end of the American war of independence. Schelbert, "Swiss Migration to America," 96; George F. Jones, *The Germans of Colonial Georgia, 1733–1783* (Baltimore, 1986).

49. The Mennonites are a case in point. Through the Committee for Foreign Needs, the Mennonites in Rotterdam and Amsterdam supported their brethren in the Palatinate and other territories along the Rhine and lent assistance to those who had decided to migrate to Pennsylvania. They were, however, reluctant to finance the move outright and discouraged large-scale migration. Many of the letters exchanged between the committee and the leaders of Mennonite communities on the Rhine are collected in the Gemeente Archief Amsterdam and have been microfilmed (European Mennonites, A[msterdam] A[rchives], #1321, Lancaster Mennonite Historical Society, Lancaster, Penn.).

50. The importance of such personal communications can hardly be overstated. An early example of a very detailed and influential report home is the letter of Francis Daniel Pastorius to his friends, dated 7 March 1684, published in part in *William Penn and the Founding of Pennsylvania, 1680–1684: A Documentary History*, ed. by Jean R. Soderlund (Philadelphia, 1983), 352–360.

51. Total relocation costs per adult probably ranged from £10 to £15 sterling, depending on the distance to be covered getting to Rotterdam and moving out from Philadelphia to settle and the overall time spent in transit. Consequently, a family of five with three young teenage children, who would pay half fare, needed at least £50 for the journey and still had to have some reserves for getting started after landing in Philadelphia. For a discussion of the cost of the transatlantic voyage, see chap. 4 of Wokeck, *The Trade in Strangers: Transporting Germans and Irish to Colonial America: Precursors of Modern Atlantic Migrations*, forthcoming (a revision and expansion of my dissertation, "A Tide of Alien Tongues: The Flow and Ebb of German Immigration to Pennsylvania," Temple University, 1982).

52. In addition, Pennsylvania rewarded such investment in the early

years of the colony with 50 acres for the master and 50 acres for the servant at the end of his or her term.

53. David W. Galenson, *White Servitude in Colonial America* (Cambridge, Mass., 1981); Wokeck, *The Trade in Strangers*, forthcoming, chap. 6.

54. In the *American Weekly Mercury* (18 December 1722), an advertisement appeared that offered "100 Palatines... for Five Years each, any one paying their Passage-Money at Ten Pounds per Head. If any of their Friends, the Dutch at Conestoga have a mind to have or clear them."

55. A report in the *Pennsylvania Gazette* (6–13 January 1729/30) gives the number of servants among Irish immigrants who arrived during the previous year, but it lists none among German arrivals in that same period.

56. See, e.g., the advertisement in English and German in the *Pennsylvania Gazette* (7 February 1739/40) asking passengers—by name—to pay their outstanding fare debts.

57. See, e.g., the contract for passengers on the ship *Pennsylvania Packet* (February 16, 1773), "Redemptioners, Philadelphia, 1750–1830" (Society Miscellaneous Collection, Historical Society of Pennsylvania, Philadelphia, Penn.)

58. See Wokeck, "The Experience of Indentured Servants from Germany and Ireland: Guaranteed Employment, Educational Opportunity, or Last Resort?" *The Report* 40 (1986): 57–76; Farley Grubb, "The Market for Indentured Immigrants: Evidence on the Efficiency of Forward-Labor Contracting in Philadelphia, 1745–1773," *Journal of Economic History* 45 (1985): 855–868.

59. For examples of creative accounting by merchants to achieve this, see Wokeck, "A Tide of Alien Tongues," 225.

60. Analysis of the records of indentures that have survived for Philadelphia suggests that masters who purchased indentured servants had definite preferences for immigrants of particular ethnic backgrounds. Wokeck, "The Experience of Indentured Servants," 73.

61. For Nova Scotia, see Bell, "*Foreign Protestants*"; for New England, see Rattermann, "Geschichte des deutschen Elements im Staate Maine"; for South Carolina, see Robert L. Meriwether, *The Expansion of South Carolina, 1729–1765* (Philadelphia, repr. ed. 1974).

62. Exceptions were the Swiss transports to the Carolinas and those of the refugees from Salzburg to Georgia.

63. Gottlieb Mittelberger's account, *Journey to Pennsylvania*, ed. by Oscar Handlin and trans. by John Clive (Cambridge, Mass., 1960), is an overpublicized case in point.

64. On application to leave the country, most territorial authorities included the value of future inheritances in the assessment when they calculated the amount of manumission and emigration tax. Given this practice, many emigrants had an interest in keeping in touch with their relatives and were eager to collect their already taxed inheritances when they fell due. Also, in this clumsy bureaucratic manner, the local authorities contributed to the maintenance of ties between Germany and America, which in turn fueled one of the most effective recruiting mechanisms for future emigration from those territories, namely, the stream of newlanders returning to collect inheritances but at the same time building the reputation of opportunities to be had in the American colonies.

65. On average, farms in the American colonies were considerably larger than those even middling farmers worked in Germany. What most reports about American farms omitted, however, was how much—or rather how little—of those impressive acreages were under cultivation.

66. See, e.g., the advertisements offering such services in *Der Hoch-Deutsch Pennsylvanische Geschichts-Schreiber* (16 November 1746, 16 November 1752) and in the bilingual *Lancaster Gazette/Lancasterische Zeitung* (3 October 1752).

67. The practice of importing goods for resale dated back to the early years of German immigration to Philadelphia. "The Palatines have brought very many goods with them so that many a man has made up to 600fl [about £45 sterling] by this trip, for everything was free, because it was not examined." Johann Christopher Sauer, 1 December 1724, *Pennsylvania Magazine of History and Biography* 45 (1921): 253.

68. The lists that form the basis of Blocher's study about the emigrants from Zurich, for example, are the result of official concern about the magnitude of the migration and the spread of the "Carolinian fever" as they called it. Blocher, *Die Eigenart der Zürcher Auswanderer*.

69. The merchants' petitions for the required bonds were subsequently published annually in *Resolutien von den Heeren Staaten von Holland en West-freisland* and *Resolutien von de H[oogh] M[ogende] H[eeren] Staaten General der Vereeinigte de Nederlandsche Provincien*.

70. For details, see Wokeck, *The Trade in Strangers*, forthcoming, chap. 5.

71. See, e.g., the advertisement in *Der Hoch-Deutsch Pennsylvanische Geschichts-Schreiber* (16 November 1752).

72. See John Dick's description of this in Bell, "*Foreign Protestants*," 135.

73. Most German settlements in the Carolinas, Georgia, New England, and Nova Scotia fall in this semiofficial category.

74. Johann Philip Buch, for instance, was a boatman of Wertheim

and also an emigrant agent. In 1754, he recruited passengers for the Hopes who paid him almost 5s. per head. Don Yoder, *Pennsylvania German Immigrants, 1709–1786: Lists Consolidated from Yearbooks of The Pennsylvania Folklore Society* (Baltimore, 1980).

75. Any kind of government redemptioner system, like the settlement project for Nova Scotia, was the exception to this scenario.

76. For a brief summary of this procedure, see Fenske, "International Migration," 342; and in more detail, Hacker, *Auswanderungen aus Baden und Breisgau*, 84–88, 107–112, 133; *Auswanderungen aus Rheinpfalz und Saarland*, 45–49, 51–54, 58–59, 83–86.

77. Consequently, territorial authorities would charge extra manumission taxes to discourage emigration or forgive the payment of taxes to encourage emigration. For some examples, see Hacker, *Auswanderungen aus Baden und Breisach*, 179–180, 192; *Auswanderungen aus Rheinpfalz und Saarland*, 108, 109, 114, 147.

78. Hacker's efforts in this regard have been particularly monumental. *Auswanderungen aud Baden und Breisach* and *Auswanderungen aus Rheinpfalz und Saarland*, which I used for my analysis, are only two of a number of regional archival studies that Hacker completed for southwestern Germany. Annette Kunselman Burgert, *Eighteenth-Century Emigrants*, 1: The Northern Kraichgau (Breiningsville, Pa., 1983), and 2: The Western Palatinate (Birdsboro, Pa., 1985), represent two studies that draw heavily on local archives, in particular church records. Don Yoder, ed., *Pennsylvania German Immigrants; Rhineland Emigrants: List of German Settlers in Colonial America* (Baltimore, repr. ed. 1981) as well as Albert B. Faust and Gaius M. Brumbaugh, eds., *Lists of Swiss Emigrants in the Eighteenth Century to the American Colonies* (Baltimore, repr. ed. 1976) conveniently gather much important information culled from many archival sources.

79. These were probably mostly young single men and women.

80. Most colonies kept no systematic records about immigrants. Newcomers can often be traced only because they applied for land or because they came as servants and their indentures were registered in the courts. See, e.g., Janie Revill, comp., *A Compilation of the Original Lists of Protestant Immigrants to South Carolina, 1763–1773* (Baltimore, repr. ed. 1968), and George W. Neible, ed., "Servants and Apprentices Bound and Assigned before James Hamilton Mayor of Philadelphia, 1745," *Pennsylvania Magazine of History and Biography* 30–32 (1906–1908).

81. Ralph Beaver Strassburger, *Pennsylvania German Pioneers: A Publication of the Original Lists of Arrivals in the Port of Philadelphia from 1727–1808*, ed. by William J. Hinke (Baltimore, repr. ed. 1966);

for an analysis of these lists, see Wokeck, "The Flow and the Composition of German Immigration to Philadelphia, 1727–1775," *Pennsylvania Magazine of History and Biography* 105 (1981): 249–278.

82. The following description of the German migration to Philadelphia is based on Wokeck, "The Flow and the Composition."

83. Wokeck, "The Flow and the Composition," figs. 2.a, b.

84. Ibid., fig. 2.c.

85. Burgert, *Eighteenth-Century Emigrants*; Hacker, *Auswanderungen aus Breisgau und Baden* and *Auswanderungen aus Rheinpfalz und Saarland*; Yoder, *Pennsylvania German Immigrants; Rhineland Emigrants*.

86. My estimates on the number of immigrants through Philadelphia and the rest of the American colonies are based on a wide variety of sources. For Philadelphia, Strassburger/Hinke's *Pennsylvania German Pioneers* forms the backbone as does the relevant secondary literature on immigration for the rest of the colonies. Systematic gleanings from colonial Pennsylvania newspapers, the charter parties registered in Rotterdam, shipping information published in *Lloyd's Lists*, and entries in English portbooks added to and corroborated details from those sources about ships and the passengers they carried. Contemporary estimates and listings of ships or passengers were an additional source of information. Drawing an all those sources, I compiled a master list of ships that carried Germans across the Atlantic and calculated the number of passengers they carried for each year. A table summarizing my estimates and detailing the sources on which they are based forms a substantial part of chap. 2 of *Trade in Strangers*, forthcoming.

87. Fenske, "International Migration," 344n; Benion, "Flight from the Reich," 196.

88. Jones, *The Germans of Colonial Georgia*, xiii.

89. Meriwether, *The Expansion of South Carolina*, 19–26, 34–35.

90. An additional 1,400 emigrants are known to have left Europe, but their ships encountered disasters along the way, and few of those migrants made it to America.

91. For instance, John Hunt of London together with James and John Pemberton of Philadelphia entered the booming German immigrant trade in the late 1740s and early 1750s, but because of the competition from the established firms, even these major commercial figures did not succeed in making a profit and withdrew from that trade. Hunt & Greenleafe Letterbook; James Pemberton to John Pemberton, Pemberton Papers, vol. 5, Historical Society of Pennsylvania, Philadelphia, Pa.

92. See comment on sources, n. 78, above.

93. For the period 1683 to 1775, 48 ships (12.9%) are not found

among the 324 ships for which immigrant lists have survived, but that includes the four decades before registration was mandatory. Evidence for the ships not included in the ship lists was derived from gleanings of the sources listed in n. 78, above.

94. See, e.g., the ships *Rachel* and *Francis & Elizabeth*; Strassburger/Hinke, *Pennsylvania German Pioneers*, 1: 409.

95. See, for example, the arrival of the survivors of the ill-fated ship *Love & Unity* wrecked off New England. Strassburger/Hinke. *Pennsylvania German Pioneers*, 1: 57.

96. The northern Kraichgau and the western Palatinate. Burgert, *Eighteenth-Century Emigrants*.

97. In this context, it is necessary to recall that the majority of ship lists omit the names of women and children.

98. Hacker, *Auswanderung aus Baden und Breisgau*.

99. Hacker, *Auswanderungen aus Rheinpfalz und Saarland*.

100. This percentage may also be too low because of the underrepresentation of women's and children's names on the ship lists, but the difference between the two regions remains significant.

101. Bureaucratic requirements to record the planned destinations of migrants varied from region to region and across time; individual officials interpreted such requirements differently, too; and migrants could be vague, if not untruthful, about their intentions.

102. In the 1730s and 1740s, the emigrants from Zurich were drawn to Carolina, not Pennsylvania. Blocher, *Die Eigenart der Zürcher Auswanderer*.

103. For a depiction of this growth pattern within and then out of the Delaware valley region, see James T. Lemon, *The Best Poor Man's Country: A Geographical Study of Early Southeastern Pennsylvania* (Baltimore, 1972).

104. For a focus on the Pennsylvania labor market, see Grubb, "The Market for Indentured Immigrants." Sharon V. Salinger, *"To Serve Well and Faithfully": Labor and Indentured Servitude in Pennsylvania, 1682–1800* (Cambridge, 1987) focuses, despite the title, on Philadelphia and does not include ethnicity in her analysis.

105. Of about 3,200 migrants known to have left the Rheinpfalz and Saarland for America between 1683 and 1776, almost three-quarters of them set out in family groups of an average of almost four persons; of about 1,100 migrants from Baden and Breisach identified with destinations in America, more than three-quarters of them left in family groups of an average of four persons. Hacker, *Auswanderungen aus Rheinpfalz und Saarland*; *Auswanderungen aus Baden und Breisach*.

106. While John Dick could persuade the English administration to pay for the fare of the Germans he shipped as government redemptioners to Nova Scotia, the majority of merchants in Rotterdam—the engine of the transportation system as a whole—relied on the willingness of American colonists, primarily previous German emigrants, to redeem the passage debts of immigrants traveling on credit.

107. In the migration of the 1770s from Great Britain, two distinct migration streams are discernible: one of young single men leaving mostly from London and one of families leaving mostly from more rural regions in the north of England and the west of Scotland. Both kinds of migration streams were represented in the German flow to the American colonies, but it still needs to be determined whether they originated from different local sources.

Contributors

Ida Altman (Ph.D., Johns Hopkins University) is associate professor of history at the University of New Orleans and author of *Emigrants and Society: Extremadura and Spanish America in the Sixteenth Century* (Los Angeles, Berkeley and Oxford, 1989).

James Horn (D.Phil, University of Sussex) is principal lecturer in history at Brighton Polytechnic in England and author of *Adapting to the New World: English Society in the Seventeenth-Century Chesapeake* (forthcoming).

A. Pieter Jacobs is completing his doctorate at the Catholic University of Nijmegen in the Netherlands. His dissertation is on migration movements between Spain and America in the early seventeenth century.

Leslie Choquette (Ph.D., Harvard University) is assistant professor of history at Assumption College in Massachusetts. Her doctoral thesis is a study of French emigration to Canada in the seventeenth and eighteenth centuries.

Christian Huetz de Lemps is professor and Director of the Tropical Space Research Center (C.R.E.T.) at the University of Bordeaux III in France. He is author of *Géographie du commerce de Bordeaux à la fin du règne de Louis XIV* (Paris and The Hague, 1975) and other works on the historical geography of tropical islands.

Marianne S. Wokeck (Ph.D., Temple University) is the founder and director of the Biographical Dictionary of Early Pennsylvania Legislators and author of a forthcoming book *The Trade in Strangers: Transporting Germans and Irish to Colonial America*.

Index

Acadia, French colonization of, 134, 136, 145, 146, 161. *See also* Nova Scotia
Acadie, Compagnie d', 144
Alsop, George, 11
Altman, Ida, 6, 20, 30
Anabaptists, 17, 216
Andalusia, 32
Anne, Queen, 215
Antilles, 137
Armadas, 75–76
Austria, 210, 211, 212

Baltimore, Lord, 93
Baptists, 17, 216
Basques, 5
Bennett, Edward, 86, 105, 106
Bennett, Richard, 106
Boleda, Mario, 162
Bordeaux, 140, 180, 185–186, 187, 188, 191, 196
Brenner, Robert, 94
Bristol, England, emigrants to Chesapeake from, 98–99
British emigrants: number of, 3, 4; socioeconomic status, 10. *See also* England; English emigrants; Irish emigrants; Scottish emigrants
British merchants: in Chesapeake, 85–87; in Rotterdam, 213, 214, 215, 216, 217–218, 219, 220, 221, 229–230
Buccaneering, by former servants, 178, 199

Cáceres, Spain, 5; economy, 33–34; effect of Peruvian conquest on, 36; emigration rates, 35–36, 40–41; emigration to Indies from, 37–53; local government, 34; return of emigrants to, from Indies, 50–51
Calvert family, 93
Canada: agricultural settlement of, 140, 145–146, 149, 150; climate of, 162; French emigration to, 18, 131–162; Québec, 134, 135, 136, 145, 146, 161
Caribbean Islands: British emigration to, 4, 5, 90; Spanish and Portuguese emigration to, 3
Castile, 31–33; emigration from, 4; Extremadura incorporated into, 35; impact of emigration on, 33. *See also* Extremadura region, Spain
Catholics, 89, 209, 210; English, 104–105; French, 140, 143, 144
Catlett, John, 113–114
Cent-Associés, Compagnie des, 135–137, 138, 140, 143
Central America, European emigration to, 3
Chesapeake, 7, 8; economic motives for emigration to, 111–116; elite of, 93–94; English emigration to, 85–118; map, 88; regional origins of free emigrants to, 96–100; religious motives for emigration to, 104–109
Child, Josiah, 9
Chile, emigration to, 5
Choquette, Leslie, 5, 7, 18, 131
Colbert, Jean Baptiste, 150, 157–158, 159
Communauté des Habitants, 137, 143
Condé, prince de, 135
Contracts, for indentured servants: French, 174–176, 192; German, 217–218

Cornwallis, Thomas, 93
Corvisier, André, 151
Council of the Indies, 60, 61
Criados. See Indentured servants, Spanish

Debien, Gabriel, 12, 178–179, 182
Delaware valley, German emigration to, 16, 216, 226, 228, 229, 230
de Monts, Pierre Du Gua, 134
d'Esnambuc, Captain, 173–174
Disease, 14, 15
Documents, falsification of, 70–74
du Tertre, Pere, 175–176, 177

Economic motives: of English emigrants, 15–17, 103–109, 111–116; of German emigrants, 209, 210; of Spanish emigrants, 33–34, 45–46
Eddis, William, 9
Emigration, European: government sanctioning of, 17–19; lack of research on, 2; magnitude of, 3–6; privately organized, 17, 19–20; timing of, 3–6; as two-stage process, 12. *See also* Migratory patterns
Engagés. *See* Indentured servants, French
England, 215; Bristol, 98–99; Germans in, 214; government policy on emigration, 19; overseas settlements of, 4; regional origin of emigrants to Chesapeake, 96–100. *See also* English emigrants
English emigrants, 231; age of, 101, 102; areas of settlement, 90; to Chesapeake, 85–118; correspondence of, 112–115; economic motives of, 15–17; family and friends of, 20, 91, 109–111, 116, 118; free, 85–118; gentry, 92, 93–94, 103, 110, 111; indentured servants, 7–12, 15, 91, 101, 117, 118, 230; merchants, 92, 93–94; motives for emigrating, 15–17, 103–109, 117–118; rates and patterns of, 16; regional origins of, 96–100; returnees, 115–117, 118; socioeconomic status of, 10; trades and professions, 91–95, 101–102; women, 90
Extremadura region, Spain, 4, 6, 20, 32, 35. *See also* Cáceres, Spain; Trujillo, Spain

Families and friends: of English emigrants to Chesapeake, 86–87, 91, 109–118; of German emigrants, 219–220, 228–229, 230–231; role in emigration, 19–20, 21; of Spanish emigrants, 37–53

Flanders, Moll, 93
Fleet, Henry, 85, 109, 110
Forgery, 70–72
France, 212, 214; Bordeaux, 140, 180, 185–186, 191, 196; first attempts to colonize America, 133–134; military recruitment of emigrants, 150–158; state's role in recruitment, 150–161. *See also* French emigrants; Indentured servants, French
François I, 133, 134
Fraud: indentured servitude and, 184–185; types of, in Spain, 70–74
Free emigrants, 6–7, 16–17; English, to Chesapeake, 85–118; French, to French West Indies, 172–173; motives for emigrating, 16–17
French Antilles. *See* French West Indies
French emigrants: to Canada, 18, 131–162; distinctive population of, 139, 141; families, 149; to French West Indies, 172–199; geographic and social origins, 133, 141, 145, 146, 147, 148, 149–150, 152, 153, 154, 155, 156, 158, 159, 160, 178–180, 188–189; indentured servants, 7, 13, 136, 138, 141, 142, 143, 146, 150, 157, 160, 172–199; merchants, 134; migratory patterns, 12–13; number of, 3, 4, 5, 161, 162, 181; recruitment of, by merchants, 140–145; recruitment of, by seigneurs, 133–134, 135, 136, 145–150; recruitment of, by state, 150–161; soldiers, 132; women, 141, 158, 159–160, 161. *See also* Indentured servants, French
French West Indies, 12; emigration of French indentured servants to, 172–199; plantation system, 199; population composition, 182; sugar crops, 181
Friends. *See* Families and friends
Furly, Benjamin, 214

Gaigneur, Pierre, 157, 158
Galenson, David, 8
Gemery, Henry, 5
Georgia, German emigration to, 215, 226
German emigrants, 13–14, 16–17, 204–231; to Delaware valley, 16, 216, 224, 225, 226, 228, 229, 230; economic motives of, 209, 210, 211, 214; family and friends of, 228–229; in Georgia, 215, 226; indentured servants, 13; legal procedures for, 223, 224–225; merchants and, 215, 216, 217–218, 219,

220, 221, 222, 229–230; newlanders, 219–222; number of, 3, 5, 206, 207, 208, 223, 224–230; Palatine (1709), 214–215, 225; to Philadelphia, 224–225, 228, 229, 230, 231; recruitment of, 211–214, 219–221, 222; redemptioners (*see* Indentured servants, German); regions of origin, 206, 208; returnees, 214; social and geographic background, 227–228
Germantown, Pennsylvania, 212, 228
Giffard, Robert, 147
Governments, sanctioning of emigration by, 17–19
Graffenried, Christoph von, 212, 214
Great Britain. *See* England; English emigrants; Irish emigrants; Scottish emigrants

Henri II, 133
Henri IV, 134
Horn, James, 16, 20, 85
House of Trade (Casa de la Contratación), 59, 60–61, 62–63, 70
Huetz de Lemps, Christian, 5, 13, 172

Ile Royale, 146
Ile Saint-Jean, 146
Iles d'Amérique, Compagnie des, 175
Illegal emigrants, Spanish, 59–80
Indentured servants, English, 4, 7–12, 15, 89, 91, 101, 117, 218, 230; women, 10–11
Indentured servants, French, 7, 13, 136, 138, 141, 142, 143, 146, 150, 157, 160, 172–199; activities after servitude, 177–178; age structure, 192–193; compulsory, 187–189; contracts of, 174–176, 192; destinations of, 198–199; emigration of, to Canada, 136, 138, 141, 142, 143, 146, 150, 157, 160; emigration of, to French West Indies, 13, 172–199; fate of, 199; geographic and social origins, 193–198; legislation regarding, 183–185, 189–192; migratory patterns of, 12–13; number of, 181, 186; origin of, 178–180; right of master to sell, 174–175; shipowners and, 18, 183–186, 187, 189–192; slavery and, 191; trades of, 193–195
Indentured servants, German, 7, 13–14, 217–218, 222, 228–229; children, 228; contracts, 217–218
Indentured servants, Irish, 230
Indentured servants, Spanish, 7, 69, 79

Indenture system, 7–12; end of, in France, 191; evolution of, 8–10; slavery and, 191
Indes Occidentales, Compagnie des, 137–138, 144, 157
Indians, American, 14, 85, 104, 162
Indies: control of emigration to, 63; Peru identified with, 36; returnees from, 50–51, 52; Spanish emigration to, 31–53, 59–80. *See also* French West Indies; West Indies
Inquisition, 70
Ireland, Germans in, 214
Irish emigrants, 5, 12, 231

Jacobs, Auke Pieter, 7, 59
Jesuits, 148–149
Jews, in Portugal, 70

Kinship ties. *See* Families and friends

La Hontan, baron de, 159
La Rochelle, 140, 146, 178, 179, 185, 187; recruitment of emigrants from, 140, 141–143
Legal procedures for emigration: from Germany, 223; from Spain, 59–65, 80
Le Havre, 140
Lejeune (Jesuit), 149
Le Royer, Jérôme, 146, 147, 148
Lesser Antilles. *See* French West Indies
Letters: from English emigrants, 112–115; from German emigrants, 219
Licenses for travel, from Spain, 63–64, 76, 80
Ligon, Richard, 9
Local society, impact of emigration on, 52–53
London: emigrants to Chesapeake from, 86, 90, 91, 94, 97, 98, 99–101, 110–111
Louis XIV, 133, 137–138, 139
Louisiana: French emigration to, 187; German emigration to, 225

Maine, 230
Market forces, 20–21, 22
Martinique, 181
Maryland: Catholic emigration to, 17; English emigration to, 85, 87, 89, 90, 93, 118; German emigration to, 226, 228. *See also* Chesapeake
Médici, Catherine de, 133
Mennonites, 214, 216
Menou d'Aulnay, Charles de, 148, 149

Merchants, 13; British, in Rotterdam, financing of German emigration by, 213, 214, 215, 216, 217–218, 219, 220, 221, 229–230; English, emigration of, to Chesapeake, 85–87; financing of emigration by, 20–21; French, 134, 138–139, 140–145, 175; Spanish, protection of, 75–76
Mesta, 32
Mexico, 14, 36; trujillano emigrants to, 39–40, 42, 43
Michel, Francis Louis, 212
Migratory patterns, 2–3; of British, 16; of Castilans, 33; of English, 90–91, 115–117; of French, 12–13; of Germans, 206–231; knowledge of, 32–33; similarities in, 21–22
Montmorency, duc de, 135
Moravians, 17, 216
Motives for emigration, 15–23; of English emigrants to Chesapeake, 103–109. See also Economic motives; Religious motives

Nantes, 180, 187
Netherlands. See Rotterdam
Networks, social: of German emigrants, 13–14; of Spanish emigrants, 19, 39–40, 47, 51–53. See also Families and friends
New England, 4, 14, 17, 89, 90, 219
Newfoundland, 136, 153, 155
New Rochelle, 196–197
New York, German emigration to, 218, 225, 226, 230
Nord, Compagnie du, 144
North Carolina, German emigration to, 215, 218, 219, 225, 226, 228, 230
Nova Scotia, 219, 226, 230. See also Acadia

Occupations. See Trades and occupations
Ochs, Johann Rudolph, 212
Ovando, Frey Nicolás de, 35

Patronage ties, 43, 47, 52
Penn, William, 212, 213
Pennsylvania, 5; English in, 212; German emigration to, 13, 14, 204–231
Percy, George, 92
Peru, 5, 14, 36, 61
Philadelphia, German emigration to, 224–225, 226, 228, 229, 230, 231
Philip III, 61
Pizarro, Francisco, 38
Plantation system: in Chesapeake, 90–118; in French West Indies, 199; and need for cheap labor, 4, 5–6, 7–8, 9, 10–11, 21; requirements of, 111–112
Port-Royal, founding of, 134
Portuguese emigrants, number of, 3, 4
Poutrincourt, Jean Biencourt de, 134–135
Poverty, in relation to emigration, 15–23
Prisoners, 218; French, 153, 157, 160, 161, 187–189
Protestants, emigration of, 204, 209–210, 212, 213
Puritans, 17, 86, 87, 89, 104, 105, 106–107, 231

Quakers, 89, 104, 107–108, 231; financing of transportation for German emigrants by, 212, 214, 216
Québec, 145, 146, 161; founding of, 134, 135, 136

Razilly, Claude de, 146, 147–148, 149
Recruitment: of French emigrants to Canada, 131–162; of German emigrants, 211–216, 219–221, 222
Redemptioners. See Indentured servants, German
Religious motives, 17; emigration to Chesapeake for, 89, 104–109. See also Catholics; Puritans; Quakers
Return migration: of English emigrants, 115–117, 118; of German emigrants, from America, 219–220, 222; of German emigrants, from Britain, 214; of Spanish emigrants, from Indies, 48–52
Revolution, American, 5, 19
Richelieu, Armand Jean du Plessis, 135–136, 137, 139, 173–174
Rolfe, John, 9
Rotterdam, 20–21; British merchants in, 213, 214, 215, 217–218, 219, 220, 221, 229–230
Rouen, 140, 142, 178
Russia, 210, 212

St. Christopher Company, 174
Sandys, George, 92–93
Santo Domingo, 181
Schwenckfelders, 216
Scottish emigrants, 5, 12, 231
Seamen, Spanish, 75–79
Seigneurial recruitment, of French emigrants to Canada, 133–134, 135, 136, 139, 140, 145–150
Servants. See Indentured servants *headings*; Slaves
Seville, 31–32; emigration from (1550–1650), 59–80

Simmonds, William, 103
Slaves, from Africa, 3, 5, 6, 8, 182–183, 191, 199, 218, 230
Smith, John, 92
Social networks: of German emigrants, 13–14; of Spanish emigrants, 19, 39–40, 47, 51–53. *See also* Families and friends
Socioeconomic status: of British emigrants, 10, 87; of French emigrants, 182; of Spanish emigrants, 40–41, 43–47
Soisson, comte de, 135
Soldiers: French, 150–158; Spanish, 75–79
Souden, David, 12
South America, European emigration to, 3
South Carolina: French emigration to, 5; German emigration to, 215, 218, 226, 228, 230
Spain: emigration regulations of, 18–19; historical development of, in relation to emigration, 31–32; licenses for travel from, 63–64, 76; servant emigrants from, 7. *See also* Spanish emigrants
Spanish emigrants, 14–15, 16; American areas settled by, 14; expenses of, 65–69, 79; family and friends of, 19–20, 37–53; illegal, 59–80; indentured servants, 7, 69, 79; to Indies, 30–53, 59–80; legal procedures for, 59–65, 80; number of, 3, 4–5, 32–33, 35–36, 64; return migration of, 48–52; seamen, 75–79; servants, 69, 79; from Seville, 59–80; socioeconomic status, 40–41, 43–47; soldiers, 75–79. *See also* Cáceres; Trujillo

Talon, Jean, 131–132, 157, 158, 159–160
Telner, Jacob, 214
Thompson, Maurice, 93
Tobacco trade, 89, 91, 94, 95, 110, 117
Traders. *See* Merchants
Trades and occupations: of English emigrants, 10, 91–95; of French emigrants, 155–156, 177, 193–194; of Spanish emigrants, 41
Trujillo, Spain, 5; economic conditions in, 33–34, 44–45; economy, 33–34; effect of Peruvian conquest on, 36; emigration rates, 35–36, 40–41; emigration to Indies from, 37–53; local government, 34; return of emigrants to, 50–51
Tucker, William, 93

Unfree emigrants. *See* Indentured servants *headings*; Slaves

Virginia, 16, 85, 86, 87, 89, 90, 109–110, 118, 226; German emigration to, 228; during tobacco boom, 111. *See also* Chesapeake

Waldo, Samuel, 219
Warner, Captain, 173–174
Wars of Religion, 134
West India Company. *See* Indes Occidentales, Compagnie des
West Indies, emigration to, 7, 11, 12, 13, 17, 19, 112, 141, 143. *See also* French West Indies
Wokeck, Marianne, 5, 13, 20, 204
Women: English, 10–11, 90; French, 136, 141, 158, 159–160, 161; Spanish, 80
Wyatt, Francis, 85

Designer: UC Press Staff
Compositor: Asco Trade Typesetting Ltd.
Text: 10/13 Sabon
Display: Sabon

www.ingramcontent.com/pod-product-compliance
Lightning Source LLC
Chambersburg PA
CBHW021700230426
43668CB00008B/684